Mary Jane

A GAME OF SHADOWS

Linden Peach

Copyright © Linden Peach 2020.

All rights reserved.

Print ISBN 978-1-8380752-8-6

The right of Linden Peach to be identified as the author of this work has been asserted by him in accordance with the Copyright Designs and Patents Act 1988

No part of this publication may be reproduced, stored in a retrieval system, or transmitted in any form or by any means without the prior permission in writing of the publisher. Nor be otherwise circulated in any form or binding or cover other than that in which it is published and without a similar condition being imposed on the subsequent purchaser.

All characters and events in this publication, other than those clearly in the public domain, are fictitious and any resemblance to real persons, living or dead, is purely coincidental.

Published by

Llyfrau Cambria Books, Wales, United Kingdom.

Cambria Books is a division of

Cambria Publishing Ltd.

Discover our other books at: www.cambriabooks.co.uk

Every snowflake that falls has the same structure but a unique identity determined by its individual descent - the time this has taken, the distance it has travelled and the friction involved.

Khaled Azzam

CONTENTS

PART ONE	1
Chapter One Endings as Beginnings	2
Chapter Two John Kelly	20
Chapter Three Holding On	28
Chapter Four The Piano	42
Chapter Five Kate Kelly	56
Chapter Six Out of Sight	59
Chapter Seven Troubled Days and Nightmares	67
PART TWO	80
Chapter Eight An Eye to a Kill	81
Chapter Ten The Whisperer and the Slaughterman	96
PART THREE	124
Chapter Nine Hand to Mouth	125
Chapter Eleven Sins of the Fathers	149
Chapter Twelve Glanders	175
Chapter Thirteen The Maid and the Princess	196
PART FOUR	227
Chapter Fourteen Widow and the Spinster	228
Chapter Fifteen New Families	249
Chapter Sixteen Fences	272
Chapter Seventeen Another Line	287
PART FIVE	306
Chapter Eighteen The Boutique	307

Chapter Nineteen Nearer?	335
Chapter Twenty Cut to the Chase	353
Chapter Twenty One Closing Frames	368

16 Tachwedd | November 1888

Carnarvon and Denbigh Herald
and North and South Wales Independent

Dorset Street, Spitalfields, the scene of the latest outrage, is the heart of a somewhat notorious neighbourhood. It is composed largely of lodging houses, which are frequented by persons of the lowest station in life, amongst them being thieves and some of the most degraded women.

Women rushed about the streets telling their neighbours the news, and giving utterances in angry voices to expressions of rage and indignation. Notwithstanding the stolid reticence of all the police engaged at the scene, the main facts of the crime soon became common knowledge, and spreading far and wide, drew a great concourse of people to the thoroughfare from which the court runs.

There are conflicting statements as to when the woman was last seen alive, but that upon which most reliance appears to be placed is that of a young woman, an associate of the deceased who states that at about half-past 10 o'clock on Thursday night, she met the murdered woman at the corner of Dorset Street. Kelly informed her that she had no money, and it was then that she said that if she could not get some, she would never go out any more but would do away with herself. Soon after they parted, a man who is described as respectably dressed came up and spoke to the murdered woman and offered her some money. The man accompanied the woman to her lodgings.

PART ONE

DAUGHTERS

Cruelty has a human heart,
And Jealousy a human face;
Terror the human form divine,
And Secrecy the human dress.

William Blake

Chapter One
Endings as Beginnings

Rhagfyr | December 2016

2016 is the year on which Dr Mary-Jane Sullivan will look back, for as long as she is able, as her "annus horribilis". While this was not when everything started to fall apart, it was the year in which she stopped pretending to herself that her mother would recover. It all begins with a three-word medical term of which Dr Sullivan has never heard; something very rare, from an obscure scientific paper that even her physician only stumbled across by chance. It refers to something which has taken root in her mother's head. There, it is slowly changing the shape of her brain, absorbing her memories, preventing her thinking, eroding her identity and transforming her personality. The rarity of the illness makes what is happening to her mother seem even more cruel. She has never been truly friends with her mother. In the last few years, as they have become older, they have become closer. She wishes that they had always been this way. But all she can see now is her mother disappearing from her.

Then there is the question which Mary-Jane cannot answer. She has no idea whether anyone else in her family might have suffered from this condition. And with this question, others arrive like summer swallows lined up on telephone wires waiting to migrate. She realises how little she really knows about her mother, her family.

Normally, if she had a query about them, she would text her

mother (her uncle, her only other living close relative, is rarely able to help in such matters). But now her mother is confused, unable to remember which day it is, even forgetting occasionally she has a daughter, as in the future Mary-Jane will forget her mother.

Mary-Jane is a veterinary surgeon. She tries to conjure up a time when she will not be able to remember enough to practice. The spectre of the black hole into which all knowledge, all achievements and all family pasts will one day sink frightens her. Terrifies her. But this year she has been dragged into a past, a story, which in her wildest dreams she would never have believed had anything to do with her.

Turning from her computer, Mary-Jane's eyes flood with tiny, microscopic bugs. They swim in front of her for several minutes and she feels the beginnings of a migraine. She shuts down the screen, turns off the desk lamp and closes her eyes. In the darkness, someone is walking with increasingly heavy footsteps inside her head. It is not for the first time. With her eyes screwed up, with all this noise inside her mind, she loses track of everything, even where she is.

Ebrill | April 1871

As one gate clashes and crashes another is dragged open, scraping a semi-circle into the earth floor. It is held wide enough for a large, black Highland bull to pass through, pulled by its owner and cajoled by a posse of others.

They manoeuvre the massive animal off a gangway that spreads in three directions, each with entrances and exists.

The auction arena is lined with wooden benches. In the centre of the ring, the bull stands gladiatorially, secure in its own mass. A large white label with a number is stuck like a shield to one of his rumps.

A face in the crowd warrants our attention. Her father is holding her on his shoulders. She is nine years old. Her hair is tied in ringlets with pieces of leather. He is terrified she will inadvertently raise a finger, scared that they might end up with a bull in their back yard in Carmarthen. He can feel her knees gripping him. He is loving this moment with her. Everything else is forgotten. Journalists and authors will write about her. But that is a long way off. She and her father are next to her sister who is a few years older and stands very erect with her hands pressed tight to her thighs. The two girls do not look alike but there is a resemblance which lies in their gestures and the secretive looks that are passed between them. The family is Irish and this is their first visit to mid-Wales. We will return to them all.

Then we might pick out another equally nervous man and someone, who appears to be his son, watching as intently next to him. Spindly bones shape their faces against taut, leathered skin giving away that they are farmers. They are several yards in front of the sisters. The girls do not know them. But no one can miss them, especially the son; he is excited and keeps biting his fist between bids. The nine-year-old can see him clearly. Later in life, she will have a faint, blurred memory of seeing him. Somewhere. Sometime. She will never place him. So much will have changed by then.

The auctioneer begins spouting numbers that fly over everyone's heads, all of them crowded into the half-moon . 940, 50, 60, 1,000 … each caught randomly it seems in different parts of the arena in patterns that only he can see.

The owner stands nervously beside his prize bull. He is trying to decipher the increasingly chaotic shouts, grunts, gestures and yells breaking out all around him.

The auctioneer shouts, 'sold.' But he doesn't exactly shout 'sold'. He shouts 'gwerddodd.' But it does not sound like 'gwerddodd.'

Suddenly, everything is silent.

The owner searches the horseshoe of faces to identify who has bought his beast.

Officials hustle the bull out of the opposite gate to the one through which he entered. His hair hangs so far over his eyes it seems that he has to rely on being led. His legs rise and fall like pistons. His footfall is mechanical and laboured. The platform outside vibrates under his enormous weight and the boots of his minders.

Here and there are small clusters of men, women and children who wait for him as if he were a crown prince. Among them is the nine-year old girl who saw him sold, her father to whose trouser legs she clings and her sister. Backs are slapped, friends greeted and the rump of the bull sporadically smacked. He stands between owners, between brands. Below him much smaller cattle wander and circle among themselves under the gaze of buyers and sellers some of whom stroll while others move quickly, striding the length and breadth of the different sized pens. There is a cacophony of noise, like the mustering for battle, and nosefuls of different urinary smells.

The new owner arrives, with his son in tow, and grabs his purchase by the thick iron ring through his nose. He raises his head to better admire the muscle spreading the length of his gigantic body and visible in the partings of his thick hair. As he does so, he and his new bull make eye contact. Each is reading the other.

Awst | August 2016

Nearly one hundred and fifty years later, Dr Mary-Jane Sullivan walks barefoot through the gates of the graveyard near Llanrwst in north Wales, swinging her walking boots nervously in one hand and carrying a leather rucksack over her shoulder. Her red hair is wrapped around her neck and held in place by a Stetson with an embroidered hat band. Her bare feet attract the attention of two elderly women, one leaning on the other's arm, as they pass her.

'Dwi' hoffi eich traed noeth chi' one of them says smiling. 'Dych chi'n cerdded mewn traed noeth llawer?' [I like your bare feet. Do you walk barefoot a lot?]

'Fel Mary Jones,' says the other enthusiastically, recalling the story of a fifteen-year-old girl who walked twenty-six miles across the countryside from her home to Bala in her bare feet to buy a Welsh Bible because she did not have one.

Mary-Jane thinks of Paul McCartney walking barefoot over the Abbey Road crossing. She does not know why this image comes to mind but believes that perhaps it should have been the white-suited John without his boots and socks.

She pauses, and replies to the women, telling them that it is in her blood, her genes. She walks barefoot whenever she can.

These days, more than others, she needs to feel connected. She doesn't say so, but it helps her with her migraines, with her concern for her mother. Without shoes, you cannot stride down country paths as if they were corridors in your workplace.

'It relieves my stress,' she tells them jocularly.

The two ladies laughingly tell each other that maybe they need to do this then.

The camera is recording.

Mary-Jane treads carefully over grass paths criss-crossed with bits of bramble and embedded with small stones stretching into the graveyard's darker reaches. In the shadows, the earth becomes colder and she can feel the damp wriggling between her toes.

She passes spindly trees, clumps of nettle and unkept graves, many with broken and lopsided crosses over them. She contemplates for a moment the stories that are in these graves, all ending in death. A few have cracked urns without rims and figures of faceless angels. Most of them are late Victorian. One stone is dedicated to a much-loved mam-gu who lived to a ripe age for her times and it makes Mary-Jane think of her own mother.

Further on, the camera follows her eyes to a commemoration of someone's sister who died in her teens in 1884 and more than one stone is erected to babies from around the same time, each only a few months old.

Eventually, she reaches an area that is more open, with fewer graves, well-trimmed grass and narrow, levelled paths that are kinder to her feet. There is nothing hidden here she thinks. She is able to walk more quickly now and makes her way toward a particular grave where she and a local historian are to have their spontaneous, rehearsed conversation.

The two women cut an interesting contrast for the screen, an earthy youngish woman in walking clothes, who looks as if she walks everywhere, and a late-middle-aged woman dressed as if for afternoon tea in chain-store blouse and trousers. She holds a small-clipboard and some loose papers.

As Mary-Jane approaches, the camera zooms in on her. The historian greets her as if they have never met before and for the benefit of the viewer reminds Mary-Jane that she is researching her ancestry, inspired by her mother who is suffering from dementia and by the realisation that there are so many gaps in her knowledge of her family. A voiceover will add that Mary-Jane is a local veterinary surgeon who is also a freelance press and tv journalist. After the two women have greeted each other, the camera focuses on a gravestone beside the historian. It has a short inscription but most of the words have been erased over the years.

Sometimes, as the novelist Charles Dickens discovered, a single name on a gravestone plunges us into reverie, allows a story to emerge. The camera picks out the letters that are left. For the fourth time that afternoon, Mary-Jane has to make her enthusiasm show in her face and sell it to the camera. The historian moves between Mary-Jane and the gravestone, pointing out what remains of a name with her forefinger and then tapping on some figures beneath.

'This is the grave of your great-great-great-grandfather,' she says.

Mary-Jane peers closely as if that were the first time she has seen it.

The historian traces the letters with her forefinger.

'There is his first name, you can see that there are four letters and the name begins with an 'M' and ends in what looks like a 'c'. The surname is Davis.'

'There must have been many Davises,' Mary-Jane surmises, remembering her prompt.

'That's right,' she replies, without laughing as she did in the rehearsal, which throws Mary-Jane slightly. 'But what really interests me is this. Can you read what it says?'

Mary-Jane couldn't make out the inscription herself but she has been told what it says and pretends to decipher it slowly as she has been instructed.

She bends down so as to be closer to the gravestone, as the director had ordered her, and reads the Welsh slowly. Then, moving back slightly, she provides a translation in much faster English.

'Died in Llanelli, February, 1880.'

'Yes, that's right,' confirms the historian with the same feigned enthusiasm she had managed to muster all afternoon. 'This is in Welsh which suggests,' she says, 'the importance of the language to those who buried him and maybe to himself.'

Mary-Jane straightens her back and steps to one side, conscious of the camera in her blind spot. The historian points her finger at

Llanelli which is Mary-Jane's cue to continue the narrative, not to camera but speaking side faced with the historian.

'So, my great-great-great-grandfather was from here, moved away and was brought back from Llanelli to be buried?'

'John Meic Davis, known as Meic,' the historian interrupts with the results of her research.

The name Meic Davis meant nothing to Mary-Jane when she first heard it. John Meic Davis even less.

The historian summarises what she thinks she knows, trying not to sound too staged, 'died, from whatever cause, in Llanelli and was returned here and buried by his Welsh-speaking family. Unusually in this part of Wales, at that time, we now know that the local school did not encourage Welsh and we know that your great-great-great-grandfather's mother came from Liverpool.'

She pauses which is Mary-Jane's cue to ask whether they knew how old he was when he died.

'The records show that Meic Davis was born in 1856.'

'So, when he died, he was,' Mary-Jane pauses, as if she were calculating, again as she has been directed, 'only 24.'

The historian agrees, pointing out that at that time, 24 was an 'older' age in terms of a person's lifespan than it is today, but even so he never had what might be called a full life.

'What was he doing in Llanelli?' Mary-Jane asks, again on cue.

'Farming was difficult in Wales generally in the 1870s and 1880s but especially so for the hill farms and, like many young people at the time, he travelled to the south for work in the new coal mines, steel mills and iron foundries. There is evidence that Meic found work in the mines in Carmarthenshire. I would like to show you this.'

Mary-Jane drops her ruck sack near to where she had placed

her boots so that she has both hands free. She is handed a facsimile of the middle page of a newspaper from south Wales. A small paragraph near the top of the page is circled in red ink. It describes an accident in a mine near Llanelli in which three men have been killed. The historian summarises it for the benefit of the camera.

'So,' Mary-Jane repeats pedestrianly, again for the camera as she has been rehearsed, 'one of these men was my great-great-great-grandfather.'

The historian draws the camera's attention to the date at the top of the page.

'It corresponds with the date on the gravestone,' she says. 'He would have been buried within four weeks of the accident, one would think.'

Mary-Jane nods, sadly. Although they have rehearsed this piece several times, the violent death of her young ancestor still makes an impression on her. There is something so intensely lonely in the way his name has been forgotten. She tries to put her feelings into words again. Each time, she expressed them differently. On this occasion, the crew seem satisfied.

The historian produces more paper. She has a death certificate and explains that the death was registered by Megan Davis, his sister, both of whom were born in Llanrwst to a John and Jane Davis. She skilfully accepts her prompt to look again at the gravestone. She draws attention to two letters beneath the line which Mary-Jane had translated. She seems genuinely excited by them despite the number of times she has already drawn attention to them.

Ebrill | *April 1871*

John Davis pulled on the nose ring and saw the look that he had seen so many times. The look that said, I have the mass, the muscle and the horns. His tail rose and John slipped to one side to avoid the crashing water fall, steam gasping from every direction.

'Amgyng.'

Megan could think of no other word. Coming up behind her father, she startled him even more than the bull's outpour. Stepping smartly forward, she helped him pull on the ring until the bull was pointing toward his paddock.

'Byth! Byth!' she hissed aloud. She had worked with some large cattle in her time but she had never seen such a crate as this.

'His coat really is amazing,' she said, as she would go on to say nearly every time she saw him. 'Y fath dduwch!' (Such blackness).

Her father was out of breath and simply nodded, watching the animal swagger through his own muck. Again, with his daughter's help, he dragged the gate shut behind him.

'I have never seen such a coat,' she continued, 'even on a horse.'

For a moment, they fell into silence.

'Have you had a good day?' he asked somewhat awkwardly.

She winced in reply.

'My head feels like it has his horns,' she said, nodding toward the bull.

'He came with a cow and calf. Let me show you,' he enthused.

He led her the familiar route to the sheds, where this time beneath a bundle of straw, in the last of the day's daylight, she fell in love.

'Mae hi'n hyfryd,' (She's gorgeous) she exclaimed, not sounding much like her usual, distant self.

The calf's mother was very different in mass from the bull but still of worrying proportions with horns like widespread arms.

When they returned to the front of the yard, Megan's father

stopped to resume inspection of his new purchase. He couldn't tell Megan, or even her mother, how much he had spent on him.

'He seems very restless,' Megan said, thoughtfully tilting her head.

'You would be, too,' he replied, 'if you had been carried from a place where you thought you belonged, across country, to these hills. I have already sensed that he picks up vibes very easily.'

'Like yourself,' teased Megan.

They studied the way the new bull circled his pen, the slate grey of the hills exaggerating the darkness of his coat.

'When he settles, families will come here,' Megan continued, 'just for the pleasure of seeing him!'

Her father swatted a miniscule, black flea that had leapt onto his forearm.

'If he settles,' he said, frowning.

'There is always an 'if' with you,' Megan chided him, which took him by surprise. His expression hardened but he said nothing in reply.

Every few minutes, the bull stopped. Staring. Swaying on his large ankles like a loaded wagon on its rear wheels.

'Highland cattle meat is so lean, the best beef you can eat,' John announced, as if justifying his purchase. 'Reared on all this Welsh hill grass ... Imagine the taste. Distinctive, succulent, Welsh.'

He seemed to be offering an apology for having bought him.

'You cannot wait to get his calves to slaughter even before they are born,' Megan laughed, noticing over her shoulder her father's dead-pan expression. It was a cruel jibe, as he was uncomfortable with this aspect of hill farming. When he was even younger than his daughter, he was taken to feast days when a bull was killed with a special tool, a pole-axe, with an axe on one side and a spike on the other. Villagers would put sixpence in a box and then work their way down a line of bowls put out on tables containing lungs, kidneys, liver, brains, and other bits of offal.

Megan knew that her father, and her brother, had fallen in love with the breed for its power and strangeness.

'Velvet,' said Megan.

Her father turned, looking her straight in the face.

'A bull was your idea. You get to name him,' he said.

'You have remembered,' she retorted sharply, then continued, 'Velvet. Makes him sound gentle.'

Daughter and father stood quietly together.

'Velvet Bull,' she mused.

'Not John Bull?' he queried thinking of his own name.

'No,' she responded quickly. 'John Bull is all about beef, men and English nationalism.'

'There is that word again,' John thought, knowing it was a word she always spat, like 'Saesneg'.

'John Velvet,' her father suggested doubtfully.

'Velvet John,' Megan countered, resting her chin on the fence and biting her arm. 'A challenge to John Bull. A kinder, more cooperative approach to farming,' she added, thinking that that would appeal to him.

Her father shook his head, laughing. Megan could not quite decide whether her father was supporting her or despairing of her. Rarely, to his mind, he was enjoying his daughter's company.

Slowly, as if waiting all the time to be summoned back, one of their sheep dogs slipped under the pen, his neck straining so as to get his nose closer to the bull's smell.

Velvet John started to drag his heavy feet toward the dog. A string of saliva hung from his rubbery mouth. He drew it up again with his thick, blue-pink tongue as if it were a piece of spaghetti.

Megan called the dog back, sounding somewhat indifferent to the danger, but he came nevertheless.

'You have done well,' she congratulated her father, looking around the yard. It was a much more visitor-friendly place. Before they arrived, any stranger who entered the farmyard would have been greeted with barks, growls and deep-throated grumbles, as dogs hauled the chains which restrained them through the cracked mud left by carts and horses.

Megan turned away and headed to the house. Her father waited with his dog. Within seconds, his daughter had gone.

Awst | August 2016

Mary-Jane can never be sure when she will have one of her migraines, when those tiny microscopic bugs will fly inside her eyes, which is one of the reasons why she finds camera work stressful. For the moment, in the outside air and feeling close to the earth, she seems free of them.

'This is what really interests me.' The historian pauses for effect. 'Look here,' she instructs Mary-Jane, who remembers to move nearer the stone again, trying not to block the camera. 'MJ.'

Mary-Jane steps back, feeling the pinpricks of some bramble thorns camouflaged by the grass beneath her feet. She stares at the stone in feigned puzzlement.

The historian suggests that they might refer to Meic's sister, Megan. Her full name was Megan Jane Davis. She explains that Megan went to live in London as a young woman and their parents are recorded as having moved to Liverpool. Obviously, they had been forced to surrender the farm.

'Little is known of Megan after her move to London,' she concludes. 'Except, there are suggestions that she returned to the farm. But the only bills of sale that relate to the farm are from much later and in the name of another family, Prothero.'

The Davises, who farmed near Llanrwst until the late 1870s, could never have imagined all of this, cameras, microphones and television.

'So,' says Mary-Jane, again on cue, 'if Meic is my great-great-great grandfather, he must have a child, presumably born in Llanelli.'

'We will come back to that,' comes the retort, gently reminding Mary-Jane not to get ahead of the script.

'Why did Megan not have her own name and those of her parents put on the stone. You know, devoted son of, beloved brother of …?'

The historian agrees that it is a puzzle.

'Perhaps,' she suggests, 'they were really poor by this time. Remember the farm has gone and Megan has left north Wales for a low paid job in London. They may only have had enough money to pay for the grave.'

From the script which she was handed earlier in the afternoon and the rehearsals, Mary-Jane knows that at this point she has to prepare herself for the first indication of the 'big' story they have uncovered.

'These initials,' says the historian with a sense of triumph as if she were laying down a flush of cards, 'are the same as yours. Maybe they are not referring to Megan Jane but a Mary Jane.'

Mary-Jane is interested in their scratchy nature. They remind her of the clawing of desperate finger nails on a dungeon door but she does not say this, it is not in the script.

'So where does Mary Jane come into the picture?' she asks, remembering her line.

'Who is she?' asks the other, as if she were thinking of this question for the first time. 'Did she have her initials carved on the stone? Or was this done by someone visiting the grave? Was she present at the burial? Was she the person who was responsible for the stone, maybe even for the burial?'

Mary-Jane runs with the script now, pointing out that the fact that no other member of the Davis family is mentioned might suggest that the gravestone was erected by someone who was not a member of the immediate family. Or maybe he was buried here and the grave stone erected years later when someone could afford it. But the mystery remains, why did they not have their name in full on the stone or even add their surname? Or has that been eroded?

The historian takes up the script again on cue. She can see that Mary-Jane is experienced in talking to camera.

'There is no sign that it has been eroded. But these are all very good questions. I cannot help think that this MJ is going to be a significant figure for you. Is Mary Jane a popular name in your family?'

Mary-Jane had not been asked this in rehearsal and she finds herself reflecting and not, she hopes, for too long. She admits that while the name was not popular in the sense of it occurring in every generation, she is aware that there had been other Mary Janes in the Sullivan family.

The historian studies Mary-Jane carefully as she answers. She has something else to say which Mary-Jane had not heard in the rehearsal and it is almost as if she is assessing how much information Mary-Jane can comfortably absorb at one time.

'Of course, before we can go on, we have to know, as you

suggested just now, how Meic Davis is connected with you. There has to be a child. But there is no mention of him being a father on the gravestone and there is no record of him having a child, even of being officially married.'

Mary-Jane's interest is captured, along with her surprise. The camera is content. The historian is signalled to reiterate the key point.

'If this Meic Davis is your great-great-great-grandfather, I suspect that MJ is not Megan Jane.'

Mary-Jane continues to look stunned, as the director, in cahoots with the historian, was hoping for. Somehow, MJ as Mary Jane or as Megan Jane worries her. It is because of the nature of these initials. Everything about them from the way they have been carved to the mystery behind them disturbs her. She does not know why but MJ is a ghost that she doesn't want in her life.

Then, everything is called to a halt. The historian collects her papers while the director, the camera crew and sound team stand around comparing notes. The director's assistant begins checking schedules. They all know things that Mary-Jane doesn't. Maybe because they do not trust her with their secrets, they leave her alone. She knows that this is only the first part of the programme and they will want her continually surprised as the broadcast unfolds in order to grab viewers. A member of the crew hands her more papers and a date for the second interview with a different historian a few weeks later in Carmarthen in south-west Wales.

Mary-Jane balances herself on the edge of a grave and gathers her boots and rucksack near her as if they were pets. The fastener of her rucksack is jammed. The strain in her attempts at releasing it, and her frustration, reveal themselves in the way she pummels the side of the bag.

Eventually, she is able to search inside and find a pair of bright red walking socks. As she does so, she thinks about Meic Davis and how his life was over almost before it had begun. So much left unfulfilled and unfinished. She thinks again of her mother and how her life is coming to an end.

Slowly, she brushes bits of leaf, grass and grit from the soles of one of her feet and pulls on the thick, Welsh wool. Then she does the same with the other, conscious that the assistant who is alternately scrolling through texts and emails on her phone is watching her. After her bare feet, the boots feel heavy but warm and comforting. It occurs to her how sore and bleeding Mary Jones's feet must have been after walking twenty-six miles each way over mountainous terrain. She yanks the laces as hard as she can, raising each foot in the air as she does so, and drawing the lines of eye holes tightly together.

She wishes that the programme was filmed last year or was scheduled for next year. There is too much trauma in her family at present. Not only is her mother very ill, but she herself is waiting for the results of tests.

Life for her at the moment is all about waiting.

Now she has this mysterious 'MJ', this great gap in her family history, to worry about. Who is she and what is her relationship, if there was one, with her great-great-great-grandfather? What is her relationship with herself? Is Meic Davis really her ancestor? Where is the missing link between Meic Davis and herself? His daughter? She is anxious now about what might be disclosed later in the programme. When the full story is revealed, she will see the connections. Truly, it is like waiting for test results. Why do test results take so long? She regrets having agreed to take part in the programme.

Thoughts come and break like waves on a beach. She remembers how her mother had always said that she would 'go' before Mary-Jane's father. 'Go', an interesting word for death she thinks. Meic, Megan and MJ, whoever she is, have all 'gone'. As a vet, she has seen her fair share of death, bereavement and the myriad of ways in which people cope with loss. She wonders how many people had attended Meic Davis's internment. At the end, were it only the two of them?

Now everyone has moved away, the gravestone looks solitary in the gathering gloom. She suddenly shivers and pulls her sleeves lower over her wrists. She imagines the young man left alone in the earth beneath the stone as everyone departed.

She remembers scattering her father's ashes in the sea at Ynys Môn with her mother. The day had been calm but the sea had been billowing and as they cast his ashes off the cliffs, the waves kept jumping like sea seals, snatching handfuls at a time and disappearing with them into the deep.

Chapter Two
John Kelly

Sometimes the future walks so close behind us that if we were to turn, we would see how our life will pan out. Meic Davis and Mary Jane Kelly thought so and Mary-Jane Sullivan came to believe her future was over her shoulder.

But as a child, Mary Jane Kelly found the present dragged around her ankles like a rabid dog that refused to be kicked away. Her relationship with her father in Carmarthen was very different from that between Megan Davis and her father on their farm in the north. Her father may not immediately be recognised as the man who took two of his children to their first cattle auction in mid-Wales. Relaxed as he was then, spontaneous amusement and ease with himself were not qualities which his family or his work colleagues would later associate with him.

Although he was not a military man, he thrived on order. Afterall, his job at the foundry involved long-term planning, balance sheets, profit and loss charts and risk assessments. Everything there was focussed, tight and efficient. His fondness for order could be seen everywhere at home, from the neatly stacked logs in the rear yard to the straight lines of vegetables and the front path raked with a special kind of gravel. Everything was functional as you might expect of a book keeper. There were a few flowers, some planted by Mary Jane's mother who forgot to care for them and others carried there on the wind like the family itself. In the house, everything was compartmentalised and tools and machinery, not his forte, were confined to the cellar. He regularly cut, tugged and tore weeds from the yard. Through the late summer, he always piled them beside the gate posts for the local farmers to collect and add to their winter feed. Mary Jane thought this was worthwhile work; she went to school with many of the children from the farms. Regularly, she took a sharp, stubby knife from the kitchen drawer.

'Nawr, dwi'n barod,' (Now, I'm ready) she said.

Enthusiastically, she joined in the digging and slicing. Her father seemed pleased, every time. They gestured to each other and looked into each other's faces as they did when he took her to the animal auction. Only occasionally, she caught him wincing as she dragged her blade carelessly against stone which made an unbearable noise as if she were scraping bones. When they completed their weeding, father and daughter often sat together and planned the rows of vegetables they would plant, potatoes, onions, leeks, green beans, a favourite of Mary Jane, cabbage and carrots. In the corner, she imagined an island of rhubarb, the only plant in the whole garden not in straight lines, and argued for some canes of currant bushes near one of the hedges. As they talked, she pictured the wigwam of sticks for the beans rising high like temples over the freshly dug earth and the strings running the whole length of the plot like laundry lines. She looked forward to the green shoots poking their way through the soil, symbols of hope and promise. This was always the most exciting and the loveliest time of year for her.

A few years later, no one ever saw her father without a frown, his forehead seemed permanently lined like graph paper. His fellow workers were perpetually disturbed by the look which his face always bore, a little secretive, a little malicious. He became a difficult man with whom to hold a conversation. He treated everyone as if they belonged in a column of figures. But life was hard for him. Every day, he sensed how he and his children were received. They were the Irish. They might have been fellow Celts of sorts, but it meant nothing in this part of Wales. Their clothes, hair and shoes were scrutinised before they left the house. They had to look better than the other children because they were instinctively seen as badly dressed. Whether they were going to school, the church or town, he would warn them, 'Do not disgrace the family. Remember you are a Kelly.' He encouraged them to speak Welsh, against their mother's wishes, and his own instincts, and to practice it among themselves. He showed interest in their progress but he also became more and more hot tempered and, outside the house, he sometimes drank more than he should have.

And so, he came to see himself as stuck in Carmarthen with a wife who was becoming more and more of a recluse, addicted to all kinds of medicines and pills, and children with no thought for their futures. Especially one daughter. She was so unlike him and his reliance on logic, decision making and mapping. Mary Jane was different. Her father believed that she should never allow herself to be held back by the past. But she always looked to him as if something were pulling her shoulders down, rounding her back as if she were an old woman. It made him angry. At other times, he thought himself responsible and felt guilty. But, although he was a Catholic, he did not have much time for guilt. Guilt he told his children would wear them out when they most needed to pull themselves up. 1872, nine years old, and she seemed to have no interest, no faith, in anything. She rarely smiled in his company anymore and, even when she did, she never looked happy. He once told her that she must live for something. And not simply for the day when she would announce she were leaving home.

There had been a time when the children were encouraged by their mother, before her ailments struck, to read and share books. They still did so of an evening without her involvement. But this was a pastime that had long since deserted him. He spent his evenings outside and as they grew darker, inside with the local newspaper or documents from the foundry.

But he enjoyed hunting, as did his father and his grandfather. He once shared with Mary Jane how when his father went round the stock, he always carried a gun to be ready if his sheepdog raised anything on the way. Hunting brought him closest to others from the town. However, the children hated looking at him when he returned, the injuries he had inflicted on another living thing were stamped on his face. They feared him then, cowering together when they heard the door being unlocked. The children whispered among themselves in Welsh, in case he overheard them, about his temper, 'ei dymer ffrwydrol', that he could not control, how he went 'o fod yn dawel i fod yn darw gwyllt mewn eiliad', from a quiet man to a wild bull on the spin of a coin. As they grew older, they despised him more. He would call them into the kitchen to see what he had shot with others or by himself. The children always arrived in the room together, as if there were safety in that. This was something he had come to recognise and expect. They did not want to see the rabbit he had hung but they knew they had to. Its face always had more shape the following day, the sockets which had appeared empty were then restored with eyes, admittedly not live brown watching eyes but black orbs. Sometimes it ended there, at others one of them was given it to skin.

Increasingly, he behaved like his own father. He became accustomed to giving orders, at work and in the home, and he expected instant obedience. He spent less and less time speaking with his wife and regarded his older children with increasing suspicion. As their Welsh developed, their English became more limited and they became increasingly reluctant to talk in their parents' tongue. He observed, scrutinised and criticised. There wasn't much he shared.

At night, when he and his wife went to their bed, she would lie beside him, silent, sullen and unresponsive. Her womb was exhausted, she could bear him no more children. As his wife's ailments, as she called them, grew worse, there were weeks on end when she barely left her room. Everything was down to him.

Increasingly undemonstrative, austere and even cruel, he found it difficult to hug or listen to his children.

But they could all remember when things were not like this. When there were early morning weekend walks to the river, passing houses where fires were being lit and the preparation for breakfast underway. In some of the cottages they heard a clattering loom making clothes. Beyond was the churning grey of an uneasy estuary and in the farther distance the chimneys of the iron works panting smoke and steam into the clouds. In summer, there would often be a haze above the mudflats where the river's mouth met the sky. Gulls wheeled overhead and screeches from far corners of the estuary became screams immediately above them. They enjoyed being frightened by them or at least having the licence to scream themselves, raise their voices and caress each other.

Their father loved to watch the sun come up; how in early spring, it shifted its position on the horizon over which it peered like a house burglar over a wall. Although they shivered slightly in the cold, the children enjoyed their father's joyousness in something so simple. They would explore the river, searching for small, white crabs among the pale pebbles. Mary Jane was always the first to enter the shallow water and the others would listen for the splash of her feet. She was taller than her sisters and all but one of her brothers. She was lanky with stork legs. Her father would watch her more than the others. They competed with each other, trying to send stone nuggets skittering along the water's surface. Mary Jane could feel tears of perspiration beneath her arms cooling in tiny rivulets. They made her armpits feel sticky. The release of body odour meant that she had to keep a distance from her father who would always make this an issue, oblivious of the stiff smell of sweat from his own work shirts. More than once, she caught him staring into the river as if he were trying to read its depth. It was not unusual for them to stay here until the new sun slunk behind gathering clouds, inconsistent in colour and texture, like an elderly man's pipe smoke, and the air grew heavy with an impending storm. One morning in late summer, they all stood together and watched jagged streaks of lightning striking the horizon. Their father said this reminded him of Ireland. Mary Jane never remembered her mother with them on any of these walks.

There were days in late spring when John Kelly would take some of his children up into the hills after mass on a Sunday. Mary Jane was invariably among them. Spring warmed him. Spring is Victory, he would always say, or something very similar. Victory over the cold east wind, the frozen ground, over death. Mary Jane loved to listen to the cold water flowing in rivulets and dropping over the grassy stones, so simple it frightened her. Years later someone who had grown up on a farm, wholly in the country, would teach her to smell and taste as well as hear the flow of water, in the trill of a stream, the slap-on-slap of a waterfall. She loved these walks. On misty days, she wished their father would take them higher into the cloud, but he knew how everything could change, how clouds might savage wayfarers who took them for granted. He would exaggeratedly inhale and exhale. There, he would say, our lungs are fully charged with fresh mountain air, now we can face that dirty, smoke-filled town. And at the end of their days out, when they re-entered the town, her father would often take her arm in his and they strolled together behind the others.

The days at home which Mary Jane hated the most were those on which rain teemed out of the sky, that kind of sullen, black rain that invaded the body and spirit alike, that slipped easily down her neck, ran along her arms and settled in her boots. Then she saw a different side to nature, narrow channels unable to contain the heavy rain overrunning drains, tearing deep grooves in the ploughed fields around their town, obliterating country paths, swamping nests of the birds along the river bank and uprooting wild flowers.

There were many days when Mary Jane was unhappy. As she became older, her sisters noticed that she smiled less and secret worries often creased her forehead and darkened her eyes. Her relationship with the rest of the family became increasingly strained. She had a habit of saving morsels of her favourite food around her plate until she had almost finished her meal. She had many quirks like this. On one occasion, at a strategic moment, one of her brothers leant over her and, using his fork, speared them and lifted them into his own mouth. Then he sat back and laughed. Her other brothers and her sisters joined in his mocking merriment, apart from her eldest sister.

Not only did family life change over the years for the worse, but Mary Jane never settled into school. Word of her apparent strangeness spread quickly among the pupils and her eldest sister had to protect her. She did not have the scabs and rashes of the other children her age. But she was decidedly aloof and preferred her own company and solitary pursuits to the rough and tumble of the school yard. Her eyes regularly travelled over the other children but she saw nothing in them to which she warmed. When she first attended school, she did not speak their language, which made all her lessons an appalling struggle, and in the yard and behind the teachers' backs, the other children mimicked her slanting Irish accent. Very few of the children in the school were Catholics which puzzled Mary Jane because a quarter of those who gathered for weekly mass, the majority of whom were of some kind of Irish descent, were no older than herself. The teachers had little sympathy with the Catholics in their school or any understanding of them. She never forgot how one girl, of about her age, was made to kneel for an hour in the entrance hall after school every day for a week. By the weekend, her knees were pockmarked by the cold uneven floor. But she never complained once and passed each second of every hour praying with her rosary beads. Her face never changed all the time Mary Jane was in school with her. It bore the serene composure of the martyr or in Mary Jane's eyes, the vacant stare of the Holy Fool.

As his children became older, Mary Jane's father did not know how to discipline them. None of the children felt comfortable with him any longer, always watching for the serpent's tail whenever he played with them. Family life became a tin toy he wound and rewound, fearing the spring might break. In later years, there was no relaxation even at Christmas. Gifts were heaped in the centre of the room. One by one, the children were summoned from the hearth and each of them had to say in turn why they deserved a present. Their faces burned under the strain.

Then the year crept up on everyone when he stopped playing with his children altogether, no longer sharing simple pleasures like he used to, and they found it hard to remember him laughing with them. He would glance endlessly at his watch, as if they were taking up too much of his time.

Chapter Three
Holding On

Awst | August 2016

Gwen Sullivan has not heard the door handle turn. Normally, she slept like a cat, eyes shut but ears awake. Like a cat, she has the ability to move one ear independently of the other. Not as obviously as a cat, of course, but it had always been her party trick. When she was young her daughter loved it. Or so she thought. She cannot understand why her ears have failed her. Every year she has needed stronger lenses in her spectacles. But she has always been confident in her hearing. It has never let her down before.

She manages to drag herself up the bed so as to rest more comfortably against the heaped pillows. It is only possible for her to move an arm, her left leg is still a dead weight. Perhaps the rain had awoken her. She has rarely known such heavy rain, even in Wales. It rains and rains. Her room is on the top floor and the gutter spouts heavy torrents of water. The troubling sound rushes down the pipes, beats indolently, mournfully, against the windows, and percolates into her mind. What was it her mam used to say? Mae hi'n bwrw hen wragedd a ffyn. Her husband always joked that if you wrote a geography of Wales, you would need a whole chapter on rain. That was a long time ago.

Her supper tray is fuller than usual. She cannot imagine how somebody could have carried it into the room without waking her.

Each dish is covered in clingfilm, and, this time, there is a small pot of tea, rather than the usual mug. What a surprise, she says to herself. Maybe they are coming to take me home. Even now she does not know who 'they' are. Or what has happened.

She peers through the film that covers each plate in turn, like looking through misty window panes. She cannot remember the last time that she has slept so deeply. Does this mean, she asks herself, that 'they' are slipping something into her hot drinks. She doesn't trust them.

There is enough late afternoon light for her to see each of the courses. One plate is antipasti, pieces of unidentifiable meat, some with small, spit-sized globules of fat in them, cut into surprisingly neat strips and mouth-sized squares. They make her think of pwdin gwaed, or what the English call black pudding. This was one of Tad's favourites. He had had pwdin gwaed with streaky bacon and cockles for his breakfast every Sunday morning. Why is it that some things which are so far away in time come back to her and others do not? Having been brought up on a farm and having lived on two farms where they knew where and how their animals were slaughtered and butchered, Gwen has always found it difficult to eat anything if she does not know where it has come from.

Her second plate is full of ravioli, dressed with garlic and gritty, finely grated Italian cheese, with a content which might be animal, vegetable or mineral. There is a bowl of chocolate ice cream to follow which has begun to melt. It reminds her of cow pat. She rebukes herself silently for being ungrateful before looking directly into Mary-Jane's face.

'Do you know what I wished they had brought me?' she asks.

But that does not mean she recognises her daughter. Mary-Jane cannot think of anything to say so she studies a small, bejewelled moth that has perched on one of her curtains.

'A nice bowl of safe, warming cawl,' her mother says, answering her own question.

Mary-Jane thinks that 'safe' is an interesting choice of word. Then she reminds herself that her mother is not talking to her or maybe to anyone. It is as if a circle has been drawn around her. She observes that her mother is still not allowed a knife and fork, only one large plastic spoon with which she is expected to eat everything.

Gwen has never liked ravioli; it has always reminded her of used tea bags at the point when they are almost cold and begin to turn yellow. Her daughter watches her touch the pasta's waxy sheen with her knuckles. It reminds her of her mother's face after the stroke. Gwen was expecting it to be colder than it is. Then, for a while, she lets her liverspotted hands fall into the blankets in which she is wrapped and sits very still.

Mary-Jane wanders around her mother's room re-ordering her cards to create a better sense of symmetry and making sure they all stand equidistant to each other. She glimpses herself in the future, in her mother's bed, as if it were a film clip. Around the insipid odours of bleach and iodine, she hobbles slowly, trailing her slippers. Then everything unspools. She finds herself wondering what kind of family the Davis's had been and if MJ were Megan Jane what possessed her to have her initials carved like that on her brother's gravestone. Or did she carve them herself? Were they a close family? After all, brother and sister went their separate ways. As did she. All she had been interested in was science and veterinary medicine. She wished now that she and her mother had been closer. She must have such a wealth of knowledge about the Sullivans. Has all that gone now, she asks herself.

Mary-Jane had always thought of ancestry as a subject for the elderly. She wished that she had taken more of an interest in her family, asked her mother more questions. Why do they not use ancestral research in schools to teach history? Perhaps they do, she argued with herself, remembering it was a while since she was in school. She notices that there are not many cards and that the family cards, from herself and her uncle, are separate from those from outside the family. She is not sure that she likes this but at least there is order in it.

She asks her mother, in Welsh, whether she knows anything about her great-great-great-grandfather Meic Davis. Her mother stares into the room. Mary-Jane cannot be sure whether she has understood her or not. She repeats the question but with no more effect. Throughout Mary-Jane's visit, her mother speaks little Welsh but when she does it is when she is most conspiratorial. She beckons her imaginary companion closer. Mary-Jane keeps her distance. Her mother addresses someone right in front of her face.

'What is it I can't remember? Has something bad happened? Is there something that is bad that I can't remember? Have I done something dreadful?'

Is she talking about herself, Mary-Jane wonders. She is so frustrated that she wants to scream. Every time she speaks with her mother, she can never be sure whether she has understood, or even heard, her. Possibly, deep in what is left of her memory, she is thinking of Meic, sifting through the remnants of her family knowledge. Maybe she knows about MJ and could tell them all who she was. Possibly, she knows about Megan Jane, too. Perhaps, her mother is the only person left who can make sense of the gravestone. Maybe she has even visited it.

Then Mary-Jane remembers the previous month. How her mother beckoned her over. Sounding more Irish than she had ever sounded in her life, she drew her daughter's attention to the corner of the room.

'They are there,' she whispered. 'Watching. Those bloody rabbits. Chase them off will you. They are eating all the lettuce. Shoot them.'

Today, she is left to think about Meic and MJ by herself. Those heartbreakingly carved initials. Why will they not leave her alone?

The worst thing of all is how the producers are keeping her waiting. What have they discovered? Have they stumbled across something terrible? Something that she will find it hard, impossible, to live with. She suspects that the next programme will not be so rehearsed, if rehearsed at all. They will want her agony on screen.

So many gaps. She has never been a person who liked gaps. She has always liked everything joined up. She can't live with this. It is all too inconclusive.

There is no record of Meic having married. That is what the historian had said. There is no evidence that he had ever become a father. He died so young. There must have been many who died young in the foundries and mines. Like being in a war. But he must have had a child and the producers must know that already otherwise why are they so confident that Meic Davis is her ancestor?

Gwen has stopped talking with her imaginary friend and is listening very intensely to the rain. Mary-Jane decides to wait in her room until the storm passes and the evening sun appears. Gwen naps fitfully and there isn't much conversation between them.

'Crazy weather here, isn't,' she says at one point but her mother does not seem to hear.

There is so much that Mary-Jane dares not think about. Would her mother suddenly stop remembering her? Will she ever have any memory again?

When the rain calms to a sleepy shower, Mary-Jane decides to leave. As she rises, her mother sits up and speaks out loud.

'Diwrnod du ond noson dawel.'

Mary-Jane barely understands what her mother has said. She repeats it again to her imaginary friend who is obviously still sat near her. Black day but a quiet night. Then her mother falls back and enters a deep sleep.

All the way home, listening to the screechy wipers against her windscreen, Mary-Jane flips the phrase over and over to herself. Diwrnod du ond noson dawel. Later that night, watching television, showering and lying in bed, contemplating her schedule for the following day, she keeps mulling over her mother's words. Turning and tossing them as if they were small pancakes, she tells herself that they may mean nothing, like her mother's rabbits. It is impossible for her to know what world her mother is in at any point in time. She has never heard her mother speak in this way before, even before her stroke. 'Diwrnod du ond noson dawel.'

Eventually, she puts it out of her mind, while thinking at least she has something else to worry about apart from Meic Davis and the enigmatic MJ.

Mawrth | March 1873

She was ten years old. The streaky sky reflected the light through different shades of various colours like slowly drying paint. There was a smell of rain in the air. But, for now, Mary Jane was content to remain outdoors, reaching deep into the pure present, the kind of moment she imagined a baby experienced when it was born.

When she sat like this, she felt herself strategically positioned between the sky and heaven, the cosmos, where there seemed light and clarity, and a chaos beneath everything where there was confusion, darkness and dissolution. If only the sky would stop moving. She concentrated her attention on the greenness of the grass in front of her. It helped her not to think about her mother. She was inside the house as she had been every afternoon that week, sprawled on a sofa in the lounge like a bundle of discarded clothes. It had been her father's weekend free of work and he had spent most of it alone in the woods and the fields. He had not stopped missing his brothers and sisters who were still in Ireland. His wife made him angry and when he was angry his children were most frightened of him. And he was most scared of himself.

Mary Jane reflected on how no blade of grass was like another. Each had its own unique shade of green. It occurred to her that she did not have to look far beyond her feet to see something small and other worldly, very close to the soil. The farther she looked into their yard, the taller the grass became. A small thistle, by thistle standards, stood out from a bundle of straight edges. It bore a tiny, purple bud above a ring of minute fish-bone thin spikes which she had overlooked at first. There were no other thistles nearby. This made her want to adopt it as her own. It seemed misplaced, as if a bottle of brown-green glass had been left there. Once she had noticed it, everything became focussed around it. She could not undo the seeing of it. The thistle had drawn her concentration away from all the greens she had been identifying. There were hair line cracks in the small bud. She had to squint to see them more clearly but they had not yet widened enough to allow her to see through them into the inside of the growing flower. The clouds had begun to move faster and in the changing light she could no longer see the bud clearly. The tips of the thistle turned slightly even though there was not much of a breeze, as if someone were gently twisting the stem at its roots. That was the trouble, if you stared at something long enough it played trick and treat with your eyes.

The room where her mother dozed was crowded with objects, each deserving of its own space. If they were not in school, or at work in the town, the children had learned to give it a wide berth when the door was firmly shut. On the garden steps, Mary Jane felt safe. She was comfortable with the back door, the kitchen, the hall and all the smaller rooms behind her. She could imagine that they all had nothing to do with her. Her mother would have one of her bottles beside her. Normally, they were hidden in the cupboard deep in the scullery behind the mops, buckets and soaps. When Mary Jane was younger, this was known as the maid's room because that was where the maid skived. But when the children became old enough to share the washing, scrubbing and polishing, there was no longer any need for their parents to keep a maid.

The secretiveness of her thistle, half-hidden in the long grass, made Mary Jane think of the Saturday when she and two of her sisters searched out her mother's bottles. The eldest of them had enough English to read one of the labels out loud although neither of the other two understood fully what they were hearing: 'Dr Hamilton's World-Famous Blood Mixture.' Mary Jane imagined Dr Hamilton. He was a man, all doctors were men, and he had a frock coat and top hat because people's blood had made him rich. Her sister said that he didn't exist but the firm had simply invented him because their quack medicine would sell better if it were associated with an imaginary doctor.

Their mother always made them take medicines, even when they were not ill. She talked a lot about the need for older people to purify and restore their blood. Mary Jane wondered what 'World Famous' meant and if Hamilton were world famous why was the bottle hidden behind all the under-house pipes. The drain smelt of dead rats and when they opened the bottle, it smelt the same. None of them wanted to taste it. Mary Jane replaced the cap while her sister retrieved a box of Clarke's 'invigorating' pills from further behind the pipes. The scullery was very damp and the cardboard packet felt clammy and soft, as if it would tear at any moment. Her elder sister struggled to read the label this time but she managed to make out that the tablets were intended for 'nervous weakness'. She couldn't read all the ailments listed but together they were able to decipher 'want of energy', 'loss of memory', 'inability to fix attention', 'unpleasant dreams' and 'depression'. She skipped to the end of the label. The box had come from Oxford Street in London. They all thought that this address sounded very expensive. The pills had to be ordered from there and the box had cost four shillings and sixpence.

'Do you think our father knows about this?' Mary Jane had asked. They all thought not, but one of them suggested that the maid probably knew about them and maybe that was why their mother dismissed her. The elder girl observed that maids who knew too much were often disposed of.

Everything at the back of the scullery was damp, grey and smelly. It reminded Mary Jane of the vestry at church. It was the kind of space that you didn't want to leave without lighting a candle.

Mary Jane realized that she had been sat by herself in the yard for most of the afternoon, waiting to catch sight of animals as they emerged at the end of the day. This was how Mary-Jane Sullivan, too, spent many hours at weekends and in school holidays, years later. One bedtime, when she was a child, Mary-Jane's mother read her a poem from the 1920s in which the poet froze in his steps before the sudden appearance of a fox. This became one of her favourite poems, the description of the fox's eyes, 'dwy sefydlog fflam' (two steady flames), his 'fflewyn cringoch' (red fur) and how, unhurried, he slipped over the ridge and disappeared 'megis seren wîb' (like a shooting star).

Mary Jane, too, would have adored this poem. Her spirit rose and fell with the different sights and smells of the country and the fields rolling away into the distance. She loved to see herds of sheep for what in her eyes they really were, family clusters, needing and depending on each other. There was love there, she was sure of that.

Suddenly, her father appeared and slapped a dead rabbit across her lap.

'Skin that,' he demanded, adding almost as an afterthought, 'I'll show you how.'

The poor creature had only recently been shot. It was warm and soft on her bare legs. She felt sick and pushed her fist into her mouth, biting down hard on her knuckles. Her father was on his knees in front of her. He pressed down on the animal's back until its underbelly squeezed Mary Jane's legs. Without averting his eyes, he handed her his hunting knife and made her cut a ring around each of the hind legs, just above the joint. Then he took her hand and moved it to make a single slice upwards from the rings along the entire line of the rabbit's under-belly.

Paradoxically, she liked his hand guiding hers. He was touching her. She had never done anything like this before and she trusted him.

'Nawr, dach chi'n barod,' (Now, you are ready) he announced. Years later, she remembered his exact words. It was a kind of initiation, into the adult world, into the real countryside, into the blood and guts of the hills. Her father removed his hand from on top of hers and instructed her, kindlier and more softly than he had spoken to her earlier, to pull back the hide. Then he told her to work it free from the carcass with her fingers through the rings that they had made.

He held her hand again in his and directed it, bringing his extra force down on the knife as it cut through the bone of the tail, making sure not to puncture the bladder. When he released his grip, the knife slipped onto the grass beside her shoes. She was left then to spread eagle the legs and slowly pull the hide from the body. The purple pink carcass underneath smelt like the stagnant water at the back of their scullery, but the hide came off easily, like a glove, until she came to the head where the hide got caught like an uplifted pullover beneath the chin.

Then he handed her the knife for a third time and made her sever the rabbit's small head, under the veil of its uplifted fur. She found herself trembling, so much that she had to push and push again with the knife until its thin tip almost snapped.

She paused again, waiting on her father. He told her, more firmly this time, to pull the rabbit's fur coat clear of its body. It was something that returned in dreams for years. She experienced nightmares, in which she pulled the hides off live rabbits, except that often it wasn't a rabbit, it was a little cat or a dog.

Her father stood over her, seemingly content, as the rabbit carcass dangled at her legs like a loose belt and the fur coiled at her feet. She wanted to vomit. But she was pleased to have satisfied him, unaware how here were sown the seeds for a pattern her life was to follow.

Mai | May 1875

For Meic and Megan Davis in another part of Wales, much more rural and mountainous, life was very different. As they became older, their father involved them in developing the farm. He trusted Meic's judgement, despite his age, ever since involving him in purchasing their prize Highland bull. None of them thought at the time that their futures, be they long or short, would lie elsewhere.

That is why John Davis took them with him to meet an elderly neighbour whom everyone rumoured was about to leave Llanrwst. Already, a sense of something coming to an end had settled inside Mrs Pryce-Evans's gates. You can smell it, some said, like you can taste death. As they made their way into her yard, they all felt the same shiver down their backs, sheep loitered behind them, keeping a mournful distance, like a ghostly gathering of lost souls. The sun was rising like a gentle cat and rubbed herself around them. Meic and Megan had not seen the widow for a while. They thought she had aged. Her face had lost its weathered, countryside appearance and had acquired a yellowish sheen. It seemed to have fallen a little on one side and her neck was scrawny. She was struggling with a bucket of feed for her chickens and was visibly relieved to have an excuse to put it down while she talked with her neighbours.

'I hear you are selling some sheep,' said John.

Mrs Pryce-Evans sighed. She looked around at the buildings and the hills as if she were done with them all and they with her, as if the soul had gone out of the place. But John had already warned his children not to be fooled by that.

'She's a canny old woman, who'll have the shirt off your back if you let her,' he had said as they set out.

'With the market as it is, all we can do is keep on keeping on. Isn't that right, children? I need to get rid. I have plenty that will pay for you if you fatten them up. Some fresh born. Best if they do not have to travel.'

She stared at Megan who suddenly felt uncomfortable.

'My dad,' said Megan as outspoken as ever, 'is wondering why your sons are not taking over the farm.'

Her father stared embarrassingly into the bucket. All three were silent, listening to the sheep beyond the house.

'It's Owen,' Mrs Pryce-Evans said at last. 'He is losing his sight. This time next year he will be blind ... But I, his brother Tomos, too, want him to have a good life. There is a School for the Blind in Birmingham. They will give him lessons and he can learn sport. It is going to be expensive. This farm pays for nothing. Tomos will get work in Birmingham.'

'How many sheep are there altogether?' asked Meic.

'I am selling forty ewes, a dozen lambs, a few rams if you want them.'

John and Meic nodded.

'How is your Highlander doing?' she asked, adding 'something of a beast I hear.'

'His first calves went six months back, on offer from a place in Monmouthshire. Somebody wanting to build a herd. We used the money to get some good Welsh blacks. We are going to cross breed if we can.'

'Cross breed,' she muttered without giving away what she thought about it.

Owen, with the aid of a stick, had come up beside them. He looked well otherwise.

'There are two cows and a calf going as well if you want them,' he said.

Brother and sister looked at each other.

'They've always given good milk,' Mrs Pryce-Evans contributed.

She watched her son thoughtfully.

'Owen, show them the stock. While you and the children give everything the once over, their father and I will go inside and talk business.'

They split up leaving the bucket of feed in the middle of the yard. John and Mrs Pryce-Evans strolled, close together, like mother and son, toward the house.

'Now what are your plans, John?' she asked.

The two had a shared toughness.

'I want to get the makings of a good herd together by three years next spring. I want something decent, a herd I can let the children develop over the next few decades, something I will have left them when I'm no more.'

Mrs Pryce-Evans winced but he didn't notice.

'You are lucky if your children want to continue. Continue where you leave off. Pick up where you have failed.'

John stared at Mrs Pryce-Evans. He wasn't sure what she was saying. There was always more to everything she said than you first heard.

'I do not think the children will ever want to leave,' he replied. 'If they ever had to move away, they would be lonesome for all of this. Meic, he's going to make a brilliant farmer. And Megan, mae hi'n gwella o naid i naid.'

'I am sure that could have been true,' she said enigmatically.

'Could have been,' he responded in a voice that had an edge as if he wanted to shout but knew they were being observed. 'I wish you would say what you mean. You are always …' He was struggling to find the right words.

They both knew what he meant. For a while, they stood on the steps in silence. Small biting flies swirled around them and the elderly lady flapped her hands as if she were buffing boots. From where they stood, they could see Megan, her brother and Mrs Pryce-Evans's Owen running their hands over the back of a calf.

'I think we had better go inside,' she said and conclude our business.

She tried to swish the flies off the door frame, not wanting them inside.

Chapter Four
The Piano

Chwefror | February 1874

'We will meet together in the parlour after supper, Mary Jane.'

He was going to hurt her. They said she was having one of her tantrums. She was like concentrated sulphuric acid. She looked lazy and innocuous, but you had to be careful how you approached her. Dilute the acid by pouring it into water and everything would be fine. But add water to the acid and the rage began. In fact, he had been waiting to hurt her. He had been ready to take her in hand for some time. That was the way he was.

The parlour was hardly used, except at Christmas or New Year or for baptisms and funerals. Sometimes the children were allowed to practice the piano. Lit only by the evening sun that sneaked in between half-drawn curtains, the room was full of shadows and pools of darkness. It was the kind of room in which her mother had told her she had been born. Her father believed that a child had to be taken upstairs before it was carried downstairs so that they would always look upward. This was a tradition, an old belief, in the home country. Around the walls, there were pictures of her ancestors from Ireland about whom she was vague. Each of them seemed very alone, looking out from their solitary darkness and their individual nightmares. It was a history from which she felt orphaned. There was a picture of a prize bull and another of three rams together.

They were so much brighter than those with people in them. But she noticed that there were no pictures of ewes. There were two china sheep dogs, almost as large as the real thing, one on each side of the fire grate. The room was cold and very quiet except for the gravelly tic-toc of a grandmother clock in a corner. Behind the casement, the pendulum swept slowly from one side to the other. The ticking was deep and ominous.

Mary Jane had only been in the room a handful of times. Her mother sat there occasionally, by herself and in the dark. They were a large family but she could never recall them being a happy family. There were moments of mirth and joy. There were Christmases that were fun, although eventually, before the children were very old, even they were to lose their joyousness, and Mary Jane could never forget that auction in mid-Wales and her father sweating in case they accidentally bought a prize bull. But they stood out like the bright pictures on the wall from what was otherwise a general gloom. She disturbed her mother in the parlour once and she remembered thinking that her mother seemed very alone and depressed. Apart from the family, her mother had few people with whom she could speak and none, Mary Jane realised, as she became older, in whom her mother might confide. She and her daughters were not close and there were no women in her life.

That evening, Mary Jane studied the large watercolour of the rabbits again. There were five of them charging through long grass. Their ears were long and strong and their eyes were wild. The hindquarters of the few at the front were thick and muscular. She remembered, on the first time she saw them, asking her mother what kind of rabbits were they. She had answered that they were 'children-book rabbits'. Now, she stared again into their eyes. They seemed angry and revengeful. Their paws were heavy like hooves. She found herself observing again that if they were children-book rabbits, it must be a very dark and violent story. It was not one which she wanted to read.

Her father entered and didn't remove his hat until he had closed the door tightly behind him. In the quiet, the latch striking its plate sounded like a hammer.

'Mary Jane,' he said.

Normally he called her Mary but when he was mad with her, he called her Mary Jane. It was like she was a different girl in his head then. A different daughter in their home. Mary Jane. Now she knew for certain he was going to hurt her. She began to steel herself, to prepare for it.

He said nothing more, making Mary Jane watch him run his fingers around the rim of his hat. She could feel the anger emanating from him. He repeated the circular motion three times as she fidgeted. He had doubts, deep misgivings about what he was thinking of doing and was about to do. Visibly, he was forcing himself to press on against his daughter's insolent resistance. If she were to shed a tear, twitch, express fear, or show remorse he might be able to change his mind, let her go, even hug her. There will come a time when he will look back to these moments in this room and wish he could go back and not do what he plans.

Slowly and deliberately, he positioned the hat on the arm of the nearest chair. Everything in the room smelt damp. He never talked with her, with any of his children in fact. Or their mother. Those days had passed. She looked back at him, dark and expressionless. There it was, the forthrightness in her face that he hated so much. Did he tell himself that only Mary Jane was like this and Mary was never like this?

He told her to go over to the piano and lift the lid. She did so reluctantly. The keys grinned malevolently. She had learned to master them. She could make them dance; she could be hard with them or she could depress them softly. Even more hesitantly, she followed his next instruction which was to place her hands on the keyboard. Her fingers were long for her age and she was able to spread them over several keys at a time.

'You enjoy crying yourself to sleep, don't you?' he said.

She had never known him be this nasty. He walked slowly to the piano and took the end of the lid nearest him in both his hands.

Mary Jane's fingers crumpled as he raised it again. Her knuckles felt as if they were punching each other as the pain pushed its way into her brain. She slowly lifted her hands to her armpits, the only comfort she could find. Under her arms, Mary Jane's hands shivered as the soft flesh and muscle there kissed them. She felt her armpits soaking up her pain as if they were blotting paper.

Her father said nothing. He watched as he might a sheep falling beneath a slaughter gun. All he did was close the lid over the black and white keys. Tears hurried into her eyes and her nose. They dripped onto the shiny reflecting wood. One drop hit the metal lock and dispersed over the maker's name, Broadwood & Sons.

Awst | August 2016

The oddest thing. Piano music is drifting from somewhere in front of them. It is coming through an open window from a courtyard below.

'You would think as a vet I would be OK with hospitals,' Mary-Jane tells a nurse who leads her down a long corridor.

The nurse makes no reaction and, as they walk together, Mary-Jane glances left and right at the notices on the walls. Some are very carefully placed, well-spaced and firmly attached to their boards. Others are more loosely pinned and one or two lift in the draught the two women create in walking past them. As they stop outside a small waiting room in which only an elderly couple, two women, are seated, there is a poster about recognising the symptoms of a stroke and the importance of acting quickly. There is a checklist of what to look for and what to do.

Among the jumble of things in her head, she half-recognises the music. It is one of Bach's cantatas. Frustrating. She knows this. Everybody does. Suddenly, Sheep May Safely Graze. Relief. But then, her lover, Amelia, and her uncle enter her mind like an incoming migraine. She winces and screws up her face.

The nurse asks her to take a seat, adding that she will not have to wait very long, the most reassuring thing she has said. But, then, Mary-Jane reminds herself that it is a nurse's job to be reassuring even though she probably knows nothing about the patient. As she lowers herself into what appears to be the least uncomfortable of the chairs, beside a table of domestic and women's magazines, Mary-Jane feels a couple watching her. They remind her of the two who commented on her bare feet when she was being filmed visiting Meic Davis's grave. She can hear their thoughts ticking over. They are surprised that a person as young as herself should be here. The older of the two has obviously had a stroke. Mary-Jane can see one of the symptoms from the checklist on the wall in her face. It has fallen on one side, albeit ever so slightly, but is still noticeable. Then she remembers that she is a vet and she is trained to look for signs. If this lady were an animal, she would be accompanied by her owner and they and the vet would discuss everything over her head and she would not have any knowledge, apart from intuitively, that anything was wrong.

A door opens and, having called a name, a doctor stands in the doorway, as Mary-Jane does countless times a week while trying to spot her next patient. She has always been amused that vets call in clients by the names of their pets. One of the elderly women rises and helps her companion, her husband or wife maybe, but Mary-Jane knows from experience not to jump to conclusions. She struggles to her feet supported in the other's arms. Now the signs of the stroke are much more visible. There seems to be no life in her one arm which has been resting in her lap. She places it carefully in a sling. Mary-Jane observes how she has to throw herself forward from the other leg in order to walk. She is reminded of her mother.

They take a while to reach the office door and pass inside. The door closes and Mary-Jane notices how much better sealed the consulting rooms are than in her own place. There, if you have anything distressing to communicate the whole waiting room can hear if you do not lower your voice.

Twenty minutes later, the couple are back in the waiting room and the patient is readjusting her dead arm in the sling which is made, Mary-Jane notices, from a cashmere scarf and still bears the John Lewis label. The consulting room door is closed again. They always do this at the vets when they have to swab down the examination table and send the cost of the consultation and the medicines which have been prescribed to reception. Their receptionists are always eagle eyed, looking to catch anyone who tries to leave without paying. She puts the magazines on the table beside her into three neat piles according to their genre then scolds herself for doing so.

The consulting room is as small as her own. But there is no examination table. There is a bed against a far wall but it does not appear to have been used much recently. She and the doctor occupy one half of the room. His desk, like her own, is against the wall but, unlike in her room where everything takes place around the table, she and the doctor sit opposite each other with nothing in between them. Nothing that is apart from the knowledge to which he is party and has yet to divulge. As he throws himself into his chair, Mary-Jane notices that his computer screen is positioned so that only he can read it. She makes a mental note of that. There is an in-tray full of folders and her file sits by itself in the centre of the desk. She wonders whether he will reorder the papers after she has left or whether he will simply toss the whole file on top of the others, relieved he has finished for the day.

As she sits erect and uncomfortably studies his desk, he opens her file and removes some papers. She wonders how well he remembers what is in them and whether, as in her meeting with the historian, this is a gesture intended for dramatic effect. It communicates the importance of the knowledge which he possesses and the authority which he has over her. She is worried and feels her heart palpitating. She has enough pills at home to remedy this and she wishes she had taken them. She would like a woman consultant. She wants a doctor like the woman who sold her tablets. She sometimes forgets how men can behave. She decides to curl up inside like a cat in her surgery.

He recalls (for whose benefit she asks herself) how many visits she has made, reminds her of what the different doctors have told her and asks her to recall that they have taken bloods for testing. The word 'bloods' she can focus on. Medics are always taking blood. She understands from being a vet that there are different bottles and they do not necessarily go to one laboratory. She also forgives him summarising everything because most of his patients probably have some form of dementia. She feels like she is in her television programme again. Everything is building up to why she is there, up to what the viewers will be watching for. Then he tells her that all but one of the tests have come back. All but one. She wants to scream. Intuitively, she knows that it is the missing piece on which the whole jigsaw is going to depend.

'They are inconclusive', he says. Inconclusive. She could have coped with anything but this. She cannot abide incomplete. Nothing around her could be allowed to be unfinished.

She is frustrated. The whole week has been nonconclusive. Who is MJ? Is it a Mary Jane or Megan Jane? Is it a woman at all? Is she related to them?

Inconclusive. Yes. She knew that was coming.

Chwefror | February 1874

Mary Jane's hands were shaking, her fingers had turned an earthworm pink. The impact of the cold water into which her sister plunged them sent shockwaves up her arms. She gasped and started shuddering from her shoulders, down through the rest of her body. Her sister placed one of her arms around her and gently kept the young girl's hands in the bowl. One of their brothers peeped through a slightly opened door, met his sister's stern stare and slithered back to the landing. Mary Jane tried to pull her hands clear of the cold that was stiffening them but surrendered to the loving pressure her sister exerted.

Outside the door, whispering speculation as to what had happened to Mary Jane brought the others together. Each constantly looked over their shoulder for a step on the stairs. Mary Jane's sister wrapped a small towel around each hand. Pausing her sobbing and temporarily ceasing the flow of tears, Mary Jane managed a short laugh at how ridiculous she must have looked trying to rub her eyes with bandaged hands the size of her whole face. Her sister brushed away as much of the wetness as she could with her own fingers. She noticed how red Mary Jane's eyes were and how her lips were quivering. Leading the child to the bed, she laid her down near the pillows. Neither spoke. Mary Jane had surrendered herself to her father whom she knew was going to hurt her, but this time she knew that she was with someone she could trust.

Mary Jane's sister used gestures and gentle touches to lead her from moment to moment, as she might have done with a sick animal. She studied her face to discern whether the cold water had eased the pain and observed how Mary Jane had crossed her towel-wrapped hands over her chest. Every thirty seconds or so, Mary Jane pulled them closer indicating how her pain must be coming intermittently in waves. Her sister let her be for a while, simply sitting beside her. Together, they listened to an owl and before too long Mary Jane seemed quieter although her chest still heaved.

After some time, Mary Jane's sister asked her how her fingers were. Her lips began shivering and her eyes welled again with tears.

Her sister hugged her, avoiding squeezing her hands. Waiting for Mary Jane to quieten herself, she lifted each hand to her chest and slowly unrolled the towels from around them. Mary Jane watched for a while, thinking it was like seeing someone unwrap a Christmas gift, but then she stared into the night outside the window. Her hands were redder than they had been and were very swollen. Blue-black bruises began to colour her skin. On some fingers, they dipped into a blood-red sheen. Her one hand seemed worse than the other and several of her fingers cast claw-like shadows in the candle light. Mary Jane winced, almost withdrawing from her sister at every touch but slowly her sister rubbed a sticky cream over the backs and palms of Mary Jane's hands. One at a time, she did the same with each finger, taking longer with some than with others, allowing the depth of the bruises to guide her, and spreading more of the ointment in layers on the ones that seemed the most injured. Then she wrapped a single cloth around each hand, noticing from her sister's face that she was experiencing some relief. Two fingers were especially difficult to close inside the glove she was making, they were already turning cobalt blue at the edges and the nails darkening. She stretched the cloth to reach and cover them so that she did not have to bend them.

'Why do you think, he did this to me?' Mary Jane asked. 'Am I so bad?'

'No, you are not bad,' her sister replied. 'Sometimes I feel our father is mad. When he is frightened, I think he finds it difficult to keep in control of himself. He is afraid of something and he takes it out on us.'

'What do you think he is afraid of?' the little girl asked.

Her sister could not answer. Mary Jane was too young to understand.

'I saw the devil in the parlour. I wanted Father to hurt me to drive him out. The devil was there because of me,' she said.

Her sister shushed her gently. 'You must never talk like that,' she said.

Minutes later, Mary Jane was quiet again and rested her head on her sister's pillow. Her sister lifted Mary Jane's legs and feet onto the bed, slipping off her shoes. It seemed to her best to let her sleep. Her father had once said to her that the way to give relief to a sick animal, after you had applied all the medication you had, was to let it sleep. Mary Jane woke for a minute or two. She brought her sister's hand close to her lips, smiled and kissed it.

'Can I spend the night in your bed?' she whispered.

She had one favourite toy, a woollen cat scarred and threadbare by the battles it had seen. One of her brothers brought it to his sister's room and tucked it between her sleeping face and the blankets heaped around her.

As Mary Jane slept, she dreamed. In her dream, she was in what she came to call 'the time before'. The time before now. Years she could barely recall but which she knew were happy years. A large, woolly mammoth, built to survive the cold, looks at her as if he recognises her.

After this punishment in the parlour, she worried about being alone. When she was by herself things began to form at the back of her mind. She always knew when they were coming because she would feel the hairs at the nape of her neck rising.

They were like dark dreams except they were not quite dreams. As she became older, they came more frequently but she found them no easier to describe. She once used the word 'visions'. But they were not visions exactly. She thought of herself as looking deep into the unimaginable past. Her fears swirled around her. One night, she dreamed she was being eaten by a rat, she could hear its teeth grinding and the twitchy movements of its jaws. She woke up screaming. Nothing after was quite the same.

'Your mother,' the doctor says 'definitely has Front Temporal Lobar Degeneration.'

'FTLD,' she says because she wants to speak with him as two scientists together and she likes her science in boxes. Science is about exactness, formulae and acronyms. This is her definition of the scientific brain. And she has a scientific brain.

'FTLD,' he repeats, and then pauses as if to check that he has satisfied her, before continuing, 'which began when she was in her 40s. You reported that, as a teenager, you yourself observed changes in her behaviour and her mood swings that were starting to cause problems in the family.'

So, she said to herself, here comes the evidence. Then the analysis. They are scientists talking together. But he is moving quickly to conclusions.

'There has been a slow but progressive atrophy of her frontal and temporal lobe cortices. While this process starting at an early age is not usual, it is not unheard of.' She wonders what 'early' means in his vocabulary. 'Similar cases have been found in young people, half your age.' He looks at her in a short, steady gaze. He has noticed her age, which is the first time Mary-Jane feels that she has registered with him as a person in her own right. Then, he continues: 'These pathological changes, if you like, have resulted in the gradual deterioration in behaviour, personality and speech which you and the rest of the family have witnessed.'

Mary-Jane begins walking through her childhood and adolescence. Her eyes are wide open. She notices, every back turned indifferently on her, every sudden shout, every uncontrolled outburst, every hurtful word, every slurring of consonants and every confusion of language. It takes her a while to return to the present. The doctor reminds her of how she sometimes addresses her clients. He sounds like a voiceover in the documentary about her family past.

'The memory is relatively preserved in the early stages of this illness. But that is only in the early stages.' There it is again. That word, 'early'. She makes a mental note to ask him to clarify this, realising that she will probably forget to do so. 'Then we have the more severe pathological occurrences which lead to overlaps with corticobasal degeneration and Parkinson syndromes.' He pauses. Fidgets. 'In your case, we would not expect to see the onset of FTLD for another fifteen or twenty years. You are physically in good shape.' Mary-Jane feels his eyes probing her. 'The tests hint of the beginnings of change in your microtubule associated protein.'

She stares at the desk as if she is finding its need of organising and tidying very distractive.

'I noticed some time ago in addition to her mood swings ... semantic dementia ...'

'And in yourself?' he asks.

She shakes her head.

'I am fine,' she says while deliberately avoiding his eyes.

He seems thoughtful, poised in his chair like a tennis umpire, about to pounce.

'It is thought to be genetic,' the doctor says. 'There may be evidence further back in your family, especially as they became older.'

'Like my mother,' she says.

'Maybe not as severe.' She notices that he is becoming more careful, choosing his words slowly. 'But at your mother's age is when people are most at risk, as we would expect.' He pauses. 'That said, there have been incidences in much younger people, where selective frontal or temporal reduction in blood flow or metabolism has resulted in changes in behaviour or mental capacity. Of course, even a short time ago none of this would have been accurately diagnosed.'

Mary-Jane notices that he has become more of a scientist. She tries to bring the doctor back into the room.

'So, what would I be looking for in the family?' she asks.

'Well, FTLD would be difficult to locate exactly even where there were serious personality changes. After all, there are so many pathological and psychological variants. But we would be talking about gradual personality and behavioural changes over a period of, say, ten years. If this occurred in people of a relatively young age, say in their early and mid-twenties, this could be a powerful indicator of FTLD in your family, especially if you were able to identify which side of the family and how it entered.'

Mary-Jane had not thought of it quite in these terms before. Family trees branch in so many different directions. Different family trees become entangled. These interconnections are often about migration. Family secrets can begin almost anywhere, in geography and time. But they must start somewhere.

'What kind of symptoms would be displayed ... in ... say younger people?'

Mary-Jane is no longer thinking about her mother or herself.

'We have not identified many cases and they are all very recent. There is a report of a young woman who began to present symptoms of anxiety, depressed mood, and frequent transitions between laughter and tears. Others have presented symptoms such as delusional ideas, bizarre behaviours especially around sexual instincts, compulsive behaviours and neglect of personal hygiene. Of course, not all of these need present themselves in any one person. They may be brought on by trauma of some kind.'

'I don't have much to look forward to it seems,' Mary-Jane quips.

'Look,' he says, 'you are a vet, a doctor yourself, you know as well as I do we catch a lot of things today which in even the recent past would have gone unnoticed. The earlier we can diagnose something, the better our chances of, at least, mitigating its effects.'

Mary-Jane notices he has returned her papers to her file. He does not toss them between the cardboard covers but he doesn't order them and ensure they are all in their right place. That really worries her. She wants to pick up the file and organise it herself. Out of the corner of her eye, she has watched him shuffling them as he talks with her, as if he is finding this conversation as uncomfortable as she is. She wants to lean over and make sure that the pages in her file follow each other consecutively.

Eventually, she looks him straight in the eye.

'But my case is inconclusive, right?'

Now 'inconclusive' is good. There is hope in the word.

She says it over to herself as she rises to leave.

After she has re-entered the waiting room and closed the door behind her, she can hear the music from outside again. She curses. She has forgotten to ask him. What is his definition of 'early'?

Chapter Five
Kate Kelly

Have you hurt her? You have hurt her, haven't you? What have you done to her? Tell me.

If you have hurt my baby Jane, it will be the worse for you. Don't you bar my way. I am going to her. You put that key away. I want to see what you have done.

Why do you hate us? You hate us, don't you? If you have hurt her, I swear I will leave this place and take the children with me. You blame us for heaven knows what but it is you who brought us to this god-for-saken town.

Our children do not even speak English anymore. We cannot understand them half the time. They talk among themselves. Every night when you are out, with your friends, pretending to be somebody, they are upstairs, in their rooms, whispering in Welsh. I can hear them. I listen to them talking about us. In Welsh because they do not trust us. Our own children do not have faith in their parents. And it is because of you. Do you not think they are plotting? No, you, too, have heard them. Is that what's wrong with you? I promise you, one more buckle belt on any one of them and you are on your own.

Get out of the way. You are not the man I married. You are your father. Mother of God. That's it, you can only hit women and children. In the way you speak and look at me. I see him in you everyday.

Open this door.

What would your fine civic friends say now if they saw how you treated your wife? Your children? If they knew what you have done to us.

Let me out.

I want to go to Mary Jane.

I am going to tell them. Can you hear me? I am going to tell them. I am going to reveal all your secrets. They will see I am not the drunkard you tell everyone I am. It is not me who is sick in the head.

Yes, I know what you say about me. They will discover what kind of man you are. Then we'll see, we'll all see, how many of their fine lunches you get invited to then? Let me out. You have broken my nose. Unlock this door at once. Do they know you in the town hall? Do they really know you, like we do?

He did not expect this outburst of vitriol. He doesn't know who she is anymore. He can hear through the locked door between them how much she is repulsed by him. Why is he so surprised? There has been nothing between them for years now. They exchange mouthfuls of words when one of them angers the other, sparing like bare-knuckle fighters. She makes him dig down to a weaponry he never knew was inside him. He doesn't think about what he has done to her. She is sick, she has always been sick. He can't get beyond that. He knows nothing of the black liquid swilling inside her head. He doesn't understand how terrible it is. How it is like being tied and gagged in a dark cellar from which there is no escape.

He wanted to love her, more than the others, differently. But she never gave him anything in return. He no longer trusts her. Then, he tells himself that he did what she wanted. She needs a father whom she can respect, who will stand up to her, whom she isn't afraid to go into the clouds with. She craves a father who is different from her mother.

But all his thoughts are ragged and unreal.

Chapter Six
Out of Sight

Tachwedd | November 1994

They became more and more unreal. That was the problem. When she was too old for stories about ponies and teens falling in and out with each other, Mary-Jane attended an after-school biology class. It gave the science department an opportunity to teach some topics more thoroughly or subjects that weren't even in the curriculum.

In one session, Mary-Jane and her fellow enthusiasts are given a sheep's eye to dissect. They have been supplied by the local slaughterhouse, owned by her uncle, and to Mary-Jane they look like stuffed mushrooms on a plate of hors d'oeuvres.

'You have a vivid imagination, Mary-Jane,' her father says when she tells him. When he was in school, they did a lot of dissection, earthworms, frogs, rats, organs.

Her teacher always wore the same disgruntled expression and Mary-Jane could never understand why she chose to become a teacher. But in these extracurricular classes, she is a different person, alive and enthusiastic, moving among the children, making her way from activity to activity, like a puppy suddenly free of its leash. Here, in this small *clwb ar ôl ysgol*, she enjoys children and she talks with them as young adults.

Mary-Jane remembers this particular club meeting. How she hesitated with a sharp scalpel in her hands, feeling a strange chill even though the laboratory was warm and fuggy with the sticky sweat of children. How it made her feel, momentarily, no longer herself. When the teacher comes to stand next to her, talking excitedly, Mary-Jane is unusually shy. She is fourteen and, of course, confusion is creeping up on her. She listens to her tutor and allows her hands to be manipulated as if she is no longer in her own body. After the teacher has made her way to another bench and another student, Mary-Jane orders and reorders her instruments, searching for an exact symmetry and insisting on the perfect pattern. She does not know why she is doing this. Perhaps it is a kind of shield to protect her from what spills out into her dissecting tray, what she has always feared was on the other side. She realises how much she she needs order, symmetry and structure. When things become difficult for her in the laboratory, when she has to work in a group where friends toss aside their knives, tweezers and needles, urgently and chaotically, she has to regulate her breathing and can be seen checking the buttons on her lab coat, over and over, pulling at loose threads.

In this particular lesson, Mary-Jane has to follow a worksheet as she does in the usual classes. But the pupils are working individually, not in groups. She likes the organisation in the worksheets, everything is carefully structured and based on observation, and she thinks they may have been used by pupils in her mother's school days. It looks like a page from a textbook belonging to one of her parents that she found at home when she was younger. It is divided into four parts: External Anatomy, Internal Posterior Anatomy, Internal Anterior Anatomy, Cornea & Lens. Not everything has to do with sheep. Beginning with pointing out signs of ageing, such as cloudiness of the cornea, it takes her into the eye from the rear to the front. The lens is compared with an onion, in that it is hard and is composed of layers. But what interests her most are the questions about cataract and glaucoma. These are terms she has heard in relation to her grandparents. Most of the pupils in the afterschool club do not know what they mean and have to call their teacher over or turn around and ask Mary-Jane. She has a reputation for her interest in medicine.

The teacher is talking over all their heads, telling them things that are not in the worksheet. She is giving them what she calls latest research and is encouraging them to think along these lines. Mary-Jane finds this exciting and reminds herself that she is happier in school now than she would have been in her mother's day. The teacher is telling them how scientists have discovered that 'eyes say it all'. Look at the eyes in front of you, she tells them. They answer questions about the creature's place in the pecking order, whether it is a hunter or hunted. Hunters who are taller and chase down their prey have round pupils. Animals, like sheep and deer, have eyes with horizontally elongated pupils. Their eyes are on the side of their head which gives them panoramic vision, so they can scan in all directions for danger. Later, Mary-Jane was to discover something unexpected that changed the way she thought about the eyes of sheep and the relationship between hunted and predator.

When she attended university, she learned that the ability to see in all directions only works if the animal's pupils are parallel with the horizon. Animals like sheep are always pitching their heads down to graze like a cleaner sloshing a floor, bopping up and down. Then they are most vulnerable to wolves, foxes and out-of-control dogs. Scientists in her veterinary school suggested that when sheep and horses lowered their heads, their eyes rotated in their skulls to maintain their parallelism with the ground. As a woman walking home alone, late of an evening, she found herself thinking about her ability to scan the environment around her and wished she, too, had pupils that rolled in her head.

Awst | August 2016

Perhaps it was because of the way she rolled her eyes. For a few moments one afternoon, Mary-Jane believes her mother remembers her. Gwen comments on her cards and seems to think that she has been taken ill and will soon recover. She is appreciative of her family and friends who have sent them. It is as if it is her birthday and she is late getting out of bed because she has been opening presents. Mary-Jane is the child again who on her mother's birthdays would bring her a cup of tea and toast. She would pour three or four cups downstairs in the kitchen and bring her the one that looked the most drinkable along with the least burnt of the toast.

Mary-Jane gathers a few cards at a time and presents her mother with them as if they are snacks. She helps her read them. Her mother nods and smiles at each one as if she recognises who has sent it. And she waits patiently while Mary-Jane rearranges them on the chest of drawers and the window sill.

When she sees her brother's card, her mother's eyes become moist. They have not got on well together for years and it is a while since she has seen him. She seems pleased to have this card, as if it is some kind of reconciliation. She does not know that her daughter has sent it, forging her uncle's writing. Then she sheds a few tears. The tears stream ceaselessly along the wrinkles beneath her eyes. They follow the line of her Sullivan nose and drip from the chisel of her country Irish chin, as Mary-Jane always describes it. She sobs softly, not for very long, but Mary-Jane finds it difficult to watch.

Mary-Jane holds her mother's hand. They are the closest they have been for some time. Her mother lets her head fall back onto her pillow and she stares at the ceiling. Mary-Jane releases her hand and adjusts herself in the arm chair beside her mother's bed. She looks at her kindly. She is not asleep. Mary-Jane doesn't know if or what her mother is thinking. Or, for sure, whether she knows where she is. Mary-Jane leans forward and touches her mother's chin. Remaining tears dissolve over her finger tips. Her mother puts them to her mouth and kisses them. Then she lets her daughter's hand fall.

Among her memories, one of her mother's friends has lit the

fire at home. Everyone is worried because her mother is sick. The side of the fire that is alight burns noisily. They are not used to making fires thinks Mary-Jane. A nugget of coal falls into the grate. It makes her jump and she looks to her mother, concerned that it might have startled her. But Gwen appears not to have heard anything. Mary-Jane rises quickly and grabs the coal in a pair of tongs. She turns toward her mother, thinking of showing it to her, as if it were a pulled tooth, before tossing it into the throat of the chimney. The heaped fire stirs slightly, moving forward as if it has suddenly come to life. Mary-Jane straightens herself and moves away, conscious of how the heat is flushing her face.

Her mother raises herself on her pillows and follows her daughter's movements around the bed. She seems receptive and looks as if she is ready to talk. Mary-Jane feels the moment is right.

'Do you remember talk of a Mary Jane Davis in the family?' she asks.

Her mother shakes her head. Mary-Jane is not sure whether she has understood her.

'Davises, from Llanrwst,' she amplifies.

'Sullivan,' her mother says in response. 'We are all Sullivans.'

Mary-Jane nods.

'Yes.' she says. 'But Meic Davis is from Denbighshire. He moved to Llanelli.'

Her mother's face is expressionless. Her brow is furrowed. She thinks again.

'Mary Jane Sullivan?'

It is a long shot but Mary-Jane thinks that she will give it a try.

'From Limerick,' her mother says.

This time she does not seem to be asking her daughter a

question. Mary-Jane knows the family came from Ireland but from Dublin. They were well-off Dubliners and bought a farm. She has never heard mention of Limerick.

'We are Dubliners,' Mary-Jane says deciding that this is the only way to keep her mother alert.

Her mother seems to understand. She nods and mentions the area of Dublin where most of their family still live.

'Mary Jane Sullivan?' she tries again now she thinks her mother can remember Dublin.

So far it has been a kind of pillow-quiet conversation, the kind of exchange shortly before sleep. Every visit, Mary-Jane watches the woman whom she had come to value too late in her life shredding like Banky's Girl with Balloon before her eyes. But Gwen suddenly turns sharp. Mary-Jane has seen this before but it still takes her by surprise.

'Dewch â gwydraid o ddŵr ataf.' (Bring me a glass of water)

She speaks quietly but demandingly. The water is in a plastic jug. It is filled with fresh water three times a day. When Mary-Jane pours out a cup full, bubbles rise as far as the water level will allow. Then they disperse and disappear. This is not something she would ordinarily notice but of late she has begun to observe all kinds of ordinary things which have previously passed her by. As she focuses on the water level, it becomes a boundary between the energy in the freshly poured water beneath it and the seemingly empty air above.

'Dewch â gwydraid o ddŵr ataf,' her mother repeats.

Mary-Jane hands her mother the drink, noticing how much more wrinkled the backs of her hands are becoming and how much rounder the mole marks as the family always called them. Gwen simply sips enough water to moisten her lips.

Mary-Jane ponders the boundary between memory and … nothing. Sometimes, the pain of trying to remember something is too hard, like punching through a brick wall.

'Kelly,' Gwen spits.

For a moment, Mary-Jane thinks her mother is remembering the ancestors no one speaks about.

'No,' her mother decides, 'we are not Kellys. We do not belong to them.'

Her mother stops listening and returns to her pillow. But she is not falling asleep. The furrows below her hair are deeper and closer together. As a teenager, Mary-Jane had learnt to read her mother's lines like the sky. She knew when a storm was coming. A cloudburst to be avoided.

'I must go now, Mam,' she says but without believing her mother is paying her much attention.

She makes her way to the door and, on looking back, she sees that her mother has closed her eyes.

'The Limericks,' her mother says.

Chwefror | February 1874

She is not recovering. Mammy, you should look at Mary Jane's hands. Two of her fingers may be broken. The swelling hasn't gone down. We need to take her to the doctor.

Wake up. Wake up. Can you hear what I am telling you? A doctor needs to look at Mary Jane's hands. Her fingers need splinting.

You have to stop him hurting us, Mammy. He is getting worse. You need to come and look at Mary Jane's hands.

What's this? Are you even conscious? Are you drinking this stuff again? Does he know?

Sweet Jesus. Don't let him find you like this when he comes in. Mammy, you cannot keep crawling into these bottles.

If he finds you like this, he will murder us.

We need you, Mammy. To be strong again. We have to stand up to him. Wake up, Mammy. So, why are you like this? Now of all times.

Can you hear me? Mary Jane has to see a doctor. They are talking about her hands in school. She cannot hold her pen. She cannot even pick anything up. Everyone can see that she has broken fingers. She's in excruciating pain.

For heaven's sake, Mammy, wake up.

Chapter Seven
Troubled Days and Nightmares

Medi | September 2016

An Indian summer they call it in English, but in this part of Wales, Haf Bach Mihangel. Cloud has started to arrive, hiding the sun, but the pressure on the street continues to build. There is no escape. People stroll in T-shirts, most of them in sandals and quite a few in shorts. This is not a day for the elderly who walk slowly between huffs and gasps. All the bench places in the shade are taken and the young do not give up their seats. Café doors are forced ajar and chairs and tables outside are at a premium. Drivers switch off their engines smartly and move into whatever shade is available. A thunder storm is on the way one says to another. Dustbin liners have been in place all day, covering windscreens in parking spaces where there are no trees. Smaller shops put bowls of water on the pavements for tongue-lolling dogs. Most conversations seem to be about the heat and where it has come from with the older folks pulling at their collars or fanning themselves beneath a dress top lifted with their other hand. Salad vegetables are stuffed into bags-for-life and hardly anyone stops by the butcher's window. Still, people sip hot coffee and tea. Hardly any of them mention climate change but the smothering temperature seems to have caught everyone out, everyone that is who has difficulty remembering the hot May a few years previously or years before that when hosepipes were banned and baths outlawed.

In the corner of a small, suffocating operating theatre, 'Cymru USA' by the Welsh-language singer Meinir Gwilym closes the radio's lunchtime show. They can all feel the heat outside pressing in. One of the animal nurses, all of them in loose-fitting blue T-shirts, flapping trousers and clogs, begins to sway at the hips while she clears up the work space around Mary-Jane. Mary-Jane's bare feet quietly squelch as the polished floor releases them. All the nurses admire her. She is a fast worker, focussed and efficient. Some of the practice's clients are not so sure. She can be brusque and impatient with them, especially with their rambling anecdotes about their special friends, their 'ffrind arbennig'. She is often better with children. They struggle to hold up their pets to her, which are often too large for their tiny hands, and keep them in mid-air as if they are an offering at harvest festival. Mary-Jane always accepts them, priestlike, with a reassuring smile. In her wider palms, their pets immediately look more comfortable. This pleases the children. They become more confident and relaxed. Half the battle she always thinks.

The creature on which Mary-Jane has been operating is as small as a tv meal. But it is some child's best friend and she will be coming in a few hours hoping to take it home. When she concentrates, Mary-Jane raises herself forward on her toes. She cannot stop thinking about MJ. She doesn't know what the evidence is for the name being Mary Jane or Megan Jane, but she feels instinctively that it is Mary Jane. The troubling nature of the way the initials have been carved, so differently from anything else on the gravestone, makes the whole figure of Mary Jane a trembling presence.

Thinking about these initials seem to summarise for her what being human means. Someone cared enough about Meic Davis to carve, or have carved, their initials on the gravestone. It makes her think of the hand of a dying person being held, a touch of bodily warmth, cynhesrwydd corfforol, to be carried forward into death. She has seen a cat who has lived all their life with a beagle curl up beside the dog as it dies, one consoling the other, a sharing of something between them at a deep, albeit primitive, level. She cannot help think about how the sympathy MJ had for Meic came from a shared knowledge of loss, agony and nightmare. She turns the words over in her mother tongue as if there is a taste to them. A taste which lingers. Deeper than this is her intuition that MJ is female and how both she and Mary-Jane share the struggle and pain in being that, a woman.

For a moment, the 2.00 pm news headlines startle everyone in the room and stops the animal nurses from gyrating as they move between cupboards and tables. The details follow quickly after the other stories in the bulletin have been briefly bullet-pointed. 'What?' they mouth as they look at each other while still listening. There are no further details but one of the nurses summarises what she can hardly believe.

'A car driven over four tents on a campsite?'

'What is our country coming to?' another despairs.

The radio moves through another story involving a fight outside a pub, nothing as shocking as the campsite incident, before the bulletin moves to report an animal market closing in a few months. This is due to rising costs, a shortage of animals and several cases of tuberculosis. When the newscaster mentions the last detail, 'achosion o'r diciâu yn yr ardal', Mary-Jane raises her eyes to the ceiling. It is as much of a shock to everyone in the room as the campsite story.

As another song starts to play at the end of the news, Mary-Jane returns to thinking about MJ.

'Who are you?' she asks herself, almost but not quite outloud. 'Do you even know who you are?'

Mary-Jane is not sure why she is asking herself this. Maybe she is more stressed than she has realised. The next piece of filming is very near now. She is worried. She has started talking to Mary Jane herself. It is haunting her, scaring her, the nature of those letters in which the initials MJ had been carved. It seems that only she has seen the desperation in them.

She scans the tray of operating instruments which has been prepared for her. She is searching for a needle fine enough to stitch a rabbit's stomach together. It is handed to her by Angharad who has been following her carefully. Angharad was bullied in school because of her high-pitched voice and strange accent. She lost all confidence. Her mother took her to a stable where riding was a kind of therapy. Contact with the non-human made her human again.

Now she is back where she wants to be. Almost. Mary-Jane knows that she should take her under her wing. But she cannot. She has lost her father and is losing her mother. She understands suffering. But she is trying to hold on to her former self. She cannot involve herself closely with another troubled soul. Besides, she has a new girl-friend who is herself complex and demanding.

Mary-Jane feels herself slipping away. She likes the operating theatre and the laboratory. She loses everything in surgery. She is never happier than when she is surrounded by instruments. She is considering an MSc in veterinary anatomy.

The rabbit's eyes are red and shiny like drops of fresh blood. Mary-Jane thinks the small creature looks like a cute piece of taxidermy, remembering how the Victorians placed even smaller animals in human scenes, such as weddings, parties, shops and living rooms. She doesn't ask Angharad what she thinks. But she beckons her to stand closer so she can see more clearly. She studies her specimen which she imagines in a bubble of sleep that she is about to burst. Like a spellbinder she will return it to life. She has always been able to understand the appeal of taxidermy, life with everything messy and rotting removed. But as soon as you remove what is distasteful and toxic from life, it ceases to be life.

As her needle makes tiny holes in the delicate flesh, Angharad would love to be invited to help with the stitching. But she is not asked. Mary-Jane thinks of the anaesthetised and the unanaesthetised rabbit as two concurrent states like her life with her mother and the life she is beginning to share with Mary Jane. She fantasises about travelling back to the past. Meic Davis and MJ are still there, standing as if on a station, waiting for time to return so that everything could start over again. Only, it does not feel like a fantasy. She wonders at the fragility of her creature's belly that is now almost zipped up the centre. It is as if the opened and closed bellies exist in different periods of time, almost able to touch each other but not quite. She watches her fingers as if they belong to someone else, pushing the needle in and out of minute tunnels, entering, emerging, and coiling the thread. This often happens when she is operating, it is the closest that she ever comes to an out-of-body experience.

There are too many thoughts in her head like too many open files on a computer. She almost pricks herself with her own needle. 'What is the matter with you?' she asks herself, usually not letting her mind wander as much as this. She shakes her head as if to refocus her brain before looking around the room, only to find that everyone is in their place and waiting for her. No one has noticed her needle slip.

At last, she decides to let Angharad take over some of the stitching. She is delighted. She has long, white fingers and Mary-Jane steps aside but observes her very closely. There is a stiffness in the way she manipulates the needle and thread which Mary-Jane finds unusual. It is one of the many things that interest her about this new nurse.

She looks to the clock, estimating how much anaesthetic time is left. It makes her think about her mother again, how all her friends are remembering her, wondering how it will all end. Then she stares at the wall itself and feels the straining immensity of time and space beyond.

Halfway along the zipline of stitches, she encourages Angharad to press the skin around it. This is something Angharad has seen Mary-Jane do on numerous occasions. Everyone has observed how Mary-Jane appears to listen to the tension in the skin, wanting to be sure that, when she had finished, the wound would not slip apart. No other vet with whom the nurses have worked studied, felt and listened to wounds as she did. They wondered whether this was something she had invented, learned in another practice or inherited.

Mary-Jane takes over again briefly, before cutting the thread with a small scissors. With gentle hands, Angharad lifts the small bloated body, like a pasty, onto a tray and then into a small cage to await consciousness. She does it all with such kindness. It makes Mary-Jane think about her again and what she might become with more support. After all, women have a shared history of oppression and must support each other. They are sisters.

As the nurses clear away the instruments, disinfect the surfaces and reorder the room, Mary-Jane ponders how different her world is from that in which the mysterious MJ had lived. Whoever MJ was, she had no understanding of air flight, motor cars, nuclear weapons, terrorism, the internet, supermarkets and self-service checkouts. She thought of how much had changed in her mother's life and about what would unfold in the future. But what really begins to worry her is that in a few decades, like her mother, she may have difficulty remembering all of this. People might still refer to her as the vet but she will only stare back, blankly.

Mai | *May 1876*

Although early summer, the kitchen floor was metal cold to Megan's feet. The unusual intensity and high pitch of the bleating had brought her to the kitchen window. It was noticeable also to the men and women herding the last few lambs together for the slaughter house and, to judge by their flattening ears, even the dogs.

Eventually, the last and most stubborn of them stood in the large wagon bleating in a slipping, accusatory kind of way. The pen doors were shut fast and the bolts slid with a screech that drowned the pleading cries of the others.

'Shall we follow behind to give you a hand when you get there?' one of the men asked.

The driver looked quizzically. 'That will not be necessary,' she said.

She wondered whether they would have asked her that if her husband had come for the lambs.

The bars in the gates rattled beside the bodies of the animals left behind. The cart swayed awkwardly as it began to grip the dried mud on the farm lane. Those watching from the yard could still hear the panicky, young sheep as they had been funnelled up the planks of wood, a few at a time. Eventually, the cart was being hauled to the better surface further along. In another few minutes, the two carthorses began to speed up which caused the lambs inside to press against each other even more tightly. For a while, the tall trees marked off its progress.

'Ten in a wagon that size is too many,' the farm staff were still telling each other. 'There is too much strain on the horses.' 'They need more horses.' 'What is she thinking?' 'They should be walked.'

Others took a different view. 'She will have them slaughtered and in the butcher's in Denbigh by tomorrow. Best lamb some will have had in a while.'

John hated this time of year. In addition to everything else, he was worried about what he had to pay. The slaughter house drove a hard bargain. 'We have our margins, like you,' they would always say. 'Everybody's eating less home-reared meat. I do not know what will become of us.' If John took them the best reared, low fat lamb Llanrwst had ever seen, the response would be the same. But he had seen the deliveries coming into Liverpool docks for himself. He knew what they were saying was true. Importing foreign carcasses made no sense to him. How could the Welsh farms afford to survive in face of this competition.

John stood at the back, behind his neighbours. Most of them were from generations of land workers. Solitary country men who lived down hidden lanes. Megan brought him a mug of tea. He was half way down it before he spoke again.

'We need to finish with them,' he said to her and placed the half-drunk tea on the kitchen window sill. 'We need to slaughter our own. We need to train up Meic.'

Megan thought it did not sound like him. He was not a man who spoke easily about this aspect of animal farming.

Medi | September 2016

Troubled day, disturbed night. That evening Mary-Jane's thoughts about Victorian taxidermist scenes return in the jumbled way things do in dreams. Her patient seems to have subdivided itself many times over and identical rabbits in corduroy trousers, heavy boots and cloth caps are laughing with female hamsters and mice whom they are hoping they can take outside. All these figures appear momentarily. Around them is the darkness that surrounds everything. On one table, gambling cards are tossed aside in despair and guinea pigs in police uniforms are slyly watching everyone from the end of the bar.

Suddenly, they all become human. A piano tune chases bar songs around the room and knocked-over bar stools trip up women dancing on and off the tables. They shatter glasses and bottles roll between their feet. Some lose their balance while others deliberately fall into the arms of a male. One of the women stands out from the rest. As a hamster, she had been there all the time in a very neat white blouse and pressed skirt but no bonnet. In human form, she slowly exposes her legs, right up to a lean mutton of thigh, as Mary-

Jane describes it to herself in her sleep, and laughs uproariously before a rabbit dressed as a man, muttering curses into her ear, drags her to a table farther away where men with rabbit and guinea pig faces, and some with tiny, pink, mice hands, throw dice.

The small cubes turn over and display numbers that, even in her dream, Mary-Jane knows are too big for them. They turn into a computer screen where numbers count themselves down in fours. In her dream, Mary-Jane realises that they are years rolling past and for a while they distract her from the singing, the boisterous laughter and the nonsensical arguments occurring everywhere in the room. The guinea pigs in police uniforms are moving towards her. Then all the animals disappear. The woman whom she had first seen as a hamster, is dancing on a table in a tight circle of men and women. She is singing an Irish song with a chorus everyone loves and everyone joins in, including Mary-Jane:

She left her home her castle great
she left her fair young lover
she left her servants and her estate
to follow the Gypsy Rover

Then the Irish singer is outside the bar with her. She has thrown-up and for a while ignores Mary-Jane, looking left and right over the pavement. Mary-Jane is suddenly worried by her. Not worried for her but scared of her. She tries to speak to her but the dream crashes like a computer in a power cut. Everything is lost. In a desperate bid to retain what she will later see in her entirely rational mind as ridiculous, she grabs a pen from her bedside table and scribbles what she can remember on the back of a drinks mat.

This isn't Mary-Jane's first nightmare of this kind. They began after her first visit to Meic's grave. She has returned several times since; the month previously, she had taken her friend, Amelia, with her.

As they enter through a gap between the closed gates and the wall, Amelia is urging her to let go of 'all of this' as she puts it. The change she has seen in her lover in only a few weeks is really bothering her. She is not sure why Mary-Jane has brought her. Or what she is expected to say.

For a moment, Mary-Jane is thinking how quiet the graveyard is, without the camera crew, the two old ladies and the passers-by attracted to the media like hornets to a beer glass. But there are quite a few glasses lying around, as if Mary-Jane and Amelia were strolling over a summer common, along with discarded wrappers, take-away tinfoil trays and assorted cans. There are two circles of ash and the remnants of burnt sticks.

'Someone has had a party,' Mary-Jane observes.

'Or a wake,' her friend replies, sardonically. 'I don't know why you want to spend so much time in grave yards. They give me the shivers,' she says.

'Irish Welsh,' Mary-Jane laughs. 'A maudlin combination.'

Amelia grunts, noticing tall grasses casting spikes of grey shadow on stone. 'How old is this graveyard?' she asks.

'Some say there are graves from the fifteenth century or there abouts, but the oldest I have seen are late eighteenth-century, there are a lot from Victorian times, many of children.'

This makes Amelia wince. Mary-Jane puts her arm around her, trying to step clear of her friend's thick-soled trainers. 'I want you to try to understand. I know it is making things difficult. But it is about my mum. She remembers so little now. I feel that it is down to me to make sure our ancestry can be recorded. It is about me, my identity, the whole family.'

Amelia explains once again how she hates what all this is doing to her friend. Mary-Jane seems tired. We can imagine how many times the two of them have been slogging around this particular circle together. Then she stops, checks her bearings and ushers Amelia onto a diagonal path. She is able to hear her own grassy tread in the silence. Not even a bird, she suddenly realises.

'The grave is over here,' she says, pointing energetically.

'You be careful,' Amelia advises. 'This grass is full of thorns.'

Then, having looked back, it strikes Amelia that they can no longer see their car. Perhaps it is all the cans, broken bottles and plastic glasses they have just seen that is worrying her.

'Will your car be alright?' she asks.

'We will not be long.' Mary-Jane wants to sound reassuring, but she is very distracted now.

As they approach the grave, the stone's lettering seems fainter than on Mary-Jane's first visit. Amelia loves archery, her eyes are keen and perfect over distance. She is unimpressed. 'What did you say his name was?' she asks, with a hint of incredulity.

'Meic Davis, apparently.' Mary-Jane adds 'apparently' as a concession to how she, too, is now seeing the letters.

'It could be anything,' Amelia sighs, a little exaggeratedly.

Mary-Jane is most interested in the 'scratched marks' as she calls them.

Amelia mutters something about that being called right. 'They could be just vertical lines,' she says, not sparing her friend's feelings.

'MJ,' Mary-Jane insists. 'You can feel they are letters with your fingers.' She sounds exasperated and Amelia realises that she has not been brought along for her scepticism.

'I am not much help, am I. Sorry,' she apologises.

'MJ could be several people. Even his sister. But I feel ....' She stops. What is the point, she thinks, and turns away.

'I don't know what I was expecting to find. Or what I was hoping for in dragging you up here.' It is obvious how dispirited she sounds.

As they pass three or four graves, a new thought seems to strike Amelia, and she turns back.

'Did you say these scratches, scratched letters, might have been added some time later?' she asks.

Mary-Jane nods. She is convinced in her own mind, for whatever reason, Meic's partner returned and tried to carve her initials on the stone.

'Why would she not have had her name carved alongside Meic's?' she asks.

'The historian suggested that it might be for want of money,' Mary-Jane says. It is the best explanation she has to offer. Amelia continues unimpressed. The more Mary-Jane thinks about it, the more she starts to convince herself that MJ could be Megan Jane. But, in terms of her coming back later, that makes even less sense.

'Why scratch just MJ? Unless you wanted to be ambiguous.'

Mary-Jane looks at Amelia sideways. She is revealing her love of conspiracy and conspiracy theories. But, yes, she has a point. Was someone being deliberately obtuse? Was there more of a story behind them?

Then, still looking back at the stone, Amelia makes another observation. One that had never occurred to Mary-Jane, but would, she thinks later, have struck an animal activist with experience of protest and break-outs.

'You couldn't have carved your initials there easily.'

Mary-Jane agreed. 'You would have to scratch as best you could. That is granite. You would have had to scratch vigorously, like a prisoner counting the days on their cell wall.'

'But to try and scratch you initials there, you would have had to have lain over the grave. Really, on top of it. Even then, it would be difficult, if not impossible. It would have been so much easier, if you didn't have the right chisels to have carved your initials higher up.'

This had not occurred to Mary-Jane. She isn't sure what to think now.

PART TWO

STRIKING BACK

*You don't get explanations in real life.
You just get moments that are absolutely, utterly,
inexplicably odd.*

Neil Gaiman

Chapter Eight
An Eye to a Kill

Hydref | October 1876

Megan had got up from her bed in the middle of the night to snatch herself a drink. She could hear her father snoring on the other side of the curtain that divided the family sleeping room, otherwise everything was quiet. The stairs were short and before she knew it, she was in the pantry pouring milk. That night there was a full moon dispelling the darkness. Its light seemed to dance around the kitchen. She always had difficulty sleeping on such nights.

Suddenly, the entire kitchen blackened. Darkness so absolute and intense, as if something had passed in front of the moon.

A large anvil of a head, sitting on a haystack of a body, filled the frame of the open door.

'Nefi blw!' she gasped.

What in heaven indeed. She felt everything around her rearranging themselves to make way for the sheer shock of his presence.

His eyes, like large shot-gun barrels, were barely visible behind the curtain of black hair but she could see they were looking right at her and, all the time, he kept moving forward.

Familiar as she was to him, they had never been confined together in such a small space.

She yelled for her father. Velvet John kept swaying, turning his massive hulk, approaching her one second and holding back the next.

Meic was already half a wake and he came down first to see the table upended and pushed to one side by Velvet's mighty bulk. His father was now beside him. He summoned the deep, inner calmness he always managed when faced with danger.

'He's looking for me,' their father explained.

With slightly quickened pace but now very gently, Velvet came nearer.

'Never, never in all my life,' Megan muttered, nervously stunned by the spell her father first, and then her brother, seemed to cast over the bull.

But she had had enough experience of animals to know how unpredictable they were. In her mind was the image of him from earlier that spring rising high on his hind pistons, his entire weight thrusting forward, trying to enter one of their cows.

One of Velvet's extraordinary long horns caught a roasting dish on the dresser. Behind her, Megan heard her mother scream.

'Go back, Mam. Leave him to Meic,' Megan whispered.

Her brother had slipped around to Velvet's side and was gently smacking his hindquarters to encourage him to retreat. As the bull moved clear of the door, Megan advised her father to fetch straw from outside which he did instantly and speedily. Slowly, without creating panic, he and Meic laid a trail for Velvet to follow. Megan found herself becoming concerned for her brother's feet which looked so vulnerable next to Velvet's hammer-like hooves.

'He's all bull, isn't he,' her brother quipped as if distracting himself from the fear of Velvet becoming wild and aggressive. The bull kept turning its head to look back at Megan and her mother. Megan studied his eyes, trying to anticipate what he would do next;

coal black orbs that never seemed to catch any light and never seemed to move.

Twenty minutes later, Velvet was back in his paddock and the downstairs door securely bolted. Megan returned to bed. She lay beside her mother shivering and shaking, trying to come to terms with the idea of such a monster making his way into the house. But she was also transfixed by the way he followed her brother more obediently even than their sheep dogs. He seemed to have two personalities, the gentle Velvet John and the terrifying Black Velvet.

Awst | August 2016

Amelia is well-and-truly inside Mary-Jane's head now. Disturbingly. Only half-awake, she is retaking their walk together through the graveyard. She is looking at Meic's stone very closely. In her imagination, she magnifies it like a picture in her smart phone, in order to focus on those initials. Amelia did not see them as initials, just vertical lines she said. She has convinced herself, or perhaps Mary Jane herself has persuaded her, that the initials stand for Mary Jane.

She conjures up Mary Jane lying on the grave as Amelia had suggested. A young married woman, pregnant with her first child, who has lost her husband. She knows what it meant to be a widow in Victorian Wales. She has a mental picture of her, heavily pregnant, her swollen belly making a shallow hollow in the loose earth. Why would she do that? Then it occurs to her that whoever is lying there, to follow Amelia's idea, probably did not set out to go there and carve their initials or even to lie on the grave. These were spontaneous actions by someone beyond themselves with grief. So distraught that they lie down on top of their husband's corpse, six feet beneath them, and then, unplanned, desperately, carve their initials in this way on his stone.

Unimaginable indeed. But then even more unbelievable,

suppose that the historians are mistaken. That this was not his wife, his partner, but Megan Jane, his sister! Everything turns upside down. Is this the hidden secret in the Sullivan family history? Is this what the television programme's great discovery will be? Not that her great-great-great-grandmother was an Irish Welsh woman from south west Wales whose partner was killed in a pit explosion, but her great-great-great-grandfather's sister who bore his child.

Mary-Jane asks herself if she can live with this, should it prove to be true. If it proves to be the case, she will not tell her mother. Instead of walking to the grave with Amelia, she is following Meic's sister to his grave. She knows nothing about this woman, but she is following her. She sees her fall down on her knees, hitch up her coat and lie down on the grave. But it doesn't necessarily mean that Meic and Megan were lovers. She tells herself not to ignore the love and dependency that can develop between siblings. But if Meic and Megan loved each other that much, what impact did it have on Mary Jane and her marriage, her husband only partly with her and she only partly with him. Which of them scratched their initials, digging and scraping over and over, until the letters formed from the pain that hollowed their hand and wrist? It was impossible to ignore the other, to see anything but the two women in them. Always there would be the other MJ.

Mary-Jane leaves Megan at her brother's grave, like a rag doll tossed out of history. She airbrushes her from her thoughts, as she had erased herself from the farm and the family when it was sold, and returns to Mary Jane. It has to be Mary Jane. She knows that from the way in which the historian spoke of her, confidently, and she's convinced that it will be shored up by what is to come. But the name has an uncomfortable ring to it. It is there in the back of her mind but her memory, as it has a tendency to do, probably out of stress, is failing her.

She reaches for her phone and googles Mary Jane, tagging her to Llanelli and then Carmarthen. The results mention a Mary Jane

Richards, a number of song lyrics and Carmarthen in the First World War. She thinks of googling the pit explosion, to see when and where it was exactly. There is a mention of a pit explosion in Risca but she doesn't know where that is. She almost presses on with the name Mary Jane. But she is too tired, it has been a long day in the surgery, and her visit with her mother has depressed her. She lets her mobile slip from her fingers onto her duvet and tries to summon up her schedule for the following day. She wonders why even that is becoming harder these days. She is exhausted. She thinks that she is operating all morning. If she had kept on searching ... Still, something she does not expect is waiting for her.

Mai | May 1874

Mary Jane's father weighed his shotgun across his upturned palms as if it were a large river trout. This was what he enjoyed doing most. It took him back to the rural life in Ireland which, despite his management job at the foundry, he missed so much. He crouched down next to his gun. The other guns were raised. From now on, no one would dare move. An hour passed. They held their positions. Then, suddenly, a patch of darkness became darker. He had taught the others how to read the darkness. That was it, the far gun thought. But you had to be sure. Everyone continued to wait. The faintest snap of a blade of grass would be enough to spoil everything.

The far gun caught his attention and nodded to an area of darkness which she thought had suddenly become deeper. If there had been more of a moon, they would have seen that he was there. He was moving stealthily beneath a nettle bush pressing into his back. The plant stems were soft and appeared to make no noise as they were moved. But hunters with guns have the sensitivity of field mice. They all thought now that they could hear plants snapping. Mary Jane's father was not sure. He was the most experienced gun and everyone looked to him. Then unmistakeably, something definite. A sound in the far-off bushes, born of movement. The trick now was to coax him forward. The small, burnt brown head, like a three-cornered hat, was studying the clearing in front of it carefully.

Now was the moment of greatest risk. To bring him forward Mary Jane's father would have to make his vixen cry. He could not afford to get this wrong. He had practised all evening in front of a mirror. As he raised his hands to his mouth, his sleeves made the slightest of noises. The fox had stopped. Listening. Kelly and the other guns were listening. The others had heard the sleeve, too. The dark patch they had been studying was subtly lighter. He had moved. Had he gone? Mary Jane's father dared not produce his vixen cry now. Even if it were only the slightest breath too human, the fox would run. He waited, like the others, scanning the darkness. The fox was sniffing the air. His nose suspicious. His ears listening.

Mary Jane's father saw that the darkness, that deep darkness that excited them all, had moved further back. Much further back. The fox would not come forward of his own now. He had never brought a fox in from this distance before. But he thought it would be worth the risk. All the other guns were watching to see what he would do. He had kept his hands near his mouth. All he had to do was get the vixen's pitch right. The dark patch was not moving. The fox was not ready to flee. Yet. The vixen cried. The dog fox heard it. He did not move. That was the sign that Mary Jane's father and all the others had been hoping for. No one, animal or human, was moving now.

He had not lost his touch. The vixen cried again. This time a little louder. Like a child being strangled. It sent insects scurrying along everyone's arms. Silence. The fox had not moved. Would she cry again? She did. Each time, Mary Jane's father was getting more accurate, less human, more animal. He and the fox had merged. A fourth time but not quite as loud as before. Silence. Then, a very timid rustling of leaves. Yes, he was coming forward.

'Reveal yourself. Come on, reveal yourself,' everyone was saying to themselves. They were all waiting on Mary Jane's father. The vixen had to make her move and she did. She cried a fifth time. A much higher pitch. The fourth gun was convinced and suddenly the dog fox was in the clearing. The vixen howled this time, distracting the fox for the split second that was needed. The fourth gun fired. The fox screamed and a second gun scored a hit, too, sending it backward with a monumental kick. Blood poured from its mouth. The fox was twisting in the long grass, turning it red. The guns were nonchalant. All that is except one who moved forward upset by the death throes he was seeing. There had been nothing clean about this kill and he fired both barrels at close range. Even then it was a few more seconds before the thrashing and turning finally came to an end.

The fox lay in front of them all, its eyes had surrendered their brown-gold to the bloated blue of blackberries. The vixen cried again this time from one of the other guns who mocked the evening's work.

'We have him at last,' someone said. Mary Jane's father did not think so. He would have preferred them to have waited longer so they could have shown off a cleaner, less shot-up body.

They broke their guns and removed the cartridges. Mary Jane's father pulled the bloody carcass up by its brush and held it so that they could all see. Then he passed it to one of the others, taking care to keep the blood from his clothes. The vixen cried louder and longer from different parts of the bush. The gun who had the fox at this time swung it at arm's length, smashing its skull against the tree so hard that one of its eyes fell out of its socket. Vixens yelled in celebration. The dog's one eye was completely hidden by blood and the other now a barely visible black hollow. No one had seen where the eye fell.

Awst | August 2016

Impatient clouds are darkening the distant mountain tops. Mary-Jane is intending to spend the night in her mother's house which for many years had been her family home although she has not been there for a while, longer in fact than she feels comfortable to admit. The kitchen has energy-saving light bulbs and when she turns them on, they do not brighten the room very much. She feels that she has to rely on what is left of the early evening sun. There are geraniums on most of the window sills and a dead bee lies on the rim of a saucer in which one of the pots rocks slightly to the touch of her fingers. At first, she thinks the insect is a leftover chocolate, the kind served in expensive hotels. It is so perfectly oval and seems to have a brown, shiny wrapping.

The very first time that Mary-Jane witnessed a serious change in her mother was when she stood in this kitchen waiting for her to come home. She waltzed through the door with an armful of reduced cat food for a pet that had died two years previously. On that occasion, her mother laughed off what she had done. She had made a joke of how she had gone back in time. Thereafter, very slowly, she became increasingly confused. Mary-Jane consulted a doctor behind her back. He advised her to agree with her mother when she was confused and not confront her. Like not waking someone who is sleepwalking, Mary-Jane thought. But the confusion came more often and lasted longer. It showed in her speech, her behaviour and in her face. It made her angry.

From the kitchen, Mary-Jane makes her way to the lounge. The room is as she has always remembered but much untidier. She wants to set about organising everything. She hates clutter. She wonders why she and her mother had fallen out. Searching for photographs that she hopes will help her mother remember things, she finds herself thinking more and more about their relationship. Visiting her in the care home is very difficult and becoming more so. She has decided that she needs to focus her, provide her with subjects around which daughter and mother might build a shared conversation, a discussion that might resuscitate her mother's dead memories. Is that even possible now?

On the fireplace there are two wooden candlesticks with whorled stems which she remembers belonged to her grandmother or even her great-grandmother. There is a Beswick corgi which she remembers her mother buying in a gift shop in Aberystwyth. It has a chip in one of its ears and the brown paint with which Mary-Jane had daubed it as a small child is still there and as an unsuccessful a camouflage as she has always remembered. A small television sits in a corner with the blankness of a dead light bulb. Everywhere the house seems sombre because the curtains are closed. She feels a pair of eyes fixed on her.

In another corner, there is a piano which is a Victorian antique. It is a family heirloom. Neither of them has played it since Mary-Jane were a child. She tries to remember what it was that she used to play when she was younger. She raises the lid and tries to arrange her fingers on the yellowing, ivory keys. Something makes her place a forefinger on a particular black key. But nothing comes to mind. There is a brick wall she cannot break through. It is excruciating. There are memories in her fingers but they remain there. It makes her realise how her mother must be feeling. She closes the lid, relieved that she at least has other paths in her mind she might follow. Not everything is blanked out. The piano has been unplayed for so long, it has acquired a waxy sheen beneath a thin layer of dust. She has a memory of the lid slamming shut but she does not know where it has come from. The piano is so old that she wonders whether the memory is in her head or in the wood itself. But the real surprise comes when she opens the piano stool. There is no sheet music, only some half-drank, miniature bottles of gin and vodka and tiny cans of bitter lemon. She has never known her mother to drink. It is as if she is a child again, discovering a family secret that has been hidden almost in view.

More hurriedly now, she selects some framed photographs from the top of the piano and the mantel piece and returns with them to the kitchen, suddenly aware how few photographs she has on display in her own home. The kitchen door is open and the room has darkened further by a new presence that she cannot decipher. She blinks. Whatever it was has gone. Back to where it had come from.

She doesn't like being alone in what has become her mother's house. It is too quiet and cavernous. She thinks that she hears the letter box open and close and mail thump onto the hall carpet. But it could not have been. It is the wrong time of day. Another slippage. She is running barefoot over the parquet hall to the front door to finally see a letter for which she has been waiting for days. An offer of a place at the veterinary school in Liverpool. She had wished to stay within commuting distance of home, but there were no veterinary colleges in Wales at that time.

The house is so much mustier than she remembers. There is a smell of damp inside the kitchen door which is warped and, now Mary-Jane has opened it, refuses to shut firmly. Her hand searches around the kettle for a plug. As she waits for the water to boil, she ponders whether to sleep over or not. The idea seems less attractive to her now than earlier. If she does so, should see search out some bedding for the sofa in the lounge or find her former bed upstairs. Underneath the breakfast table, there is a pair of her mother's shoes. They remind her of her mother's birdlike fragility. She looks away from them. Three of the drawers in the Welsh dresser are so crammed with papers that they cannot be closed. Before the end of the year, she would have emptied them into a cardboard box file and would be sat at the table sorting through them. There would be a stack of unopened Christmas cards, most of them addressed only to her mother, which would have to be read and acknowledged. There would be a few that had been sent to both of them. She would be spending more time here than in her own home. But she doesn't know that yet.

Ebrill | April 1875

Mary Jane's uncle Fergal was very different from her father. He was studious but always genial and he and Mary Jane enjoyed the occasions when she holidayed with him in Liverpool. One weekend, at breakfast, he watched her peel the shell from a hard-boiled egg and hold it in the sunlight. This was shortly after she had returned from accompanying her sister for almost a year in Paris.

'Which organ in our bodies, apart from the brain,' she asked him, 'do you think is the most awesome?'

'Oh really!' his wife exclaimed, clearly believing such a question was well beyond a girl of her age. But they both noticed that her education in Paris had changed her.

'This is a difficult question to answer,' he reassured her following his wife's reaction. But the fifteen-year-old didn't give him a chance to brush her off.

'I think it might be the eye,' she suggested, turning her egg over and over in her fingers. 'An eye is smaller than this egg,' she continued, 'but it enables us to see the world and make sense … or nonsense … of everything around us.'

'Yes,' Fergal answered enthusiastically. 'It sends all that information to the brain.'

'How does it do that?' Mary Jane asked herself as much as her uncle.

As she did so, she sliced up her egg on her plate. Then she let the slices domino against each other, turning over one of the most evenly circular rings of egg to prod its centre. Although it was mainly hard-boiled, the yellow yoke wept ever so slightly onto the tip of her fork. For a moment, she enjoyed watching the miniscule tension between the solid and the ever so slight liquid.

'Do you think it would be possible to dissect an eye?' she asked him.

Fergal, who had been studying her carefully, put down his tea cup.

'We had to dissect an eye when I was in college,' he said, continuing to explain: 'Not a human eye, of course, but a bull's eye.'

Mary Jane's own eyes opened wide.

'Did you have to do it in a laboratory?' she asked, almost disbelievingly.

'Yes,' he said 'and, secretly, in my lodgings. I still have my old dissection kit. Everything I needed in fact to cut up anything I wanted.'

That was an exaggeration, of course, but Mary Jane looked really interested.

'Do you still dissect eyes?' she asked.

'Of course not,' he laughed. 'But I do still have pictures and some drawings.' Then he paused. 'Would you like to dissect an eye with me?'

Mary Jane was taken by surprise.

'When?' she asked.

Mary Jane's aunt dropped her knife and fork. She rose to gather as many plates and cups from the table as noisily as she could. Her husband ignored her.

'This afternoon. No time like the present. We can go into town and see if the butcher has a couple of eyes. I still have the scalpels and tweezers ... everything we need.'

'A bull's eye isn't like a human eye, is it?' she asked later, as they stood around the table in his study.

'It most certainly is,' he replied. 'It is the closest you can get to a human eye.'

A little later, a bull's eye sat on Mary Jane's dissecting tray swaddled in a coat of fat and tissue. It was greyish white, the colour of an uncooked prawn.

'Nawr, dan ni'n barod,' she said aloud to herself.

Mary Jane remembered her life in scattered images. This particular mind picture stayed with her all her life. Slowly, carefully, following her uncle's instructions, she pierced the muscle with the tip of her knife. Occasionally, he guided her hand as her father had done when she skinned her first rabbit. He used the delicate tweezers to help lift away the thick covering which she sliced through with her scalpel. She commented how very sharp it was and imagined how much it would sting if she cut herself. He noticed how confident she was.

The eyeball became so much more visible with the tissue removed. Fergal pointed out the muscles attached to the outer layer of the eyeball – what he told her was the sclera – and to what he called the optic nerve.

'These muscles,' he explained, 'enable the bull to move its eyes up and down and to left and right. Now move in closer with your scalpel, and gently, very gently, cut away as much of the muscle as you can.'

She was enjoying this. But she didn't like to get too close. The eye smelt like an uncooked pork chop that was, as her mother used to say, on the turn.

'There,' her uncle sighed. 'Come here, stand back. Now you can really see the sclera and the optic nerve.' He paused while she stood beside him and tried to see what he could.

'The next task,' he explained, 'is for you to cut through the sclera around the middle of the eye so that we have two halves.'

As she did so, Fergal again observed how careful she was, almost respectful. As the sclera divided into two parts, she could see what her uncle would soon identify as the cornea and iris attached to one half and the optic nerve to the other. Fergal held up a labelled drawing he had made in college and pointed out what she should now be able to see in the dissected eyeball.

As she studied it, she was impressed by how much colour there was. The mass of tissue at the back of the eye was grey but the cornea was much more bluish in colour. Fergal pointed to the optic nerve with his scalpel.

'This,' he said, with real wonder in his voice, 'is what sends the images which the eye collects to the brain.'

Mary Jane noticed that the eye was full of a dark fluid. Fergal explained that in the living eye all this liquid would be clearer. Then he took over from her for a while and with a pair of long, thin scissors cut away the cornea. He asked Mary Jane to hold out her hands. She did so timidly and he noticed she was trembling. She had been so confident until this point and he couldn't understand the tremors in her fingers. He had never seen her hands up close before and he noticed that she seemed unable to close all of her fingers on her one hand as tightly as the others. He placed the cornea in one of her palms. He wondered how many children might scream and drop the cornea if they were asked to do this but Mary Jane was clearly fascinated as if the cornea were a small ladybird. She touched it with the finger tips of her other hand, as if prodding it to move. It was much tougher and stronger than she expected.

Fergal had successfully avoided cutting the iris or damaging the lens. He lifted the cornea from his niece's hand and returned it gently to the tray. He drew her attention to how the iris overlapped the lens so that it was positioned to control the amount of light entering the eye. He explained how it contracts in bright light and expands in fading light. Then he directed her to remove the Iris. In the dead eye, it had yellowed and become very hard.

'Have you heard the word 'retina'?' he asked her.

She had but she didn't know what it was or what it did. He pointed it out to her. It was thin, tissue-like and slid in the sclera. But she noticed how it was attached in one place to the optic nerve and pointed this out with her scalpel. Fergal nodded, pleased how quickly she had grasped that the eye was all about collecting information and sending it to the brain and how everything was structured to assist and protect this function. He handed her the tweezers and let her lift the retina off the inside wall of the eye. As she did so, she felt that she was looking into a small sea creature. Underneath the retina, the tissue was shiny and colourful.

'This is what enables bulls to see at night. They see much better at night than we do. But because everything is reflected, so much is also distorted.'

In her operating theatre, one hundred and fifty years later, Dr Mary-Jane Sullivan is studying an eye of one of her patients and thinks to herself that life is all mirrors and reflections.

Mehefin | June 1906

We run to the Taff to swim. It is swollen at this point from the summer rain in the hills but not so much that it is flowing fast. The trees protect us and we watch each other openly. I love the play of dappled light on his back and his legs. Later, we lie on the river bank, learning the lines of each other's bodies. We see nothing but each other.

I wonder if my mother will notice a change in us and whether she will be angry. My father is away on a business trip, as he often is, this time searching for new silks in India. What can she do? I am twenty-three years of age. She had left home by then and moved to the city. The breeze is too kind and the sun too gentle to have these thoughts. We take pictures of each other on a box camera. How will we develop them?

Chapter Ten
The Whisperer and the Slaughterman

Mai | May 1878

Meic Davis tried to spend as little time as possible of an evening near the mines and the iron works. He had taken a room above a bakery in the town. It turned out to be suffocatingly hot and he had to have the windows open all the time, even at night. He had bites along the inside of his arms and around his ankles but he wasn't sure whether they were from midges or bed fleas. This was the first time he had had a bedroom to himself. He had been looking forward to that, longing for it, but now he was lonely, missing the warmth and comfort of his family around him and the curtain just beyond which his sister and his mother slept.

Memories of his sister and he together preoccupied him as he walked the hills near Llanelli. Their shared childhood seemed so far away, but still he knew it was there, somewhere. He and Megan playing, quarrelling and fighting, laughing and, like himself now, trampling the hills. She always had confidence, as if she were ready to take on the entire world and knew that she would win. As they lay together as children separated by a flimsy curtain in summer and a hanging, heavy rug in winter, he would dream of them running the farm together after their parents had retired, his father advising them when they needed his help. Sometimes, he remembered an evening while he rested after a day in the hills with the sheep and his father, she came onto his bed with the smell of school and ink-stained fingers. He missed her.

One of his evening walks, led him past a small field of sheep attached to an old farm house. It reminded him of home. He stopped to study them and gradually they made their way toward him. It was as if they wanted something from him. He found himself staring into their faces, as his father used to do, believing that they could read his face too.

'What do you see in my face?' he asked them.

His eyes wandered over the fleece of those closest to him. Three or four of them had been attacked by the fly, none hopelessly yet but it was only a matter of time before the field would be full of half-eaten, dying sheep. The way in which they were neglected made him angry.

He strode to the house. It was quiet and there was no one in the yard. He knocked and then knocked another two or three times. Eventually, reluctantly, a youngish woman came to the door. Apologising for the interruption, he explained what he had seen on the sheep. She seemed not to understand and he wished that he could speak Welsh more fluently, like his sister. An older man, better dressed than many he had seen in these parts and much better attired than himself, appeared behind her. He had come from upstairs and gave Meic the impression that he had just finished dressing. She moved to one side to let him through into the small front garden. He explained in English that her husband was away on business. He spoke in an accent that Meic had never heard before.

'These people,' he said, distancing himself from them, 'know as much about sheep as I do. I expect he will be sending them to slaughter. They came with the house you see and he has no intention of farming. He is in shipping and spends weeks at a time on the continent. You had best come back next month.'

He stood defiantly with his legs slightly apart suggesting that he knew how to take a body blow and deliver one straight from his shoulder. Meic made his way back to the road. The sheep were still gathered together where he had left them. In his room above the bakery, he had a very small medicine chest that his father had given him when he left, just in case he ever returned to farming. At the time, it exasperated him how his father refused to understand that his animal husbandry days were over and he was going to be a miner or a foundryman, not a farmer.

But now he was glad that he had his father's box. He cast his eye over the sheep one more time under the gaze of the commercial traveller, or whoever, and continued his walk. He would return with his chest later in the week.

Mehefin | June 1878

Mary Jane suffered frequently from headaches as her mother did. Serious excruciating headaches. She had long since given up trying to ascertain the cause. What she did regularly, so that it became part of her daily existence, was try to prepare herself for them. She started massaging the edges of her temples, pressing firmly. She sat in the dark for an hour or two each day; drank as much water as she could manage; and lay in lavender-scented baths imagining waves slapping distant shores. For a while, her self-concocted remedies seemed to work. She went about the house with a gentle hum like organ music. But nothing that she did brought her permanent relief. Before very long, pain would possess her and become increasingly intense until her head felt that it would burst. One day, it was so unbearable that she took her thinnest, sharpest kitchen knife and pushed it into her arm.

Awst | August 2016

Mary-Jane finds a table in the café at Cwm Garreg overlooking the hills. Cwm Garreg is a new type of farm. 'Diversified farming' they call it. It is a working farm, a children's zoo, an agricultural centre preserving traditional farming tools and machinery, and a farm shop promising organic, nutritious products. There is a visitor centre selling T-shirts with slogans about enjoying the outdoors and a timetable of activities, 'calendr digwyddiadau'. Mary-Jane notices that all the activities are organised around families and children such as 'Noson Tân Gwyllt' (Bonfire Night), 'Ffair Nadolig' (Christmas Fair), 'Penwythnos Gŵyl Ddewi' (St David's Festival Weekend), 'Sul y Tadau' (Father's Sunday), 'Calan Gaeaf (Wythnos Hanner Tymor)' (Harvest Half-term Festival). It reminds her of *Fferm Ffion* (Ffion's Farm), a novel she bought for one of her nurse's children because of her interest in farming and in animals but which to her mind flagged the end of animal farming in Wales. There are maps of Cwm Garreg everywhere and they might have all have been drawn by Ffion. The car park leads to the main entrance and shop, 'Prif Fynedfa a Siop', next to 'Caffi Cwm Garreg' and, beyond that, exhibitions of the past, 'Tractors Bach a Beiciau Cwad' (Small Tractors and Quad Bikes), 'Sied Beiriannau' (Engine Shed), 'Ysgubor Wair' (Hay Barn) and further still 'Corlan Cwningod' (Rabbits Pen), 'Stablau' (Stables), and 'Cae Ceffylau' (Horses' Field). Everything is geared to families with children, including its zoo, which consists of small animals, the kind Mary-Jane treats every day, and pens of chickens, goats, sheep, lambs in spring, a few pigs and a donkey. There is a picnic area and a small train. While visitors can picnic, horse ride or travel on the small train, most of the large, some people woul say 'real', farm animals are kept at a distance. Behind them, there is a caravan park and something slightly menacing, designed for children's interest in the Gothic, and perhaps adults, too, 'Yr Ardd Ddirgel' (The Secret Garden).

Cwm Garreg is a place that Mary-Jane has been meaning to visit for some time, ever since she had heard an argument among her colleagues in the surgery. They were debating whether it was a good thing for children to be able to see where their food came from. What worried some of them was that Cwm Garreg encouraged children to adopt an animal, as a kind of vicarious pet, and visit it regularly, keep a diary of how it grew and changed over time and receive information as to what the farm was doing to preserve the countryside. Some of her colleagues felt that it was wicked to encourage children to befriend an animal and then risk them turning up one day to find an empty pen after it had been taken to slaughter, probably at the meat processing plant owned by Mary-Jane's uncle, Edward 'Ned' Sullivan.

The view from the window is more comforting than Mary-Jane had expected. In the distance, she can make out the roofs of the village. A waitress moves some of the empty chairs to get nearer her with coffee and some vegan cookies. Vegan cookies in a farm shop. You would not have seen that ten years ago Mary-Jane says to herself. There is a menu on the table which offers Highland breakfasts with black pudding and the best haggis and vegetarian breakfasts where sausage and bacon all come from plants. Having lifted the lid on her laptop, Mary-Jane signs in, scrolls and clicks and finds herself in accounts. Pushing the machine to the edge of the table, she reaches for an envelope from among her papers and slides it open with the blade of a knife which is blunt and makes an untidy, ragged edge. Inside, she searches for a cheque. This must be one of the few parts of the world where people pay their bills with cheques she thinks. She enters the details, then moves the mouse to her mail box with her coffee cup raised to her lips in the other hand. Depressingly, there are over twenty emails waiting her.

Completely absorbed, she does not notice a large man striding up to her table, followed by his wife and two children. Each of them carries a hill-walking stick with a head illustrating the Llandudno promenade, identifying them as tourists.

'Excuse me,' he says, not impolitely but with a tone and loudness that offends her, 'I wonder if we could have this table, since there is only one of you and there is a smaller table over there.'

Mary-Jane looks toward where he is pointing. A small table

with two chairs is crammed into a corner next to the toilet door. There is no window.

'Dyma fy mwrdd a dyma fy marn i. Byddaf yma ychydig'

(This is my table and this is my view. I will be here awhile)

He turns to the woman he is with and then looks at his children. None of them seem ready to help him in the argument he has got himself into. A few tables away a child, of about his children's age, explains what is happening for her grandparents who have difficulty hearing but are very interested in the events unfolding in front of them.

'Maen nhw eisiau iddi symud oherwydd bod mwy ohonyn nhw.'

(They want her to move because there are more of them)

'You do not understand,' he says, as his wife, aware that most of the customers in the café are watching them, tugs at his sleeve as surreptitiously as she can, 'we have ordered dinners and we need a larger table than the one over there which is intended for one or two customers like yourself who have only ordered coffee.'

'A chwci,' she corrects him, then stares at him. A waitress is hovering behind the family with three of their dinners, one balanced on her arm.

'Gallwch fynd â'r cadeiriau. Nid oes eu hangen arnaf. Ond mae angen y bwrdd a'r ffenestr arnaf'.

(You can take the chairs, I do not need them, but I want the table and the window)

The waitress says she will take the meals to the empty table. The family take some steps away from Mary-Jane while the waitress, having put down the food on the other table, returns and gathers the two extra chairs. Mary-Jane thanks her, all the while watching the man who is left deserted by his family who have seated themselves behind their meals.

Eventually, he moves away to join them and occupies the seat which his family have left him nearest the toilet door.

'Did you hear that. She refused to talk with me in English for fuck's safe.'

'Not in front of our children,' their mother hisses.

The children exchange knowing glances and one stifles a giggle.

The waitress leans over his shoulder and puts down some extra cutlery.

'Dyma rai cyllyll a ffyrc ychwanegol,' she says pointedly.

(Here are some additional knives and forks)

Mary-Jane returns to her laptop and waits while she calms herself.

Mehefin | June 1878

Late afternoon, just before the evening sky slid over the sheep, Meic set out to return to them. He took an early evening meal in the Stepney Arms, reading his medical book and checking his small veterinary chest more times than were needed. It was still warm for the time of year, but he carried a coat under his arm just in case it rained. Over the hills, the sun was beginning to set and, in the distance, toward the sea, the sky was streaky and darkening. He decided to hurry, dodging groups of men snatching quick drinks before heading home.

'Excuse me,' someone shouted behind him. He did not turn or even slow down, not expecting anyone to be calling him. He felt a tug at his arm. Someone had caught up with him.

'Excuse me,' a young woman about sixteen or seventeen repeated, holding up a book, 'you left this on your table.'

He had made her run and she was slightly out of breath. As she handed him the volume, she read the title outloud.

'Y Meddyg Anifeiliaid: Yn Cynnwys Achosion, Arwyddion, A Thrinieath Afiechyd.' Then, she asked him, ' Dych chi'h Meddyg Anifeiliaid?' (Are you an animal doctor?)

'Diolch yn fawr iawn.' He could not have been more grateful. He glanced at her quickly before tightening his fingers around what must have been his most precious possession, his bible, explaining that he was not a vet but that he used to work on his parents' farm in the north and, when he had left, his father had given it to him, along with the chest of medicines.

'Na, dwi ddim yn feddyg anifeiliaid. Ond mae llyfr hwn yn fy beibl. Roeddwn i'n arfer gweithio ar fferm fy rhieni yn y gogledd. Pan adawais fy nhad rhoddodd i mi. Mae'r llyfr hwn yn werthfawr i mi.'

He studied her carefully. He could see that beneath her overcoat, she was still in her Stepney Arms Hotel uniform. She carried a handbag and had clearly just finished her shift. He was proud of how the book had been published when Victoria had come to the throne.

She took a book from her bag and held it out so that he could see it.

'Dyma fy hoff lyfr. Menywod Gorllewin America.'

(Here is my favourite book. Women of the American West).

She explained that in ysgol dydd Sul (Sunday School) in Carmarthen, the only books that she could read in Welsh were commentaries on the Bible and some books of poetry. One day, she found this.

'Pwy yw'ch hoff fenyw?' (Who is your favourite woman of the west?) he asked.

She answered immediately.

'Martha Jane Cannary. Mae hi'n chwedlonol'. She recognised that Meic's Welsh was failing him. She sorted around in her English for the right word, 'legendary'. 'Mae hi'n fenyw Americanaidd fodern'. Meic could see that she, too, thought of herself as a modern woman. 'Mae hi'n gwneud yr holl bethau mae dynion yn eu gwneud'. So, he thought, this woman, like Martha Jane Cannary, probably wanted to do all the things that men do, too. She proceeded to give him some examples, all the time watching his eyes to see if his Welsh was keeping up, and sometimes struggling to find the English word to help him.

'Sgowtiaid y fyddin (army scout), ymladdwr Indiaidd (Indian fighter), atodeg merlen mynigi ... pony express rider, a llwythlong wagenni ... wagon freighter'.

She did not expect him to have heard of Martha Jane Canary but she realised he might have heard of Wild Bill Hickok. 'Mae hi'n gwisgo fel dyn ac yn bartner i Wild Bill.' (She dresses like a man and is the partner of Wild Bill Hickok)

She seemed to think that he would be interested in, or perhaps was testing his interest in, women who dressed like men. Martha Jane Canary was a chameleon. She was one, too.

'One is not born a chameleon, one becomes one,' she would tell him later.

As she watched his eyes to see if he were keeping up in Welsh, he was afraid to look away and ended up staring into her eyes, too. They were large, excitable and compelling and reminded him of his sister. She had disclosed a lot about herself, may be more than she realised. He explained that he would often take an evening walk away from the town and a few evenings before, he had found a field full of sheep that needed treating for the fly. Hence, he needed his book and his case.

'A yw'n ddifrifol iawn?' she asked. [Is it very serious?]

Meic was surprised that she had heard of it let alone that she knew it was serious.

'Roedd gan fy nhad ddefaid unwaith'. [My father's sheep had it once]

To his further astonishment, she asked if she could accompany him. They both seemed in the same position with no one waiting for them and only a lonely room to return to.

'Nid oes gennyf unman i fynd ac eithrio i ystafell unig. Mae'n noson resymol.'

Meic accepted the offer of company immediately. However, when she mentioned a reasonable evening, 'noson resymol', he did look up at the sky and out toward the sea. The streaky red had disappeared beneath a developing blanket of cloud.

'Bydd yn rhaid i ni frysio,' (We have to hurry) he urged, hoping that hurrying would not put her off.

She slipped her book back into her bag as if to convince him she was ready.

'Fi yw Meic, Meic Davis,' he said, adding in laughter, 'gyda llaw' (by the way).

She hesitated, as if she were a gambler deciding which card to draw.

'Mary ... Mary Jane.'

He hurried her along Church Street into Market Street, crossed Queen Victoria Road, eventually leaving the town between a small row of derelict cottages and heading to a lane that took them to the small field of sheep.

Along the way, occasionally pausing to allow her to take gasps of breath, he told her how the sheep in the south grazed differently from those in the north. In the hill country where he came from, they gathered at most in twos or threes, many remained alone. He directed her attention to the fields in the distance where the sheep stood in small groups.

As they made their way into the field beside the house, the sheep moved agitatedly from them, some ambling and others jumping. He watched them gather in small groups of three or four and wished he had had Spike, his father's prize sheepdog, with him. He went as close as he dared to three of them, gathered in the corner of the field between the fence and a tree. As he had watched his father do on many occasions, he lay bottles, cloths, a lump of camphor and scissors out on the grass. Glancing nervously at the house, he prepared to take one sheep at a time.

He doubted whether Mary Jane had much familiarity with sheep, but as he watched her slowly work them with him, he was impressed. She seemed to know exactly from which angle to approach them and was obviously not afraid to hold them. They in turn responded calmly. She stood over each one as he treated them, patting their backs and letting them rub their noses in her hands. She seemed to be able to anticipate a change in their mood and when a kick was coming. When he watched her, he could only see a half-outline of her face in the dwindling light. All the time she hummed songs which appeared to come somewhere from deep inside her and he noticed the calming effect they had on the sheep.

'You are happy in this work, aren't you?' he said.

'You seem to relate to them so well, and they to you,' she returned the compliment.

Meic laughed. 'Dyna ddywedodd y chwaer bob amser.' [That is what my sister always said.]

The mention of his sister made Mary Jane think of her own. He hadn't said much about her, but there was an intonation in his voice that conveyed his warmth for her, and, of course, she had noted how he turned to Welsh in remembering her. Clearly, he felt about his sister as she did about hers. That he was a man who cared for his sister made him all the more attractive to her. It was a further bond between them, she thought.

'Did you learn all of this from your father?' she asked, realising she knew so little about him.

'The specifics, this kind of thing, treatments,' he answered with his fingers buried in a fleece.

He was interesting her now. 'And the non-specifics?'

She had not heard the word 'specifics' before and delighted in bouncing it back.

'I think … it flows in the family, from my great-great-grandparents.' He raised his eyes toward her and joyously stressed the 'great'. 'I believe it would have touched my sister, too, if she were to let it.'

'Do you really believe that there are things that flow from generation to generation?' she asked thoughtfully.

'Definitely,' he said. There was no doubt in his mind. 'Like blood. Don't you?'

She pursed her lips and hummed in partial agreement. Possibly. He could not work out whether she shared his view or not or even whether it was a perspective that troubled her.

'A yw'ch chwaer wedi etifeddu'r pethau penodol hyn hefyd?' she asked [Has your sister inherited these 'specifics', too?']

He seemed not to have heard her or to have noticed her shift to Welsh in talking of his sister as he had done in speaking of her. He was straightening himself and stretching his muscles as far as he could. He scanned the field. It was slippery in parts with green-yellow shit. He wondered, despite his early optimism, whether he was too late to save them. But he did not pass this on to Mary Jane.

After an hour or so, she, too, felt the pressure of crouching for so long and standing upright, craving the relief which he had sought in stretching the lines of his body, thumped her back several times to ease the pain.

On the whole, the evening turned out better than he had anticipated. The sun, setting throughout their work, now sent up a vertical beam of light which created a rainbow arc across the large clouds rolling in above them. The beam was white at first and then deepened in colour casting a pink hue over the wider, green landscape.

There was no denying what a filthy and tiresome job this was. He had already had a long day in the mine. There were some sheep they had to really struggle with and the sweat beaded on their foreheads although the evening was becoming cooler. Slowly, the sheep became used to their presence, gradually moving closer together. Some were more nervous than others but he found that with Mary Jane's help, he could creep among them.

Yes, something instinctual, hereditary, was returning to him. Once again, he felt that he was where he should be, free of those long cavernous tunnels where you started upright like a man, before stooping, slouching, bending low, then crawling like a beast. Without the miners' lamps, the blackness was of a kind that he had never seen before, even in the isolated hills of north Wales, without moon or starlight. The light from the lamps was yellow and never stopped quivering. It rose, dipped and shrivelled. There was no air, nothing any one would think of as air, only a heavy soup of coal dust, sweat and damp. Within the darkness, there was the interminable unsteady scrape of boot on stone, of iron hollowing coal, and of heavy gasping and cursing ricocheting off the walls and landing in pools of spit. The blind or near-blind pit ponies dragging wagons of coal distressed him. He would run his fingers around their black, delicate orbs so that they might know him. They had names taken from the world above which had nothing to do with the life they spent so far beneath, where they hauled all day and were stabled all night in the infernal blackness. He wanted to wrap their eyes and bring them up where they might feel the sun and breathe fresh air.

Through a round window, like a porthole in an old ship, someone was watching them. For a second, he thought it was his sister and he was at home again. He tried to imagine what lay behind the cottage walls. A simply furnished room, with a single bed and a night-table, perhaps, or a small cupboard spilling children's toys and crayons around the feet of a rocking horse? Or a desk weighed down with accounts? Maybe there was a brass swivel calendar where you changed the dates with your fingers like they had at home. If you forgot to change the date, the same day could stay for an entire week or if you mistook the numbers, as he sometimes did, you could slip accidently into another time.

As he moved around the field, he could hear loose coins jingling in his jacket pockets. The half-moon gave him a little light but darkness was seeping in from the countryside around, filling quickly now with the shadows of houses, trees and farms. He found himself relying, perilously, on the lamps burning in the windows of the house to see, conscious that anyone looking out would see him and Mary Jane bobbing about the sheep. Before long, it became too dark to continue.

'What about your mother?' she asked suddenly, maybe aware as a woman that he had not mentioned her, or maybe trying to encourage him to ask about her family.

He thought for a while, as if wondering what to say or deciding how much he was willing to share. But as she would come to learn, conversations with him, deeply personal exchanges, would always be a little slow.

'She loves my father, but hates the marriage.'

There were a few moments of silence, before he added, 'I think she finds the marriage limiting, Llanrwst where our farm is (she noticed he said 'our') is suffocating, which is why she has always been so keen for my father to sell and move to Liverpool where she came from and run a shop.'

Then he bent over and gathered his last few things together. Closing his veterinary chest, he wondered what Hill House would look like now. The floor covered no doubt with bits of paper, auction leaflets, invoices and advertising bills, like all empty houses.

Making sure that all the maggots were killed meant that he would have to return at the beginning of the following week and then the week after. The early moon made a thin curve above the sheep. Those nearest the house stood together in the stronger yellow light cast from its upstairs windows. It made him think of how Hill House had always looked when he came down from the hills. One of the sheep was resting its chin on the neck of another. They were like statues. It was a beautiful sight. He and Mary Jane caught the way each was feeling and laughed together. On a fine day, we invite the sky into our souls, on a dark, gloomy day we close as much of ourselves to it as we can. When rain comes in heavy downpours, it enters our bodies and seeps through all our veins.

Meic felt linked again in natural sympathy with the world around him. He didn't want to leave but at least he had reasons to return. Blood trickled a little on his lower arm. He dabbed at it with his sleeve. Mary Jane produced a silk handkerchief from her bag and tried to stem the tiny red droplets. It was a strange experience for her. Sometimes when you do something you see yourself doing it and you know that what is happening has occurred before even though it is unfolding in front of you.

For Mary Jane, imagination was about calling up pictures. She saw the edge of her silk handkerchief becoming bloodied and for a few seconds this seemed to be an image that had come not from the past but from the future. She always seemed caught between her past and a future that was this much again in front of her. In fact, she lived most of her time, as Meic were to discover, in this giddying confusion.

'What will happen to them?' she asked as they both cast their last glances over the sheep they had treated.

He shrugged.

'Will they go to auction?' she suggested.

Meic nodded.

'I have only ever been to one auction,' she said. 'Tad took us. Just to see it. We weren't looking to buy. I was eight years old. But I will never forget it. I expect you have been to lots,' she prodded.

He nodded in agreement. 'But I still remember my first. Tad and I bought our first Highlander. A massive bull. He will hate to be separated from it.'

'Naw,' she said. 'What did you call it ... a Highlander?'

'A Highland bull, from the Highlands of Scotland. They are a distinct breed. You would know one if you saw it. Really heavy with shaggy coats and horns that are longer than your outstretched arm. You can barely see their faces because they have hair falling down like a widow's veil from the crown of their heads.'

'I think I saw one, in the auction we went to. Like a mammoth?'

That they may have been at the same auction years before as children stunned Mary Jane. But Meic laughed, a little dismissively. Then, seeing he may have offended her, added, 'maybe, it is possible, you do not see them much in Wales, Tad and I wanted to introduce them to the hills, breed a strong herd.'

She liked the way he talked about his father and himself, as if they were responsible for everything. There was something 'royal' about it, she thought.

As she pondered this, he suddenly started laughing.

'It nearly killed my sister.'

Mary Jane was shocked by this. Her jaw dropped and her

mouth fell open giving her face an unusual vacantness.

'We had all gone to bed,' he continued, 'and we had left the door open. Somehow his paddock gate was not fully locked either and he got into the house when Megan Jane was downstairs, she was terrified.'

'Roedd ofn am ei bywyd arni, yea?' she said.

'We were all scared for our lives,' he responded and laughed as if to make light of the memory.

'Not you,' she said. 'From what I have seen this evening, I bet you had it in a trance in no time.'

His pursed lips formed a slight smile.

'Still, all that is in the past,' he concluded, as if a line had long since been drawn. 'I am here now, a miner.'

'I think not for long,' she said, slapping him on the back. It made him feel good. She seemed so sure there were ways forward. Maybe, he thought, he had not betrayed himself … or his family … and especially his father.

Awst | August 2016

'Bradwr a welaf o fy mlaen.' (A traitor I see before me)

Mary-Jane looks up from entering another of her emails to see who is calling her a traitor.

Her uncle, Ned Sullivan, slaps down a bundle of papers and asks if he can join her. She notices that on top of his folders there is a novel by Louis L'Amour. He is an avid reader of western fiction and Mary-Jane has always believed that in his own mind he lives in the wild west more than Wales or Wales is his frontier. She turns the book at an angle so that she can read the publisher's blurb.

> *Hondo Lane is a quintessential man of the southwest, shaped as much by the desert landscape as anything else. A former cavalry officer, Lane has to learn the Apache ways in order to survive the harsh environment.*

She scoffs and returns the book to its original alignment.

Her uncle has always regarded Cwm Garreg as a betrayal of real farming and thinks that, as a local vet, his niece should not be supporting them. Mary-Jane is a little irritated because she has wanted to be alone but she suddenly feels less obvious in a crowded café at lunchtime with someone beside her. He drags a chair from another table without asking the two people sitting around it, which makes her question to herself why everything seems so much easier for men.

'Pwy sy'n fy ngalw i'n fradwr?' she says smirking. [Who are you calling a traitor?]

She makes her uncle feel that he is something of a hypocrite in being there, too. He orders them both coffees but she interrupts when he begins to explain why he is there, announcing she has more exciting information that might interest him from her research into their family.

But Ned, as she expected, is not willing to let her continue. There is anger in the way he speaks and in the way he curls his lips as his words seethe from them. He has been to the surgery hoping to meet with her where 'they' (the receptionists, she presumes) had told him that she was snooping around the farm of the future. 'Fferm y dyfodol', he says, in a way that makes her think he wants to spit something nasty from his mouth. She knows why he is angry, his slaughter house is on its knees and the decision to leave the EU earlier that summer will not help him.

The elderly couple a few tables away ignore their meal and listen.

'Nid ydym ni'n cael digon i ladd'. (We do not have enough to kill).

Mary-Jane feels sick; she does not want to want to have to think about farming and killing when her mother is dying.

She repeats what he has said. 'Nid ydw ti ddim yn cael digon o anifeiliaid i ladd.' Then she adds, trying to better his snarl: 'Dwi ddim yn cael digon o anifeiliaid arbed.'([I do not have enough animals to save)

The evident tension between them causes ears on the surrounding tables to prick up. A young girl screws up her face and moves the bits of beef left on her plate to one side, choosing to tuck into the potatoes instead which she mashes firmly with the back of her fork.

Mary-Jane hates the whole idea of the slaughter house and she has never been especially fond of Ned. She has always felt that there was something edgy about him. She couldn't put her finger on exactly what he meant, but on two occasions when they were together he referred, she thought, to the 'Dublin boys' and in a way that was rather menacing.

One elderly lady, who is trying to decipher their conversation over the rattle of cutlery and voices in the café, seems struck when Mary-Jane's uncle mentions bringing in stock for slaughter from elsewhere. It is something which Mary-Jane, who is distracted by his anger and her own rising annoyance, fails to pick up as she might have done at another time. This she will come to regret.

'Your programme next week is hardly going to help me,' he says, 'on top of this horrendous referendum result.'

'What do you know about my programme?' she asks, somewhat stunned and refusing to talk about this other thing.

He slips that morning's Metro from his file of papers. It is open to the third page and folded neatly around a particular feature. She doesn't have to peer to see the headline, 'Superbugs in Raw Pet Food'. Next to it, there is a large picture of herself, straight to camera, looking much younger, astride a chair turned around, mirroring the famous Christine Keeler photograph. Unlike Keeler, she is clothed, but still it is a photograph she had not wanted to see again, dating from her vet school student days. She wonders why the paper had chosen to use it. In addition to this picture, there is a photograph, clearly photoshopped, of a smooth-haired fox terrier looking plaintively up at the reader, its paws strategically placed in front of a bowl of what looks like raw, minced meat. Above it, is the strapline which her uncle reads to her: 'Dog foods made up of raw meats can carry deadly bacteria including salmonella and E coli.' He tosses the paper to her and, from even a cursory glance, she can see that this sentence is part of a quotation from an unnamed scientist, lifted from the body of the article.

'Is that what you say in your programme?' he asks.

'That is what we have discovered,' she confirms.

'We?'

She ignores this.

Although the article does not acknowledge the fact, it quotes the voice-over of the programme exactly: 'People buy brands of dog food made from raw meat because they believe they are more natural and healthier, but bugs have been found in some of them that are antibiotic resistant.'

Ned stares at her, expecting a response. When none comes, he continues putting the statistics from the paper to her: 'Of 51 raw meat dog foods tested, 37 did not meet EU standards.'

'Standards,' he scoffs with a particular emphasis. Then there is silence between them, until he engages in a more sustained and personal verbal assault.

'This is another nail in my coffin. Only last year we signed a contract with a major pet food supplier. Do you ever think about the consequences of your journalism? We are a farming community for heaven's sake.'

His voice rises. Mary-Jane is concerned that her uncle seems to have forgotten that they are in the café at Cwm Garreg and that, as a vet, all her business is local. People even at the far end of the room are staring at them now and nodding which makes Mary-Jane think that they have recognised her. She tries to shush her uncle.

'Bydda ofalus beth rywt ti'n dy ddweud yma. Cofia ble rydyn ni.'

(Be careful what you say here. Remember where we are.)

Mary-Jane half closes the lid of her lap top to lean over the table as far as she can to whisper this and, as she does so, her eyes meet those of a woman watching them from behind the serving counter.

'My report will lead to fewer sick dogs and fewer animals in misery. As a vet, my role is to protect people's pets. Do you ever think of the consequences of what Llanrwst Slaughter and Food Processing Unit produces?'

She sits back in her chair. Again, there is silence for a while.

'Is that it, have you finished with me now,' she hisses. The sunlight glints in her eyes as if they are made of broken glass.

The coffees he has ordered arrive at the moment she begins to draw out some papers from her case which she was about to do at the beginning of their conversation. It is not easy for her to continue now. Her hands are trembling a little. She closes her eyes. Could he be more conspicuous, she asks herself.

Another waitress, young enough to be his daughter, brings him a steak sandwich. He lifts one of the pieces of bread and peers at the meat. It is medium rare but quite bloody in places. Mary-Jane notices how thick and viscous the slices are. He turns his head to watch the young woman slip away from him, squeezing between tables and adjusting chairs as she goes. The smell of the slaughter house rises from the meat and lingers in Mary-Jane's nostrils even when the sandwich has been closed.

'What about the small herd of Highland cattle, I keep hearing about, that you and your partner Prothero have on the farm you share?' she asks, this time with a note of concern.

Again, he scoffs, letting some globules of steak fall from his mouth.

'We do not share anything,' he says. 'It is his place, to be left to his daughter when she is older. He just lets me stay in one of the barn conversions in exchange for my butchering skills.' He seems to enjoy reminding her that these are the skills of which he is proud.

'Does that not bring you income?' she persists, still uncertain as to the relationship between Ned and Prothero.

He shakes his head, and puts down his sandwich so that Mary-Jane no longer feels in range should he become emotional and start spitting again like his cattle.

'Prothero, if he had any sense, would be building up a strong Highland herd. They do well in the hills. I do not need to tell you that. The market for beef is strong, it wants tasty, lean meat. That is what the Highlands give you. But he can't see that. He is all about milk. Milk he transports to Denbigh, Llandudno, and even Rhyl. It might all change, though, when we leave the EU and she takes over the farm.'

'She?' Mary-Jane queries.

'The daughter, Megyn. I don't have much to do with her. He keeps her well hid. It is going to be hard for her now.'

'Hey,' he suddenly exclaims as a thought strikes him. 'You haven't heard about any of those, what do they call them, animal rights groups turning up around here, have you?'

Mary-Jane shakes her head, not wishing to mention her lover. But then, she is never sure from one week to the next what Amelia is protesting about exactly.

That seems to satisfy him. He splutters over his coffee and then offers one of his typically brief explanations.

'Some of the guys at the plant have seen a bike.'

'A bike?' Mary-Jane asks.

'You know,' he says, irritated at having to clarify himself, 'one of those off-road motor thingies. The guys say they heard it up in the streets near the plant and Prothero says they heard one, possibly more, in the hills above his place the other night. Frightening the cattle, he said, not forgetting the sheep and the lambs.'

Mary-Jane looks interested. But she is thinking of youths from the town.

'I am relying on them lambs,' he quips.

Her uncle's integrity is not something Mary-Jane would trust and, if she had noticed what he had said about bringing in animals to slaughter from outside the area, she would trust him even less.

He is sceptical of her research into their family history but she is not sure why. Is there something which will bring him bad publicity, she muses, worrying herself further. Although she is not comfortable in involving him in her research, he is probably the only member of the family left who might have the kind of information she is seeking.

She feels that the producers of her programme are playing a game with her. They feed her small bites of information at the end of a thin line, enough to lure her, watch her bite, and then they will reel her in.

She wants to be at least one step ahead of them. Although she doesn't like Ned, fair play, she says to herself, she cannot imagine him letting others control him this way.

Given their argument over her forthcoming programme, Mary-Jane expects her uncle to leave. He has had his say. But, to her surprise, he stays, apparently interested in what she has discovered. She hands him a photograph of a large town house. Its walls are a lighter shade of grey within the oyster-clouded picture.

'This is because they are painted yellow and always have been, apparently,' she explains.

As a child, Mary-Jane and her friends hung around houses like this in Denbigh. They used to imagine living in them and having servants. The people who lived there would watch them as if they were burglars.

'This is where, I believe, MJ lived with her family in Carmarthen before she went to live with my great-great-great-grandfather,' she says.

Ned pushes his mouth to one side in an expression of incredulity. But this was what the Carmarthen historian had told her. She shares the questions she had for him with her uncle.

'She left a house like this and went to live with a miner in rooms in Llanelli,' she says, taking Ned by surprise and suggesting she had discovered more than he had expected.

Together, they pause over the picture.

'You are right, that is peculiar,' he admits. 'You said, last time we spoke about her, that her shadowy life is a mystery. What made her leave her home and her family? That is a question. But how do you know she lived here?'

'This is where a family, the Kellys, or at least one part of the family, lived when they first came to Wales from Ireland,' she tells him, turning from supposition to fact. Before he has an opportunity to pursue his interrogation of her, she hands him a second picture, even more cloudy and dark. Above the copy of the article, she has scrawled in spidery handwriting, befitting of a doctor, the name of the paper and a date. Ned sees it was published in 1879. Four men are seated on a platform before a large meeting of what looks to him like miners or iron workers. She explains that such meetings occurred in south-west Wales throughout the 1870s and into the 1880s and points to a figure on the platform who is second from the left. Ned looks at him carefully. He is vague, no more than a silhouette from the distance the picture was taken. He peers very closely to make out some detail, wishing he had a magnifying glass. He takes off his reading spectacles and holds the lens close to the paper as if he were trying to set fire to it. The image is a little clearer.

'This is my great-great-great-great-grandfather,' she says.

'Meic's father?' he asks.

She shakes her head wistfully.

'On my great-great-great-grandmother's side,' she clarifies.

But before he says anything more about this, she returns to the subject of the meeting: 'This was a miner's protest meeting,' she explains as he continues to study her ancestor. He can see that the man is well dressed, one of only four men on the platform who are wearing hats. Even in the ash-coloured picture, his collar stands out; it is very large and white, exaggerating his dark tie. His face is unsmiling and expressionless.

She lets her uncle study him in silence for a while. He searches for his name among those listed below the picture. Very few of them on the platform have conspicuously Welsh names. When he looks back to the picture, he sees that two of the other men in hats are not simply well, but elegantly, dressed. Mary-Jane's great-great-great-great-grandfather appears superior to many of the men in the photograph and subordinate to a few of them. Ned lives his life almost entirely in a man's world. He thinks he knows what men are like. He imagines them whispering with each other in private and slapping each other's backs in public. He does not need to bet with himself that they were used to kickbacks and backhanders. It is an observation he shares with his niece. She pulls the paper closer so that she can see it more clearly and, once again, studies her ancestor, imagining him slicking down his moustache and shifting awkwardly in his stiff-backed chair beside men he knew would tolerate him as long as they needed him but would never fully accept him.

'John Edward Kelly,' she reads outloud. 'Were we Kellys before we were Sullivans?' she asks, without giving away that she has already discovered the answer and in a tone of voice which she has learned to assume from the rehearsals for her programme.

She reads aloud more of the story below the picture, how after the meeting a number of the men visited a neighbouring colliery. The word 'visited' stops her for a moment but she continues, to discover that these men were loading coal from the stock. The 'visitors' compelled them to cease their work, the paper says, breaking up their tools, smashing the pit drains and doing considerable damage. The remainder of the page is less legible, she had copied it primarily for the photograph, but she is able to make out that, on leaving the premises, they took some of the small pit wagons and left them a quarter of a mile from the colliery.

'Difficult times,' her uncle observes when he sees that she has finished reading.

'It is no wonder,' she says, 'that he looks so hard.'

'I suspect,' he says, 'that this is something that may not be brought out in your programme.'

'Nid fy rhaglen', (not my programme) she snaps irritatedly, concerned that he understands that she has little control over the direction the programme is taking.

He seems to be grasping the point.

'As far as I know,' she says, 'historians have missed this.'

'Why should historians be interested in your great-great-great-grandmother's father?' he asks, testing out how much she knows and how much she may be keeping from him.

The historians in the programme are looking at her family tree, she tells him, because the producers are interested in a local vet who is desperate to understand where her family has come from because her mother has dementia and is very ill. They are looking at her ancestors and tracing her family tree because they have been paid to do so. She does not expect her family, she presses, to have had great historical significance.

She withholds what she has been told by the historians about MJ.

'What they do want, of course, is something ...' she flaps about like a netted fish, searching for the right word, 'some scandal perhaps to satisfy the television audience.' She stares into his face to see if she can detect any sign that the word 'scandal' is making him uncomfortable. He is thinking to himself, if she has found the house, the family name, one of her great-great-great-great-grandfathers, surely, she must know who MJ was. He sits quietly for a while. Come on, he is thinking to himself, tell me what you really have discovered.

'But you are interested,' he says 'in your MJ and how you are linked to these, what did you call them, Kellys.'

The way in which he pretends to have forgotten the name is not convincing. She ducks under his stare, unsettled by this.

'Of course,' she recapitulates, reining in her emotions. She realises how devastating he, too, must be about his sister's dementia.

He summarises where he thinks they stand now: 'Your ancestor who was a Kelly, lived in this house. MJ now appear to be his daughter's initials. Maybe,' he suggests, 'the scandal in the family that your programme (at the repetition of this again she winces in irritation but he appears not to notice) will reveal is that your great-great-great-great-grandfather and his daughter were ... shall we say ... unusually close.'

Too cliched, Mary-Jane thinks, and adds, wide of the mark, too.

She has some idea of what is coming but she is sure that it will amount to more than a father and daughter relationship, scandalous as that might be. But she accepts that at the end, her story might come down to some illicit relationships. What has always been on her mind is what if MJ is Megan Jane. It is only her historians, and her own, intuitions that MJ is Mary Jane Kelly. She closes her eyes.

'What is the matter?' he asks. 'One of your migraines?'

She shakes her head.

The conclusion of the programme is swimming before her eyes.

PART THREE

TOGETHER ... AND APART

I love to hear you laugh
It takes the world away
I live to hear you laugh
I don't even have to pray
But now the world is coming back
It's coming back to stay.

Leonard Cohen

Chapter Nine
Hand to Mouth

Mehefin | June 1913

This summer is too hot. Branwen Siân has been playing at the bottom of her grandmother's garden. Her face is scratched and she has sweated through her cotton dress her grandfather has bought her from Asia. The flowers on it are curled and moist now like buds in the early dawn. Her grandmother pulls her close to her, as she used to do with me, moistens her handkerchief with her lips and dabs the feathery cuts. As they are not looking at the camera, I take a photograph of them together.

I notice there is a small scar on Branwen Siân's leg. Why have I not seen this before? I have a most peculiar, momentary feeling I am somewhere else. Her father always calls her a tomboy. I wish he wouldn't do that. He encourages her to think she isn't a girl. 'She will grow up confused,' I tell him. My mother asks her whom she has been playing with today. She says that she and Jason have been chasing each other. I wonder what kind of dog Jason is this afternoon, a spaniel, a fox terrier or a hound. 'You must not let him take you too far into the bushes,' I hear my mam calling after her as she runs off again. She calls back to us something about what Jason is doing but I do not understand it.

Mawrth | March 1876

Mary Jane's year in Paris with her eldest sister proved the happiest in her young life. Years later, she would tell her best friend how she remembered her aunt in what she called her 'visit home' in Paris, how she recalled sitting opposite her as the elderly woman sang traditional French songs. Her voice was melodic and soothing and had such a special effect on Mary Jane. She soon started to teach her young visitor to sing and listened intently to her melancholic Irish ballads of love and separation, and her lyrical Welsh lullabies. Mary Jane loved an audience, however small. She danced among the chairs while her sister and aunt whooped encouragement and applauded.

'She will make a fine dancer and singer,' they said.

When the newspapers came to the house, Mary Jane's aunt read them aloud, translating the occasional sentence or phrase. Mary Jane knew too little French to understand fully what her aunt was reading but she built up a hotpot vocabulary that served her well in the future. As the elderly lady summarised the troubles of Paris in 1874, she held her fingers to her temples and squinted as she spoke, weaving between her French and her English. When Mary-Jane returned to Carmarthen, everyone knew that it was only a matter of time before she would leave the family altogether.

Tachwedd | November 1878

Carnarvon and Denbigh Herald and North and South Wales Independent

---

TO BE SOLD

Lot 32

A Farm, containing 63a, with Dwelling-house and Farm Buildings thereon, called 'Fferm Tŷ Bryn', formerly 'Caerffynon', situate in the parish of Llanrwst immediately above the Conway Valley, 25 miles from Llandudno and the railway station. The property might be rent to a yearly tenant at an annual rent of £30.00.

Hill House Farm stood on an upland slope where the best that anyone could usually look forward to in late October was a watery sunlight squeezed out of a tube of grey sky. Most of the year, it seemed to the family that the land was cold and wet. Hill House was a small farm, even by hill farm standards.

During the week of the yard sale, the days seemed not to become light. When the neighbours came for the bull in the late afternoon, it was led away by lanterns. From inside the kitchen, John Davis could hear Llwyd Morgan and his sons shouting and whistling. He stared at the empty dresser.

Seven years ago, Davis's bull had stood alone in the corner of a field. Everyone was afraid to approach him. But all the time there was something about him that attracted John. Several times, a day he made a point of seeking him out and talking with him. John knew that the animal could not understand what he was saying. He was a farmer, he could never be that simple. But he believed that the bull felt the rhythms in his voice and was calmed by the way his sentences curled through his local lilt. As he spoke to the bull, John believed that the half-hidden eyes, peering through a curtain of hair, lost a lot of their anger. John knew that others might laugh at him if he ever told them, but he was convinced that the animal's eyes became kinder. Velvet looked forward to John's coming, he would nestle his nostrils deep into the palm of his hand.

'I think you're falling for each other,' his wife spiked at him one evening.

'It is important to keep checking him over,' he replied curtly, adding, 'to make sure that he is not carrying disease.'

'Who knows what an outsider might bring here,' she hit back, perhaps reading more into John's words than he intended.

The once comfortable atmosphere between them as a family had long begun to dissipate.

'Mam sold her plates for more than you've got for your bull,' said Megan sharply from the kitchen table where she had been sitting for the past hour to avoid the Llwyd Morgan's. Her father turned quickly to face her. She was in the middle of reading a letter from her brother who had left Hill House over a year ago for a job in a colliery in south Wales. Megan stared back at him. There was no remorse in her face.

'You should have bought a red one not a black one,' she said.

'In the Highlands, where they come from, they are black,' he insisted. 'You always loved his coat, as we all did.'

'But that was when we didn't have to resell him.' She sounded tearful but held on to her words as if they were pieces of rock.

'Everyone now wants a brown herd like the Queen has,' she said, hoping to say no more and wishing she had not said anything.

'But that is not what they are,' he replied, less willing to let things go.

To his mind, the black Highland bull had a beauty from generations of careful breeding and selection. His bull was the result of a long journey which had come down to this very moment in time. He wished that she could see that, regretting that he had ever told her how farmers in Scotland had shifted to breeding those with red coats, thus breeding out, as it were, their natural colour. She used everything against him, eventually.

He could no longer hear the Llwyd Morgans.

'At least his family have stayed together,' he said bitterly.

Megan did not answer.

At the end of the month, his daughter would be going to London to work with the new St John Ambulance Association. All her father had said when she told him was, 'Nid ydynt yn siarad Cymraeg yn Llundain' ('They don't speak Welsh in London').

'Mae llawer ohonom ni'n Llundain nawr ('There are a lot of us in London now'), she had said slowly and coldly. 'Ydych chi erioed wedi clywed am Y Gymraeg Llundain?' ('Have you never heard of the London Welsh?')

Her mother, who was originally from Liverpool, tried to rein in their tempers. 'Stop bickering about the Welsh,' she said, 'you'll all find soon enough how important the English is when you are gone from here.'

Without looking at either of them, she took the last of the utensils into the yard. O law i law (from hand to hand). How humiliating it was that she had to put all their belongings on display like this. Everything they had accumulated as a family. Everything that had been a part of their home. When the neighbours came with their prying eyes, she did not want them to have to come into the house again. The tables, chairs and dresser were already promised. There were a lot of small plates stacked on some chairs and boxes. They seemed to have had so much more than she thought. One large plate commemorated the wedding of Prince Edward and the young Princess Alexandra of Denmark in 1863. The plate showed her in a flounced dress, with a low neckline. She was beautiful, a lot of people said.

Megan turned to a passage in her brother's letter which she knew would upset her mother and raised her voice loud enough for it to be heard in the yard. He was getting married to a girl in Llanelli, a young woman from Limerick in Ireland who had been brought up in Carmarthen. She is a maid in a high-class hotel in Llanelli. She speaks Welsh and French. She can draw as well and is something of an artist. Her mother bustled back inside, her face flushed and drawn into deep lines.

'He has never told us about her,' she said.

'He's telling us now,' Megan snapped. 'Mae o wedi gwrioni ar y ferch.' [He loves her passionately]

'Irish,' repeated her father.

'If you had been listening,' his wife chided him, 'they were talking last week at Chapel about the numbers of Irish who are still coming into the south. Does he say when ... when this is going to happen?'

'No,' said Megan, keeping the blade between her teeth and knowing that she would probably be starting her new life in London by then.

There was little but hostility between them as a family now. It was Megan's brother who had told her about St Johns. From the many accidents he had witnessed in the colliery, where there were no doctors on hand to treat the injured, he believed that having a body of people to train some of the ordinary workers to help the injured was an excellent idea.

She never thought her brother looked like a miner or a foundry man. To her eyes, he had the face of a shepherd: a long, sharp nose, sunken cheeks, eyes set deep in his skull and prematurely thinning hair. That was how all the sheep men she had ever seen seemed to look. If either of them had an interest in continuing with the farm, she would have thought it was her brother. He was forever reading books about farming and animal treatments. He was always interested in what his father and their neighbours had to say, residues of a once potent knowledge.

Awst | August 2016

'Irish,' he says. 'Catholics. From rural Ireland.'

Mary-Jane is sat on a bench near the river. In the background, there is a small seafood restaurant and there are people parking and setting off on walks. She catches sight of a boat lilted sideways on a bank beside white bones of seagulls. The day is colder than she expected and there is a distinct chill in the wind. She pulls her fleece jacket closer around her and tries to warm her hands in its pockets. The local historian is a tall, studious-looking man with a bald scalp but long strands of hair on the side reaching past the hockey sticks of his spectacles and, at the back, over the collar of his jacket. Mary-Jane feels there is something of the eccentric hobbyist about him. He sits next to her with a clipboard which he hardly ever consults.

They have introduced themselves to each other and now the camera crew have moved much nearer. The microphone hovers above them and at times becomes irritatingly close to their foreheads. For the first part of their meeting, Mary-Jane's role is to listen. She is not a good listener, she always has a point of view. The historian explains that there is anecdotal evidence that Mary Jane arrived in the town in the early or mid-1860s with her family. They are filming the interview near the river because Mary-Jane's namesake seems likely to have lived among a community of fisher folk who spoke a form of medieval Welsh according to this local historian.

He explains that she told her friends when she lived in east London that she was one of seven children and the family came from Limerick in Ireland. Her father found a job working in an iron foundry he explained, looking away from Mary-Jane down along the coast as if he could see the works from where they were seated. Mary-Jane nodded. She cannot see far, a mist is beginning to roll in from the estuary. But some historians, he says, with a deferential air as if they were more professional than himself, believe that her father was a foreman — she apparently referred to him among her London friends as a 'gaffer' — but there are those who think he was more than that, perhaps even an accountant. So, he says, this is where she was brought up to speak and read Welsh. She is believed to have married a coal miner from the Llanelli area when she was sixteen.

At this point, the conversation between them will be interrupted when the programme is broadcast with a flashback to Mary-Jane at Meic's grave. Mary-Jane is looking for evidence that the Meic whose grave they found was Mary Jane's husband or partner. The historian seems very confident that he was. He tells her that much of this is borne out by what she told a young man called Joseph Barnett who lived with her in London for a short time before her death. Mary-Jane thinks she can hear the electricity flowing softly through the camera. There is a short silence while her reaction is monitored. The historian is about to speak again but gives way to Mary-Jane who questions how reliable this information is. The tall man leans forward and almost doubles himself over his clipboard which he now clutches much closer to his chest.

'That is the problem,' he says. 'Her friend may well have embellished Mary Jane's story to earn a few extra shillings when talking with journalists.' He pauses to study the intrigue on Mary-

Jane's face. This is what has been kept from her. Like one of the sewin in the Victorian river, Mary-Jane leaps into the net they have laid out.

'Why were journalists interested in her?' she asks naively.

As has happened so many times in her interviews where she has been the inquisitor, she is drawn into close up. There is a slightly patronising hint of satisfaction in the way in which the historian leans back from her. Something, she notes, that she would never do. He does so to allow the camera in and maintain the focus on Mary-Jane's face.

'You do not know, do you, who this Mary Jane is?' he suggests dramatically, hoping that at least some of the viewers will know.

Pleasing the director and the camera crew, Mary-Jane continues to look puzzled. The local historian milks these moments for every drop of suspense.

'The Ripper. Jack the Ripper?' he suggests.

Mary-Jane recognises the name Jack the Ripper, but she has never been an addict of horror stories or serial killer narratives. Gore has never had an appeal for her.

'Mary Jane Kelly, your Mary Jane, who lived here as a Welsh woman in Carmarthen, and then Llanelli, was the last victim of one of England's,' he corrects himself, 'Britain's most notorious serial killers who preyed on prostitutes in London's East End, in Whitechapel. That is if her own life stories, from the patches of information we have, can be believed.'

Mary-Jane notes that he says 'life stories' not 'life story'. The cameras continue to record. All the lenses are on Mary-Jane's face and they look through her eyes to another Mary Jane. This is the moment toward which the team has been building.

'So, Mary Jane,' says her descendant, stating the obvious, 'was a prostitute. How did that come about? What happened to her?'

This time the camera is closing in on the historian. He furrows his brow and nods. The camera can see that he has more to reveal. Mary-Jane is staring, waiting for him to continue. But she knows how to play the camera.

'What happened to Mary Jane? Why did she become a prostitute in Whitechapel?' she repeats.

'She didn't become a prostitute there.' His reply is short and sharp. The scene is brought to a temporary close. The conversation is to continue in the graveyard of St Peter's Church. They walk together toward a rectanglular stonewall around a grave on which they will sit. This time the director wants them to face each other more. She regards this as a key scene and she wants them to be fully engaged. She wants to remind viewers that Mary-Jane is someone getting closer to an ancestral past that she never expected and about which even her mother has no inkling.

The historian slowly unfurls a picture of Victorian Carmarthen. Having been born and brought up in north Wales, and educated in Liverpool because Wales at that time did not have a veterinary school of its own, Mary-Jane knows little about Carmarthen.

Carmarthen, as the historian explains, was known in the Victorian period, throughout the nineteenth century in fact, for its brothels and prostitution. It was a centre of military life, a busy port and a thriving market town, notorious for drunkenness, riotous behaviour and loose morals. The desperate conditions in which the poor lived helped swell the number of women involved in selling themselves for money and there was a keen demand for sex, of all kinds, from men who came to the town for business and pleasure. Historians have identified how the prostitutes were referred to as 'nymphs of the pavement' or the 'frail sisterhood'.

'The frail sisterhood,' Mary-Jane chooses to repeat, rather icily, before asking, 'So, where did Mary Jane belong in all of this?'

As Mary Jane emerges in, and from, this Carmarthen, Dr

Sullivan's ancestral past begins to darken. There is so much that she needs to take away and try to digest, so much she doubts that even her mother knows, or knew before her dementia. Her namesake was a prostitute and the last victim of a notorious serial killer who preyed on street women. She rests her chin in the palms of her hands, facing the camera. The director is whispering to her team to hold the shot. This is the kind of drama that has made the series popular with the public. Eventually, Mary-Jane drops her hands to her waist and, taking a deep and exasperated breath, asks again how Mary Jane fitted into all of this. She asks him pointedly whether he is saying that Mary Jane entered prostitution in Carmarthen and moved as a prostitute to London.

'Mary Jane,' he explains, 'worked as a maid in the Stepney Arms Hotel in Llanelli, certainly after (he paused for a second and placed a pointed inflexion on the next words) her husband's death and maybe while they lived together. The hotel in which she was employed was an established coaching house, popular with business people, commercial travellers and so forth,' he added. 'From the 1860s, it was a very prosperous hotel in which not only gentlemen but royalty, such as Napoleon's nephew and our own Princess of Wales at the time, stayed. It was a prestigious place to work but it also provided its staff like Mary Jane with an opportunity to eke out their income by providing additional services for guests.'

'So,' says Mary-Jane sharply, 'my namesake became a nymph of the street.'

Again, the historian is quick to correct her.

'Not exactly. As a prostitute working covertly in a hotel, Mary Jane would have been a higher class of working-girl than those on the streets, the knee-tremblers as they were also known as, and even those working in the brothels among the cottages, lodging houses and pubs.'

Mary-Jane is still puzzled. As she gathers her thoughts, she looks at the buildings around them, reflecting that they may look now as they did in Mary Jane's day. The paint is peeling as a result of the scouring sea winds coming inshore and on some of them there are large patches of damp.

'You said earlier,' she reminds her historian 'that her father was a foreman, maybe an accountant even.' She then continues, 'I do not understand how the daughter of a foreman or bookkeeper ends up in prostitution or, for that matter, married to a collier.'

The historian sits back, it is clear he likes to rock and roll with the interview, placing his clip board on the grass beside Mary-Jane's feet. He spreads his arms with his palms open. The camera relishes his gesture.

'These are important questions,' he says, returning to the rather patronising tone to which he was prone. 'We need,' he says emphatically, as if stressing that he has not been caught out, 'for you to take a trip to Cardiff, a journey which Mary Jane herself took. One that changed her life and that of her sister.'

The director indicates a cut. She gives Mary-Jane, still sitting somewhat non-plussed on the stone wall, the thumbs up. But the filming does not cease immediately, absorbing Mary-Jane for a little longer while she thoughtfully studies the clipboard beneath her knees. Her mobile phone dances to a jazz suite by Shostakovich. She is horrified at her own forgetfulness, that it might have rang when they were filming. It slips off the nearby grave where she had placed it and where three generations are buried and into the long grass which muffles its ringing tone. She does not pick it up immediately. Waiting for the ringtone to cease, she adjusts one of her socks which is being dragged beneath her heel by the weight of the boot. The top of the sock forms a noose around her calf muscle and she tries to stretch its elastic. As she lifts the phone gently from the grass, as if she were rescuing a small bird fallen from its nest, she knows it is her uncle trying to phone her.

He wonders if she is at home, he would like to visit her. Mary-Jane explains that she has just finished filming. Her phrasing makes it sound as if she is involved in the running of the project. If it were true, her uncle would not have been surprised. She jogs his memory. He did not know for certain she was going through with the programme. He had warned her that it was dangerous to start roaming around among the ghosts of the past. At the time, she did not understand what he meant. She understands now. He advises her again that she does not know what she will discover. She smiles to herself, thinking about what has just been revealed, wondering if her uncle knows about a family connection with Jack the Ripper's so-called last victim.

She cannot absorb and filter all the new information and her head feels like an overloaded computer drive. She sees the scrawled initials of MJ through a different lens. But there is so much that does not make sense. So many questions unanswered. There is nothing that allows MJ to be her ancestor. She cannot wait to travel to Cardiff. As if uncertain as to whether she has heard him, her uncle repeats his warning. She does not know whether his concern is for her or for himself.

Tachwedd | November 1878

In the Davises' last few weeks at Hill House, Megan thought a lot about their life there, as a family, and especially remembered her brother. She recalled the spring there, her brother's favourite time of year. She remembered how every spring, once the mud had dried, usually alone but sometimes with her brother, she would venture out more boldly than in the winter months, happy to drop in at a hamlet and wander over to the quarry where the work had only stopped a few years previously. Now, she could not recall the quarry without thinking of Meic as a miner. She could not imagine him away from the farm, without his animals.

Half reluctantly, but needing to get away from her parents, she retraced many of her favourite walks. As ever, even on a clear, fine November day, the hills were an astonishing sight. Mellow green grass, so brilliant in the spring, under a sheet of slate blue sky. In February and March, thankful to leave the village with its houses behind, she would always try to count the wild daffodils making yellow spots into the distance. There were too many of them, of course, and too many too far away. She would give up and let the deep seams of the quarry remind her of her family and her own life. So much pressing against another. There had been talk of the quarry reopening. She thought of the large hole expanding, swallowing the hills, devouring the farms one at a time. There are places we do not choose to visit, she said to herself, but to which something draws us.

Then there were the summers. She had always looked forward to them. She and her brother always enjoyed them together. One evening in June, five years ago, and long before their parents had made the decision to sell the farm, she had demonstrated her scything skills to him. There can be few things that look more effortless than the slow rhythmic swing of the scythe. Her curling hair gleamed in the sun and the bright daylight picked out a small, jagged scar on the back of one of her legs, its feathered edges stitched into her brown skin.

Meic watched the grass sigh and fall into swathes. Megan had made it look so easy that Meic began to believe that he could do it. He only attempted to do so once. His sister tried to teach him her lovely swinging movements but, in his hands, they disintegrated into a sequence of stiff, awkward jerks. She remembered the steel blade jarring against the roots, its point jabbing into the earth. After a few minutes, her brother was short of breath, red in the face, and aching in most of his muscles. He stood out the rest of the evening and watched Megan enviously.

Meic spent much of his time with his father over where the

sheep settled in the lower hills. It seemed in those years as if he would never lose his excitement for farming. He was forever reading, talking and planning. Megan always remembered him helping her stack the scythed hay in the barn. She could hardly stand upright at the end of those days. She cursed now how she could ever have been so trite, worrying about the farm work attacking her hands. She remembered the frivolous health and beauty advertisements in the local gazette for preparations 'unequalled for softening and beautifying the skin'. One line had really made her laugh and still did every time she recalled it: 'The most delicate needlework may be undertaken without washing the hands after using it.' She often sat and studied her mother's hands in the muscles and veins of her own. Her hands were broad across their knuckles and her fingers seemed to be getting shorter and fatter. Five years later, when everything was being packed for them to leave, the newspaper pages they used to protect the crockery carried the same kind of advertisements, maybe the same ones. In such large capitals that she had to hold them at more of a distance to read them, one screamed 'NEITHER STICKY NOR GREASY'. Then she had to bring it nearer to help it into focus, 'remove and prevents chapped hands, sunburn and freckles'.

There were evenings when she had sat with her mother waiting for Meic to come in from tending the sheep. If a few of them were heard coughing, he and his father were soon out among them with a mixture of turpentine and linseed oil from Meurig Thomas MRCVS in Denbigh, pouring it into their throats and nostrils. MRCVS. Megan wondered what kind of a vet Meic would have made. Their father followed his father's practice of dipping the sheep twice a year. She remembered the week that news came from over Cwm Garreg way, that sheep had died from scab. The men confided in each other, their whispers carried an apocalyptic chill. Women were kept out of it, except by her father and Meic who shared everything.

***

Soon, no one from this particular Davis family would be left in this part of north Wales. Their parents would be running a small shop in Liverpool, something Megan's mother always wanted.

'Well, he will not be able to come back here to be wed amongst his own family,' her mother said when Megan read her Meic's letter. 'What a mess, now of all times, when he has no home from where to set off to chapel.' She stared at her husband as if this were all his fault.

'His home is in Carmarthenshire now,' Megan insisted. She was gloomy and disappointed but found a kind of solace in hurting her mother, a nastiness to which she rose at times. Part of her nature, her father told himself.

'What kind of home can he have on a miner's wages,' her mother retorted, almost in tears.

Megan swallowed another thought in order to spare her mother for the moment. She knew how to be kind, too. Meic's wife-to-be was probably Catholic. She realised that her father had not missed this point, repeating the word 'Irish' as if it were a spell or a curse.

Their neighbours gathering in the gloom outside in the yard brought them all back to the task at hand. Megan noticed what she had been fearing for days. Elin Jones had finally turned up and was being led around the yard by her mother who was making a point of studying everything closely. Everyone else seemed embarrassed and sorry for the Davises.

'And the shame of it,' one elderly woman could be heard muttering as she moved around in a group of her friends from the chapel.

Elin and Megan did not meet each other's eyes. Although it had been ten years since Elin had betrayed her, Megan had never forgiven her. At the end of a school day, she had exposed her for speaking 'the Welsh' and the 'Not' – a wooden sign painted with the words 'Welsh Not' in large capitals – was taken from Elin by their teacher and hung around Megan's neck. There was only one way she could escape the punishment that the pupil wearing the 'Not' received at the end of the day and that was to betray another Welsh-speaker. That Megan would never do.

Megan remembered how she and Miss Hughes, her teacher, studied each other. The one, a middle-aged woman who lived in Denbigh, and had just learned that she was pregnant, and the other, a spirited girl from a local farm. Megan had felt every one of the forty pairs of eyes fearfully concentrated on her. She had expected to be told to turn and face them. But that didn't happen. The senior pupils, including her brother, had been brought in and lined along the back wall of the classroom to witness her punishment.

The cane was two feet long and frayed at one end like an unravelling hem. Miss Hughes, standing in Megan's blind spot, rolled it in her hands. Megan's skirt had fallen slightly and, defiantly, she hoisted it higher.

The first stroke had felt like a slap. Some of the pupils cast their eyes downward. Her brother made a fist of his hand. An eternity later, the second was truly a cut. Megan winced and brought her lower lip beneath her teeth. She bit it as the rattan bit. Her brother had closed his eyes. He told her afterwards that he couldn't watch. She hadn't known how many strokes were in store, whether she was still at the beginning or nearer the end. Each successive stroke sliced deeper than the one before. She had thought she felt a trickle of blood. Eventually, the strokes came quicker, she bit down harder, her eyes became wild, and she started to shake from her shoulders to her heels. The class had begun to stare at Elin. A few looked at Megan's brother as if they expected him to do something but, of course, she had not seen that. Just before what would turn out to be the last cut, Miss Hughes whispered something into Megan's ear. Her voice resembled barbed wire. It was in Welsh and it would stay with her, and with her brother when she told him, forever.

The humiliation of the caning, of having to hoist up her skirt in front of the whole school, and her brother, still lingered. But her mother's approval of the punishment, because she wanted her children to speak English and 'get on in life', and the spinelessness of her father who always said he wished he was more Welsh, left deeper wounds.

Standing beside her mother in the yard, Megan endured public shame again, this time as part of a family of debtors. Her father stayed inside the house. She felt that she and her mother, the women in the family, had been left to face the community alone. They stood upright before everyone as if they had been ordered to a platform to wear a wooded letter 'D', dyled (debt), clumsily carved by her father, around their necks.

As Elin came closer to them, Megan noticed how she kept her head bowed as she had done on that other ignominious day and every occasion when they saw each other since. Megan raised her own face as high as she could, just as she had done ten years before.

'Mae'r holl Nots Cymreig wedi'u gwerthu' (all the Welsh Nots have been sold) she hissed pointedly in Welsh, noticing with satisfaction Elin's cheeks turning crimson.

When the neighbours had left the yard, Megan returned inside. She could hear her father moving about upstairs. She remembered discovering her brother, the day before he left, sat on the floor with his arms clasped around his knees. She could see that he was tearful. She ignored him for a few seconds, uncertain as to what to say to him. But she wanted, needed, to talk with him. She had no idea when, if ever, they would have the opportunity to speak with each other again, as they used to in those spring and summer days among the hills, their mountains.

***

Megan picked up her brother's letter and began folding it, uncertain now where to put it.

'This house is too small, the plaster is peeling and the damp is rising from deep down in the earth.' She remembered him nodding. 'You sleep with tad and I sleep with mam,' she said to him that day.

She stood by herself now, trying to remember that there had been good days: watching the sky over the hills, gathering berries, loving the different colours of the leaves, the copper amber of early autumn, and the russet radiance of living in the country. Her father seemed much more upset today than ever. He said very little to anybody, even the neighbours who returned to linger with offers of help. She wondered what London would be like.

The noise around her changed. For a second or two there was silence, unusual in the countryside which is much noisier with bird calls, movement and rustling than townsfolk imagine. Her father had stopped moving about, but then she could hear that her mother, outside in the yard, had finally caught their last escaped chicken. 'It is lucky a fox did not get her,' she said as she struggled through the door. Megan noticed how content she was with leaving, so unlike her father.

Her brother had remarked to her once how their father got on better with his bull than their neighbours.

'Piedwch â bod yn chwerthinllyd' (Don't be ridiculous), she had snapped as if he were a stranger.

In his letter, in a part that she did not read aloud, he confided that he realised how terrible it will be for their father to see the animal sold. 'You should be here,' Megan said to herself, despising him for his absence.

She remembered her father saying to their mother, shortly after the bull had arrived that he could read its eyes and the bull could read his face. 'Nonsense,' her mother had said, raising her eyes to the damp patch in the ceiling. 'You are talking nonsense.' Then she turned to the children, 'You shouldn't listen to everything your father says.'

Mawrth | March 1878

'Gwiriondeb' (nonsense), she would say right away. In working as a maid in the Stepney Arms and sharing a room in the town, Mary Jane entered a world of rumour and whispers, many of which found their way back to Carmarthen and her father. Her father told anyone who would listen that his daughter had become what he always knew she would.

Her life in Llanelli was hard but it was easier than at home. She wore the old strained expression less and her fresh face and her new sense of fun was welcomed by guests and staff at the Arms and in the pubs when her shifts had ended. Her pretensions and her stories irritated some and amused others. Many in the taverns were bemused by the different ways in which she presented herself from week to week, sometimes from night to night. They observed how she would shift the register of her voice and speak in different languages, sometimes in the same conversation. But Llanelli was becoming crowded and for all her garrulousness and the company she enjoyed, it was not difficult to imagine her, as the Carmarthen historian later suggested to Mary-Jane, becoming lonelier and lonelier. There were days, slate-grey days, when she felt that she was not really living her life, only surviving. Above all, she missed her sister. There was a gap in her life which she desperately needed to fill. She found herself moving around in this sense of emptiness, assuming odd ways of behaviour to help her cope with it.

As she went from room to room in the Stepney Arms, Mary Jane created mounds of sheets that stood alongside the beds like shovelled heaps of snow beside a hedgerow. This was the life of a maid. All the time, she prayed that she would not find anything too horrendous or disgusting under a pillow, in the bottom of a water jug, or beneath the rugs. She prayed that something good would happen. Day followed day and evening chased the night with little sense of progress. At night, she dreamed of changing beds, pulling the sheets off her own bed, leaving her ffrind ystafell (room mate) naked as a streak of graphite. She longed for change. That was how her great-great-great-granddaughter, Mary-Jane, imagined her.

In a small room at the bottom of the basement stairs in the Stepney Arms Hotel which the female staff had purloined as their own, Ginger, one of the hotel cooks, kicked a large, straw-filled cushion. Her foot created craters in the round, smiling face of a complaining guest. The way the fabric fell inward pleased her but it didn't exhaust her contempt. She had served liver for breakfast, strong in flavour, cut from large half-moon slices that she had bought from her favourite butcher that very morning. The guest had held his plate close to his nose and shouted at the top of his voice so that everyone else at breakfast could hear: 'This has the acrid smell of an old Tom cat.' When Mary Jane entered, she heard the straw crackling beneath the cook's feet like broken cheek bones.

Ginger was a tall, skinny woman, taller than even Mary Jane. Her long, narrow hands, cut through with white scars and threaded with black veins that looked like strings of liquorice, extended well beyond her sleeves. Her face was pock-marked and, released from her cap, her hair would defeat a matchbox of pins.

In need of a sit down, as she said, Mary Jane fell into the other of only two chairs. When both chairs were occupied, staff sat on the floor cushions or bare boards.

'Bad morning?' Mary Jane asked, somewhat blithely but the cook did not notice.

'I never expected him to open his mouth to Llewellyn the dragon. I'll be lucky if I am 'ere tomorrow.' Her lips remained pursed in the anger that had driven her kicks.

Mary Jane fell further back into her chair.

'One of my reglars,' cook added, stirring the shillings in her small, black, pocket bag as if she were trying to calculate the income she had lost. Suddenly, she stared, knowingly like a spiritual medium, into Mary Jane's face.

'Have you a bob or few yet. I bet you 'ave.'

Mary Jane shook her head.

'You know what I means?' Ginger queried.

Mary Jane nodded. She knew the hotel parlance. She understood what 'bob' meant.

'But why are they called 'bobs'?' she asked.

'A bob is a shilling, right?'

Mary Jane looked a little blank.

'Swllt. A bob is a swllt an' we call 'em that because what they are willing to pay is in bobs.' Then she paused for a while. 'We all of us 'ave our bobs you know. Well, those of us who can still offer summit. The bobs do not just take anyone you know. Well some 'ill take anyone for a feel and a quick trick 'cos they are away from 'ome. 'Bob a nob, yes?' She laughed hoarsely at her own joke, like she was scouring the grease from a frying pan. 'Some 'as done it down 'ere, against them pipes no doubt. But you do not want to do the likes of 'em, give you the pox they will before you get your skirts straight.'

Mary Jane was mesmerised by the cook's salt collection as she called it. She tried to count how many coins were in there.

'Look at my 'ands, Ginger, demanded thrusting them under Mary Jane's nose, 'I don't believe I can take many more years in the kitchen. Not unless they put me on dinners. Then you really do get the posh. The evening nosh is what brings 'em in.' She cackled gravelly again at her own joke, spitting into Mary Jane's lap as she moved even further forward. Mary Jane wiped her maid's apron but the cook failed to notice. She held her hands even nearer Mary Jane's face.

'Look at these fingers. I got strong nails. I can crucify a back if they like that kind of thing. Or if I have a mind to. Take my advice, get yourself some reglars. Cawse, they ain't pleasant, none of 'em are, well, one or two is, if you're lucky like, but they all 'as to be very quick, they all understand that. With the right reglars, not that they are easy to catch, you have to cultivate 'em, understand? You can treble what you earns in a week. An' it is our money, like. You get what I am saying? We don't 'ave to 'and it in at 'ome or anything. You understand me, don't you?'

She drew the string around her bag, closing it as tightly as a laced boot, then hid it deep in her skirt pockets. Mary Jane's mind is gurgling like the water in the pipes behind her.

' 'ere,' Ginger whispered, encouraging Mary Jane to come nearer her until she could smell sweet onion, garlic and gin in her breath. 'Third floor, on the 'ospital side, there's a small room that Llewellyn can't use for bobs. They expects a decent-sized bed and a window you can see out of. That's where you take 'em, right? Don't do it in their rooms. The headmistress knows the stink of each of us, smells us before she sees us, that one! There's always a brush outside. See, you move it to the left then the rest of us knows there is a bit of yearning and earning going on inside. See? Then we know to wait a dog's lunchtime. That's as long as it takes. You don't give 'em more and they don't expects it.'

With that, cook rose to her feet. 'It's my fault when I think about it. I should have sussed 'im. It was cheap, like. If it's cheap, there's a reason for it. Mark my words. An' I've been going to 'im for nearly three years now. I even thought of bringing 'im around to our ystafell ysgubell, our broom room. As soon as I opened 'is package and saw 'ow it was all sliced, I really should 'ave known. 'Orse, I bet you. I wouldn't be surprised.'

Leaving that thought hanging, Ginger hastened to the door,

looking down at Mary Jane as she passed her as if she were wishing her to move so she might deliver the floor cushion one last hefty kick. Then, turning back, she closed her hands into large cat's paws and clawed at Mary Jane.

'Yes, I do 'ave 'em. I'd like to leave 'im with a tapestry of half-moons. All over 'is back, 'is belly and 'is truncheon, like 'e was one of those foreign carpets. I'd leave 'em so deep you could plant your seed potatoes in 'em.'

While holding the door open to the damp stink of the basement, Ginger mouthed to Mary Jane, 'Make a bob while you still got what they want. Fill yourself a purse, girl.'

Mary Jane closed her eyes and listened to cook's feet on the stone steps and the creak in her knees. She imagined the varicose veins, of which she often complained to all and sundry, misshaping her calves into badly turned table legs. When Mary Jane lifted her eyelids and tried to stand, her head wheeled like a spinning top she had had as a child. Guiltily and quickly, as if someone might look inside her head, she stuffed what thoughts Ginger had left for her in the back of her mind, like herrings stolen from the market.

Chapter Eleven
Sins of the Fathers

Ebrill | April 1879

Two months into living with Meic, Mary Jane was looking at a bonnet in a small shop in Llanelli. The regularity with which she frequented shops on a maid's money secretly annoyed him. In Lanrwst, he had been used to the perpetual movement of clothes *o law i law*, from one generation to the next, one family to another, one child to their younger sibling. In Denbigh, their nearest town, there was a large wholesaler to which second-hand clothes dealers re-sold old clothes. Many of these clothes were bought for making good and repairing. Most agricultural families wore patched garments which when they had really had their day were put to other uses. Farmers and labourers wore more or less the same kind of clothing as their grandparents: leather breeches, gaiters, hobnailed boots, a coarse smock, and a round black felt hat. Just before Meic left, things were changing and in west Wales he dressed differently, in stiff, brown corduroy trousers and sloppy loose jackets of unbleached drill. His mother and sister dressed in cotton or fustian, but Mary Jane seemed to be able to buy the occasional skirt in wool or linen. In the nearby towns of Swansea and Cardiff, cheaper clothes were available for women, usually imported, like much of the meat, from Europe. She spent many late evenings and most weekends altering what she bought so that it was more to her taste. She hankered after a sewing machine which had been developed in

America and which she had seen in the Stepney Arms where she worked.

For a moment, Meic wondered once again how his parents were getting on in their shop. He could not see his father closeted behind a counter day after day. But mostly, he thought about his sister. He missed her very much. He could not imagine her enjoying London. True, she was ambitious. But she was Welsh through and through.

'Go on buy it for me. I need it,' urged Mary Jane pressing Meic's forearm.

'You don't need it,' he said. 'You just want it. What we need is to save our money so that we can afford better rooms when we start our family.'

Mary Jane huffed quietly. Although she was very young, it slightly concerned him that she never warmed to any mention of a family. In that respect, she was very different from his sister. There were days, when they wandered the fields around Hill House that that was all she talked about. How she wanted children and a family. In truth, he could not see Mary Jane as a mother and that tore him apart at the very times he felt closer to her than to anyone else. She never envied her friends who were pregnant and could be nasty about them, whispering to Meic when they were alone that mothers wanted to be babies themselves and brazenly announcing, when they were not, that she would never be able to cope with fractious children. In the pub, after a few drinks, she could take lullabies with her onto a table top, whirling her skirt and clicking her heels, making innocent verses obscener than those around her might ever have imagined. She had a gift for remembering songs, albeit not entirely in their original, and a flare for surprise. When she performed, her audience did not fall silent and listen, they whooped, screeched and joined in with one bawdy song and one desperate rhyme after another. She always ended in a catfight of cheers and jeers.

'You spend all your wages, and half of mine, too, on clothes,' he decided to chide her after thinking of how things were where he had been brought up.

'Mae rhaid i mi gael llawer o ddillad' (I need to have lots of clothes) she argued softly, turning to Welsh as she often did when she wanted to bend him to her will, adding, 'dillad yw fy symbol statws'.

'Symbol statws, status symbol, where did you pick up words like that. From the guests in the hotel, I dare say,' he replied in genuine astonishment.

It was true, of course, that the Arms encouraged its staff, especially those who might come in contact with the guests, to meet their clientele's expectations and mirror something of the way they dressed. They were expected to be, as Mary Jane said, 'a cut above' the staff you would find in the public house. In the Arms, she studied what people wore and into what they changed at different times of the day so that she knew how to be correctly dressed. In her own family, she and her sisters were instructed by their father in the dress codes of the middle class to which he aspired. He would snap at his daughters, and at their mother, insisting that they understand that there were moments for wearing or discarding gloves and bonnets, how there were colours and fabrics appropriate to an occasion, how there were very precise differences between formal and informal events, and that there were ways of handing over coats, hats, parasols and canes in cafes and theatres. As they became older, he bought the children dolmans, paletots and muffs and dressed them above their class and their age.

Mary Jane was very different from Meic's sister and Megan was the only woman of about Mary Jane's age that Meic could say he knew really well. Assuming the airs and graces with which he had become very familiar in a short time, she took her opportunity to tease him.

'De mon temps à Paris. Besides,' she added, 'you want your wife to look,' she paused, then pressing as close to him as she could, so that no one else could hear, and shifting back to her Welsh, 'yn rhyfeddu' (astonishing).

She smiled smugly into his face, leaving him uncertain which she enjoyed most, slipping between languages in neither of which he was fluent or slipping between the sheets in their bed. Then she pulled away from him, as if she were becoming irritable with what she liked to describe as his 'ffyrdd gwledig crintachlyd' (rural miserly ways).

'I want all the other maids to know that I am not like them,' she whispered, not wanting to be overheard in the tiny shop.

'The way I dress says that one day I am going to be somebody. One day, I will run my own hotel, right here in the middle of Llanelli. The grandest hotel anyone has ever seen,' she continued, moving teasingly away from him again and, excitedly, trying on the bonnet and holding a hand mirror to her face. It had a black ostrich feather and tiny buttons around one side of the brim like the mouse eyes on a domino tile.

'It suits you, madam,' said the assistant who could not have been many years older than Mary Jane herself.

Meic was impressed to hear her partner addressed as 'madam'. Truth be told, he loved Mary Jane. She was bricky and full of stories that would make a stuffed bird laugh.

'One day you will come to a sticky end,' he often retorted, before slowly giving into her.

As Mary Jane wore her new status symbol out on the streets, Meic followed slightly behind. She seemed to float on air as if she didn't care about anything. He liked to be seen on the street with her. He was the jammiest of the jam he could hear the young men in the doorways say. She had etiquette, especially in the eyes of those who had no etiquette. But in company, she could be too outspoken and too direct. She had never learned the essential skill of curving the truth to make it more palatable. As he caught up with her, she saw two of the cooks from the hotel where she worked. At the exact moment that they noticed her, she clasped Meic's arm tightly, lifted her head as high as she could in a manner that reminded him of his sister, and ignored them.

'You know what I am going to do as soon as I get you home,' she whispered. He pretended not to hear.

Much more slowly and emphatically, she spelt out how she was going to reward him.

'Reward me?' he questioned with feigned innocence, as if forgetting what he had just bought her.

More intimately, and in a return to her seductive, whispering voice that she assumed when she wanted something, she elaborated: 'For being the most generous husband a woman has ever had.'

They laughed together on the same breath. The mild-mannered farmer's son made her feel positive about the world. Suddenly, she stopped and looked across the street at three large houses owned by merchants and bankers.

'There,' she said, 'I will have my hotel. Right in the centre of Market Street. Just like the one I saw in Paris, with a man in a top hat greeting all the guests, carrying their bags for them and calling the best horses and cabs. Grand horses, polished and proud.'

'In Llanelli!' Meic mocked her.

As she fantasised, he watched commercial travellers turning into Pembrey Street on their way to the Arms. One of them stopped as if he recognised her and seemed about to say something but thought better of it.

The Stepney Arms Hotel was the most prestigious in the area. Meic pondered to himself that whatever Mary Jane said, Llanelli did not need another. He had seen the new owner, Mary Llewellyn, a few times, reminding himself that she must be doing very well. He tried to imagine Mary Jane running a hotel. He knew she believed she would be very good at it as he once believed he would be a farmer.

Meic said to himself that Mary Llewellyn was a very special type of woman. As his father had always told him, such women were rare. Meic had always thought his sister was one of them. Meic did not know much about hotels but he had heard this much. Like almost everyone else in Llanelli, he knew how, on a journey through west Wales to Milford, about fifteen years previously, the last Prince Napoleon had stayed there with the Princess who was reported standing on the inn steps engaging in conversation with its staff. Among colliery workers like himself, it was referred to as the Slaughter House on account of the price and strength of its drink.

In the midst of these thoughts, he was interrupted. Mary Jane pulled her husband toward a pie shop, opening her purse and counting out a few pennies: 'For later, this evening,' she said, 'with some gin,' handing him the money as if, with her new hat, she was too important to enter a pie shop.

As she waited outside, he mingled with the wives of some of his fellow colliery workers. One or two of them commented on how elegant his wife was and how he himself scrubbed up well. As they did so, they exchanged meaningful glances with each other which passed over him. This pleased Mary Jane who listened intently at the open door. She was better dressed than them and everyone knew it. Meic and Mary Jane Davis would be the subject of supper talk and door-step gossip that evening. That really satisfied her. Some of it would be malicious, a concoction laced with bitters, but she realised that you had to expect that kind of thing.

'Merci,' she said playfully, and loudly enough for the others to hear, as he handed her the pie for her handbag. She was glad of Meic's company. There had been so many evenings and late nights when she had walked home alone from the hotel in which she worked. She had always felt conspicuous like an unattended meal in a café. A single, respectable woman had no place in 1870s Llanelli. People would pass in pairs or small groups and she believed that they could smell her loneliness. One evening, when she felt a little unwell, she had to stop and lean against a wall. A sharp pain jabbed upwards from her abdomen into her heart. It was like the stab she sometimes received from one of the whale bones when she wore her corset very tight. That was the moment when her eyes caught those of an elderly woman who always sat in one of the passages which Mary Jane took to and from the hotel. She gave Mary Jane a wide, black-toothed grin and rested her heavy tongue on her lower lip. She was ready for friendship and talk. But Mary Jane was frightened of her, as if she had extraordinary things to tell her. Despite the pain and the heaving in her chest, she pulled her coat around her and hurried past. When Meic began meeting her at the end of her shifts, they walked together, and she barely went that way. When she did, she rarely noticed the old woman. But she did not entirely forget her.

Meic was popular among the colliers and the iron workers – Welsh, English, Irish – even if some of them thought Mary Jane a little stuck up. Not that many did not like her. She put on airs and graces, but she spoke Welsh, while many of them couldn't, and they admired the way in which she turned from English to Welsh to French, and even to some German, and back again. She knew how to dance on a table, her party piece, which they loved on a Saturday night in the pubs. She flirted with them like their wives used to do and a few of them fantasised about her behind Meic's back. One of them even suggested to his friends that before she and Meic became a couple, he had taken her into the yard.

Awst | August 2016

Mary-Jane is beginning to see more of her uncle than she would like: once or twice in the surgery; more often when she is sitting in a café, waiting for her girlfriend, which she regards as definitely off limits; and sometimes when she is walking to her car. Usually, he has nothing to tell her that is of interest to her. But he seems to have more time than herself to comb the local newspaper archives. One morning, she is surprised, and dismayed, to find him at the surgery before it has opened, queuing behind an elderly couple with an equally elderly spaniel and a child holding a small rodent cage. Inside her consulting room, he reveals a newspaper cutting as if he is trying to trump what she had shown him the other day.

'You will not believe this,' he says, reminding her that they have been puzzled, quite rightly he insists, as to why Mary Jane had left a fairly grand house in Carmarthen for rooms in Llanelli. 'There may have been trouble in the home,' he suggests.

As he does so, he fumbles around inside a plastic paper wallet. He is never very organised. This irritates her immensely. In her life everything has to be systematized. She thumbs through the carefully arranged files on her table as if to make the point. She is already tired of everything about her ancestry being revealed to her in a piecemeal fashion, depressed by the way in which her producers are approaching things, as if they are some kind of dripping tap in her life. And now there is her uncle.

'Tell me, everything,' she says slowly, menacingly. She repeated it in Welsh: 'Dyweda wrthyf bopeth.'

Her mother often told him that she could be forceful like this. It is not the first time he has seen it. Her face is very close to his.

'Bopeth,' (Everything) she repeats, in a tone that makes him think she is going to pick up a scalpel and hold it to his throat.

'I do not want to tell you things that will confuse matters more if I can help it, especially if they might not be true. Trust me, I understand that you are entering very murky waters.' Almost, she thinks, an apology. 'If the initials on the gravestone you mentioned in your emails are those of Mary Jane Kelly maybe you have to think about her mother and not just her father.'

His voice is smug, as is often the case, and his awkward fingers retrieve a newspaper cutting from the chaos of invoices and business letters in his folder, some of which Mary-Jane notices are conspicuously red, final demands. He has written on it, in handwriting as illegible as her own, the name of a newspaper. While most of it is unreadable, she is able to decipher 'Swansea', and the date 1876. 1876 makes her think; that would be a few years before Mary Jane moved in with Meic Davis.

As Mary-Jane is reading, Ned explains how he thought that he would try to research the mother. 'Just for a bit of entertainment,' he adds. Then he waits, partly to allow her some time to digest the contents but also as if he wishes her to thank him. She doesn't.

The story from the paper is headed 'Mother Kelly's Drop':

> *Martha Kate Kelly (52) has fallen upon evil times. Brought before Carmarthen stipendiary (Mr W. T. Prynne) for being disorderly and using bad language outside the Ivy Hotel, Carmarthen, and pleading guilty to a 'little drop' too much over the festive season she was fined ten shillings and costs.*

Mary-Jane sinks her head into her hands. She has already begun to develop considerable sympathy for Mary Jane.

'Is this my great-great-great-great-grandmother?' she sighs. 'Is this what the producers are going to spring on me when we resume filming next week?'

'I feel sorry for her,' her uncle says. 'Evil times.'

'Disorderly and using bad language,' she interjects. 'Hardly "evil".'

'Prynne came down hard on her,' he agrees. 'Ten shillings was a lot of money in those days. But maybe they took into account that she came from a well-to-do family.'

'That is because she is a woman and a mother,' says Mary-Jane who is still struggling in the largely male world of hill farms and agriculture. 'But they call her "Mother Kelly". Is that for real or are they introducing an Irish stereotype here?'

'I think her husband may have brought some influence to bear on what happened to your MJ's mother. It seems that shortly afterwards, she was back in Ireland, in Dublin, and the children remained here with him. (As he talked, Mary-Jane thought to herself that it would take a man to think she had gone to pot, but she lets him continue). A lot of my research (an afternoon in the public library she thinks to herself, a little bitterly, and aware that she is being unfair) has involved discovering more about him. His daughter, your great-great-great-grandmother, seems to have been orphaned from the family either before or after her marriage with a coal miner.'

'Well, I suspected as much,' she says. 'But whether it is before or after her meeting Meic is important.'

She says this with an air that suggests that she may have a number of theories as to why MJ left her family home and speaks as if she is briefing her trainee veterinary assistants on the dangers of jumping to conclusions.

'I should be very interested in what your historians,' he stops, quickly correcting himself, 'the historians who are making the programme with you, come up with.'

His phone rings. On seeing the number, he becomes suddenly agitated, making his excuses.

'The slaughterhouse,' he says, appearing very flustered. What else, she thinks. 'I have to arrange a meeting with some guys. Dubliners. We will talk again.'

'Dubliners?' she says to herself, wondering if she has heard him correctly. He always seems frenetic these days. She wonders what he is up to now.

Awst | August 1879

Mary Jane threw herself onto a mattress someone had left by the side of the road and stretched out. They talk a lot these days, there is so much for them to discover about each other.

'Mary Jane,' Meic reprimanded her, 'you'll attract the constable.'

He watched his wife, saying nothing, following her gaze up into the sky. Eventually, he asked her whether she was studying the stars. This is the kind of question you ask each other when you are both drunk.

'Nade,' (No) she replied, 'nade', as if she were talking as much to herself as him. 'I am looking beyond the stars,' she said. Then she paused. 'Oblivion.' One word. But not that word. 'Ebargofiant.' He sat next to her feet and took the bottle she offered. He expected the conversation to turn to Welsh. But that did not happen. At least not immediately.

'Have I told you about Sioned?' she asked him.

He shook his head and returned her the bottle. Feeling confident enough in Meic to confide in him about Sioned was an important indicator of how close to him she had become. From the way in which she started to speak about this Sioned, Meic thought she must be another sister or a girlfriend. It was obvious that whatever relationship they had, Mary Jane was very fond of her.

'What about Sioned then?' he encouraged her.

She didn't speak for a while. Then the full story came very quickly.

'Sioned,' she explained, 'had brown feathers.' Then she sucked on the bottle, much more deeply this time. He laughed. He had not seen that coming.

He was afraid that her memory stream would suddenly cease – they often did. But she continued.

'Plu melfedaidd,' (velvety feathers) she whispered, as if they were in a conspiracy together. She hesitated, as if trying to find the right word. 'Beautiful. Coeth,' (Exquisite) she said, as if 'beautiful' were not enough.

'I never thought I would say that about a chicken,' she said. Meic wanted to laugh again, but checked himself. There was something about the way she was speaking that really disturbed him. She went on to describe how, every morning, Sioned would wait at the back door for her to be given a handful of corn. Sioned had plenty of corn but it was as if the food from her hand tasted better.

She took another long, deep intake of breath. Then she led Meic back through her memories into a particular Sunday lunch. 'Cinio dydd Sul.' She spoke these words slowly, prayerfully, as if to bring out some special meaning they had for her.

Although Meic had not met all her family, he saw them around the table. Mary Jane, not much more than a child, was aligning her knife and fork on each side of the plate so that they were equidistant from the other and were aligned exactly.

'Cinio dydd Sul.' (Sunday lunch). She repeated the words differently now. More like a curse.

She began to describe in careful detail, how her father meticulously carved broad, thin slices from the roast chicken's breast. Sleisiau gwyn.(White slices). Eventually, he came to Mary Jane's plate. Meic could see them all tackle the vegetables, leaving enough space on their plates for plenty of poultry. Mary Jane's eldest sister, who had already been served, was pushing the chicken slices around her plate as if she were reluctant to eat them. Her father studied Mary Jane. He sat at one end of the table, her mother at the other. Her sister who seemed not to want to be there was opposite her.

Eventually, it was her mother who slipped the secret. Mary Jane's face froze. She brought her hands up to her mouth and coughed into them as if trying to make herself sick. Her brothers giggled and looked from Mary Jane to themselves and back to her again. She tried to rush from the table but her father held her fast by that glare of his. Inhaling deeply, exhaling very slowly, getting ready, she told Meic how her father made her sit there, as they went back to Sioned's breast for seconds, leaving a mottled grey, reddish carcass at the centre of the table. Sgerbwd. (A skeleton). It was all she could do to keep from rolling up everything on the table in the preciously white cloth and crashing it all into pieces and splinters.

Meic could not watch them all sat around the table anymore and opened his eyes. Mary Jane brought her feet up under her thighs. Another drunken young couple went by on the opposite side of the road.

'Roedd sgerbwd Sioned.' (There was Sioned's skeleton)

Then Mary Jane described how her father and mother between them broke what she called 'yr asgwrn tynnu' but in English is known as the 'wishbone'. You know, she said to him, it is like a large letter Y. Her mother won the longest arm, leaving her father with the small stub.

Then Mary Jane's mother moved around the table, her piece of bone raised triumphantly in the air and when she reached her daughter, held it over her head. She was drunk, very drunk. 'Fel mae'r grym y groes,' (Like the force of the cross) she said, as if all this was some kind of baptism, seemingly unaware of the horrible thing they had done.

Killing a child's favourite pet and making her eat it, like Tereus made to feast on his own son's flesh.

Meic could understand Mary Jane's father doing this, from everything she had said about him, but what kind of poison had filled her mother's veins that she would have been party to such a thing?

Chwefror | *February 1879*

Mary Jane was concentrating on tipping salt into one and half pints of warm blood. She didn't hear someone enter the building below her rooms and pause to inhale the smell of damp and observe the mildew on the walls, the grimy floor and the peeling paint on the staircase. Or hesitate before the nasty darkness into which the stairs ascended. She missed the heavy footsteps threatening the thinning boards beneath them and eventually stopping outside her door.

A succession of sharp knocks made the door shudder in its frame and caused Mary Jane to jump, spilling beads of white grain over her work surface. Rubbing her hands in a cloth, she crossed to the door and yanked it open.

The figure, who had stepped back into the shadow of the landing as he heard her approaching, took her by surprise. He was stockier than when she last saw him, dressed in a stout corduroy suit and tweed cap. His face was hard and flushed like a sucked gobstopper. There were the same cold eyes that she had found it so difficult to brave as a child. But she was no longer a child.

She wondered whether he had come to tell her never to come home again. But it was too late for that.

'I was not expecting to see you again,' she said. Her eyes were sharp like pieces of broken bone.

His reply was equally terse and unforgiving, 'I was not expecting that you would be seeing me again.'

They stared at each other. Seconds passed, almost half-a-minute, before she invited him into her rooms. When she did, she strode ahead, leaving the door ajar for him to close. As he moved further into her room, he thought, for a moment, that there was someone else there, not Meic but another woman with whom Mary Jane and Meic were sharing. But it was a trick of the mind.

He stood and faced his daughter for the first time for many months since he had given her notice to leave their house. He seemed to have acquired a slight stoop, she thought to herself. He had not forgotten how she had called him pathetic and nauseating and he still remembered how she sneered, laughed and then turned her back on him for all time. Now they faced each other again. He was as well dressed as always. There was a silk handkerchief peeping out of his breast pocket and his shoes had an impeccable shine. He had taken off his hat and was turning it in a circle through both his hands, a habit of his she certainly remembered.

His eyes wandered around the room. The furniture was older and heavier than he had expected and he could just see the bed in the next room. He believed he saw a broken window but that was another mistake. He told himself it was because he was anxious. Behind Mary Jane, he recognised a jar of blood, registering that she must be making pwdin gwaed. There was rice, too, which made him think that if that was their supper, they may be struggling a bit, as he had expected. One part of her was thinking about offering him a drink, the other cursing him for turning up like this. She turned, passing from one intention to another, eventually freezing the moment.

'What do you want?' she asked.

Of all his children, she was the greatest puzzle. He had rehearsed what he would say on his way there. He had no intention of asking how she was coping; in truth he did not care. He didn't like her and he certainly didn't love her. At least, that is what he told himself.

'You are a Kelly,' he said.

Mary Jane did not understand what he was meaning so she let him continue.

'You have my name as your mother has.' Clearly, he had not forgiven either of them. When their mother became ill, her behaviour embarrassed him, especially when she drank. He had forbidden the children to talk about it and if someone were to ask after their mother, they were ordered to give an answer to another question as if they did not understand what they were being asked. Was this what had brought him here, she wondered, that she might damage the family name, his reputation.

She had not forgiven him, and would never forgive him, for what he did to her hands. Wondering what he thought of her brothers and sisters now that they were older, and what they now thought of him, she let herself be transfixed by the twirling hat, which was moving faster and faster. It reminded her of the large wooden circle at the fair that she and Meic had visited the previous week where a woman of her age had been strapped to a large revolving table while a man outlined her body in knives which he threw, supposedly, blindfolded. It was one of the scariest things that either of them had ever seen. She could not understand why the girl allowed herself to be used in this way.

'May I sit down?' he asked. She did not answer but simply watched her father sit. When she was a child, he scared her witless. Now she enjoyed standing over him. But she hated the way he still felt he had the right to run his eyes slowly and calculatingly around the contours of her body as the knife thrower did with his assistant.

'I saw your picture in the paper the other week,' she told him. 'Well, Meic spotted it.'

That seemed to shake him. For a minute or so, he looked quite frightened. When she thought about it again, he often acted as if he were scared of something. One day when they lived in Cardigan, she arrived home from school to be told suddenly that they were moving to Carmarthen. It was as if the family had been discovered by people he knew were after him and they had to flee quickly.

After he had actually looked at the picture, he seemed to relax.

'The miners' gathering,' he recognised.

'How is Meic?' he asked. 'I saw him only a short while ago emerging from the bath house. At least, I think it was him.'

He was interrupted for a moment by scratching from behind the wall or underneath the floorboards. They both heard it.

'Mice?' he suggested.

'Rats,' she said, unashamedly.

It pleased her for him to know that she was living in a place with rats.

'Is he doing anything about them?'

'He will do,' she said but not defensively.

'Has he thought about going back to the farm?' was the next question. Mary Jane was not sure where this was coming from. Why had he come around, searched her out, to ask this?

'It has been sold. His parents have a shop in Liverpool,' she said, cursing herself that she was telling him all this.

'I have never been up north,' he sighed. 'Do you remember the auction I took you to in mid-Wales?' Then he stopped, suddenly realising what he was doing. Yes, there had been love between them once. There had been times when he had acted as a father should. 'Cardigan Bay is enough for me,' he said, changing track.

There was another pause before he asked her whether she had heard from her mother. Obviously, he had not done so. She admitted that she had which, judging from the expression on his face, was not welcome news. She decided not to say much other than letting him know that she was more lucid. He sniffed in that way he always did when he did not believe what he was being told. She tried to read his face. She wasn't sure whether he didn't believe that his wife was recovering or that she was writing to his daughter.

'I heard talk the other day,' he confided, not unkindly, 'that your Meic has a way with animals, well, sheep at least. He's becoming known as the "sheep whisperer".' Then he laughed the way men in his circle did when they heard that one of them had been cuckolded. 'That's where he belongs on a farm, on top, not underground.'

'I told you, there is no farm, anymore,' she spat back.

It still wasn't clear where this conversation was going. She was reminded of how he would hover around the subject when any of his children had done wrong, before striking, like he once said his adder of a father always did.

'So, you know, he is making himself unpopular in the pit?'

At last, the bite.

'How so?' she asked. He had taken her by surprise, as his slaps always did when she was a child, even though she should have known they were coming.

'All his talk about unionism. You must have heard him. Or has he not spoken with you about this.' The fangs sank deeper. 'He's a north Welshie bringing ideas about how dangerous mines are into the south. Of course, the mines are fecking dangerous. But they put money in the pockets and food on the tables of more families than they break up.' Any hint of kindness had gone, as so often had been the case at home.

Mary Jane tried to contradict him. But he was having none of it. 'How do you think it looks like for me, when a Kelly man is heard mouthing off in the bathhouse?'

A Kelly man. Meic was never a Kelly man, she thought. He is a Davis, as she was now. But the truth was that she had heard Meic talk about all the local lodges coming together. It was often when he talked about his sister in London with the St John's people and the need for more of them at the pit to be trained to help when somebody was hurt.

'A miner's wife,' he scoffed again. 'So, this is where all your airs and graces have brought you. What now the year in Paris I bought you?'

'I,' then she rapidly corrected herself 'we have plans. We will not be stuck here for fifteen years.' The number of years was deliberate, she knew what it would mean for him. She had lost neither her ability to identify targets or her skill in scoring direct hits.

She always thought she would do better than anyone else in the family, he believed, except maybe for her sister who had recently married into what he regarded as an appropriate family and now lived in a big house in Cardiff. There was a talk of Cardiff becoming a civic centre and he could imagine how that would benefit municipal men there. He saw no such future for Llanelli, or for himself. The scratching began again, this time from under the floorboards, he thought, which made him notice how uneven the boards leading into the bedroom were.

'I will tell Meic what you said when he is back home tonight.'

Over his black pudding and rice, he thought to himself.

He had had his signal to leave. He rose on cue and retrieved his hat from the edge of the table. He felt that they needed money. That brought him a modicum of satisfaction. He noticed that, with their moving around, the bedroom door had slipped farther ajar, revealing more of the bed. It was as if there were a spirit in the room. At least that is what his wife and his eldest daughter would have said. They used to attend spirit gatherings together. He looked at Mary Jane and thought how she seemed taller and plumper. He could see now that the sheets on the bed were folded back like the half-read pages of a newspaper, the way they do in the more expensive hotels. As he turned to watch her stroll to the door and let him out onto the landing, he thought to himself 'you and your plans'. It was a thought he did not want to let go off but expressed slightly differently as she stood aside and let him pass her.

'I wish you pob lwc with your plans whatever they may be.'

He paused on the landing, glancing up at her a final time and twirling his hat again but in a much more relaxed way than when he had first entered.

'Merci. Bon soir,' she said pointedly

He slowly descended the stairs, slipping slightly on the steps in the gloom, and he heard the door close heavily above him.

For some men that would have been the end of things. But not for John Kelly. He had got his message over, he told himself. But it was not long before his temper flared again. She was a disgrace, she cared for nothing and for no-one but herself. How could she cling on to a man like that? Then he stopped the onslaught of thoughts. A vein throbbed in his temple like a fire that burned low. Deep inside his head, memories, regrets, were heaving, like pebble-laden waves over a beach.

Medi | September 1879

He heard the school before he saw it. It was the mid-morning break and the children emerged a few at a time, dropping exhausted around the school steps like empty sacks. A cloud struggled from behind the building which the children's listlessness seemed to make heavier. It was the kind of cloud that hung over towns and villages when something bad had happened. Mary Jane's father stopped at the gates on his way to the colliery office, trying to catch sight of the few children he now had of school age. He saw the two of them but they were not together, standing instead in groups of their own friends. None of the children were running, skipping or chasing each other. They all stood around like old men and women in serious conversation. There was a definite mood in the yard which slipped between the various groups like a vagrant begging money, insisting that he be noticed. Mary Jane's father reflected on how his own school days in Limerick had ended a few years earlier than those of the eldest children here, loitering beneath the school windows. A group edged further toward where he was standing as if their talk had become such that it needed to be out of earshot of the others. He could overhear them but none of them were speaking English at that moment. He still hated the way in which his children were able to speak together at home in a language which excluded him even though he was the one who had encouraged them to become fluent in Welsh.

The teacher appeared at the top of the steps and he noticed how the different groups drew together as happens at a funeral when the coffin arrives. A small, scruffily dressed boy slipped from behind her skirts and skipped down the steps two at a time. The children parted, like the Red Sea, to enable him to pass through them and reach the far corner wall where he slumped, hung his head and hugged his knees. He sat there totally alone, all shadow and misery. If Mary Jane's father were nearer, he would have heard the boy sobbing and swallowing spit. The children who had not been speaking anywhere above a whisper became silent. They avoided looking at the boy or moving near him as if he were the bearer of some contagious disease. Their teacher turned into the school and the children began to file in behind her, slowly, as if they were walking into church. Eventually, the small boy rose and reluctantly joined them.

When the moment came for him to place his own feet upon the bottom step, he turned suddenly and, like a startled hare, headed for the gates and bolted into the road, almost felling Mary Jane's father, and swerving at the last minute to avoid a team of cart horses. Oblivious of the startled animals and of the wagon driver's insults, he stumbled over ruts of dried mud, almost breaking his ankle. He lay there for a while, panting like a frightened animal himself, his eyes were wild and cheeks tear-stained. Eventually, scrambling to his knees, he struggled to find surer footing and stared at John Kelly as if everything that had happened that morning were his fault. Mary Jane's father, who believed himself to have a nose for transgression, knew instinctively that the boy had committed a grievous sin. He saw himself in the boy, years ago, angry and ashamed, running from his father's strap. He knew what it was like to be lost and alone among hills and backyards, knowing that, at nightfall, he would have to return. The accused child became an accuser. John Kelly, aged 9, ran with him, toward what he was running away from.

Awst | August 1879

As Meic reached their door, the smell of Mary Jane's cooking chased the acrid dampness from their landing. Inside, the penetrating scent from bunches of herbs, some intended for the cooking pot, others destined for pestle and mortar as a pain relief, filled the room. She stood at a pan in which sizzling fat, and odd droplets of blood, leapt around in the flames. A rabbit had been skinned, boned and cut into pieces. It was cooking in its own blood, flavoured with herbs and other ingredients. A half sack of strong, earthy root vegetables, obtained cheaply from a local shop, stood beside her.

At first, he thought she was cooking cubes of chicken and expressed surprise.

'No, not chicken. I will never eat chicken, right?'

'Understandable,' he said.

'I have added red wine to the sauce,' she explained. 'The best French cooks say it makes a family of all the different flavours.'

Meic watched her crush a cocktail of herbs in the heel of her hands before stirring them into the simmering pot. She was so calm and efficient, he thought. He had never heard anyone talk about food in the way Mary Jane did. His own mother, like thousands of Victorian housewives, had a copy of Mrs Beeton's *Household Management*. He noticed that Mary Jane did not have a copy but relied on works by a celebrated chef, Alexis Soyer, which did not surprise him. This evening, *The Gastronomic Regenerator* lay open on her work surface, a book she used when she wished to impress. At other times, with less fanfare, she dipped into *A Shilling Cookery for the People*. It impressed him that she read so widely but sometimes her English failed her and he was asked to read parts of recipes to her. She seemed more comfortable with *Llyfr Coginio a Chadw Tŷ*, a cookery and house-keeping book, not only because it was in Welsh but because it was published 'gyda darluniau eclurhaol' (with explanatory pictures). Thinking of her relying on illustrations placated his jealousy over her knowledge of France and its ways.

She had once told him that she had come from a farming family but she seemed to have no sense, as he did, of the history and struggle that went into bringing foods to the market. Or, perhaps she did, he couldn't make up his mind, as was the case with a lot about her. Perhaps this was her way of escaping all of that. He remembered saying to his father, when they first started to worry about the future of their farm, food is everywhere, everyone loves food.

How many of his mates in the colliery were arriving home to French rabbit, he wondered, while laying down his snap box and tugging at his heavy, collier's jacket. He retained the Davis family's suspicion of foreign food and when he arrived in the south, until he met Mary-Jane, he lived off the street stalls, and occasionally one of the chop houses in Llanelli, on a diet of liver, bacon, lamb cutlets, bread and potatoes.

'I thought you were making pwdin gwaed for supper tonight,' he murmured gently, thinking of his mother's black pudding which he had loved. He expected a sharp rebuke but she responded kindly, lovingly, but perhaps with a suggestion that there was something else on her mind.

'I thought after a day underground you deserved better.'

Mary Jane prepared meals that were very different from those he had eaten at home. She introduced him to mulligatawny soup, eels matelot, ham with madeira sauce and what she said the ladies who came to the Arms with their gentlemen were served, *grisailles au vin blanche*. She liked cooking things slowly in their own juices, something she said she had learned from Soyer but he had noticed was repeatedly recommended in *Llyfr Coginio*. She loved her cast-iron digester in which she made all kinds of delicious soups and jellies. Unlike his mother, she talked all the way through everything, slipping, as was often her habit, into French and Welsh before returning to English as it pleased her.

'If you are trying to teach me to cook,' he once told her, 'you must use English or a bit of Welsh. I might understand you then.'

In the kitchen at Hill House, everything was sliced, sealed, slipped in and out of pans, and scooped onto plates in silence until the meal came to the table and woe-be-tide any of them who were late. Meals at home had always been a respite in a long day of endless tasks, like herding, milking and feeding. For Meic's mother, cooking was a duty. For her family, meals were a ritual.

As Meic watched Mary Jane, he could not help think about the bloodiness and butchery in which women were involved in the kitchen. Earlier that week, he and his fellow miners had been guffawing over a cartoon aimed at the new women's movement in Wales. A familiar Welsh politician's head dangled at the cook's waist while her other hand searched behind her back for a knife conveniently placed at the edge of a table. Heads were pickled in jars and displayed on a Welsh dresser while those of other politicians, which the group had tried hard to identify, were attached to chickens clucking around her feet. They had laughed with each other but there was a dark undercurrent. The woman, they noticed, had a mouthful of dagger-like teeth, sharp, awkwardly aligned and pointed. Their homes suddenly became but a veneer, like a seemingly calm sea, beneath which raged a deeper ocean of violence. Now in their kitchen, he needed to express his love for Mary Jane. So, he could see only her soft red, inviting lips.

Mary Jane put so much of herself in their meals and brought so much of herself to their table that he loved their suppers together, even though he was often too shattered from the coal face to really enjoy them. But there was one thing that worried him about them. In her cooking, as in the way she flirted with him and danced around their friends, there was too much foreignness, too much performance, too much having to be special. Some of this came from the Stepney Arms in which she worked which prided itself on keeping a good table and, on some weekend evenings, hosted table d'hôte which offered a choice of six main dishes including salmon and quail for three shillings. There were times when he wanted to shout at her, 'Why cannot you just speak English or Welsh? Why do you have to wriggle about so much?' And he thought of suggesting, 'Can't we once in a while just have a piece of mutton with nothing extra done to it?' But he had to be careful. He knew that if he said something like this, just once, it would be the end of them.

'Nawr, dyn ni'n barod' (Now, we are ready) she said, bringing their supper to the table.

His plate was nothing like anything served in a pub or at Hill House. At home, the most luxurious meal his mother served was saddle of mutton, a side order of tongue, potatoes and sprouts. He imagined that if they ate in a fancy restaurant, they would have what was now put before him. He did not know because he had never eaten in a restaurant. Mary Jane said she had.

She spread pork and mushroom pate on bread in front of him, like poultice on a bandage, as an hors d'oeuvres. The pieces of rabbit were wrapped in ham and stuffed with pieces of the creature's kidneys and liver. It made him think of her story about her father making her skin a rabbit for the first time. Fragments of the leftover offal dressed the outer rim of the stew. She had arranged them carefully so that they were consistent. They contrasted with the rabbit pieces themselves which were heaped on top of each other.

He lifted his knife and fork toward the plate, gently raising the ham which enveloped each piece of rabbit as if he were not sure what to find there exactly. She watched him intensely, leaving her own knife and fork on the table. He worked a mouthful of rabbit behind his teeth. He did not like the way she stared and felt forced to nod in approving grunts as he ate. The offal intensified the taste of the cooked rabbit bringing back to it, he thought, something of the living body.

Eventually, Mary Jane returned the smile he had cast her, picking up her own utensils. She had prepared this dish patiently, precisely and carefully. Disrobing, disjointing and dicing a small, furred creature still bothered her. Usually, she pushed it to the back of her mind. But this time, disembowelling and displaying what she found in its torso did worry her more than ever and she didn't know why. She watched Meic tuck into the centre of the stew, folding pieces of meat and shards of vegetables on his fork. He was clearly hungry and ate quickly as if at any moment he would be called back underground.

Mary Jane normally chattered excitedly when they had supper but this time, she progressed with her own plate more slowly than usual. It was as if she were trying to understand something. And around this time, Meic began to learn there were different sides to her. He discovered she had what in those days they called the morbs. Because he was tired, on this particular evening, he welcomed the quiet.

Chapter Twelve
Glanders

Look back with Meic now, over the short time that he and Mary Jane have been together. Think with him about her. What is he worrying about? What is he asking himself? Who is she? No, who is she, really? She was sixteen when they met. What experience had she had? Who will she grow into?

These kind of questions keep Dr Mary-Jane Sullivan awake. Always thinking about her great-great-great-grandmother. Some days, she seems so far away from her work. Her colleagues have noticed because it is so unusual for her. One and a half centuries have passed since Mary Jane and Meic lived together. Dr Sullivan thinks about her mother, then herself. Will someone's sleep be disturbed by questions about herself in some distant future? Will someone lie awake trying to imagine her, putting fragments together, trying to recreate her story. And will they be featured themselves in someone's memories in the future?

She is trying to see her great-great-great-grandmother as Meic saw her. Later, she will find it difficult to distinguish what she is reading from what she is imagining and from what she is dreaming.

Mawrth | March 1879

Those who looked up that morning would have seen a reddening sky as if the furnaces of hell hung over the town. A few hours previously, sheep and cattle had been driven into Llanelli's Market Street. People pressed forward, picking their way around mole-hills of crust-covered dung and between ink-black sheep's droppings, avoiding the green-brown rivulets that ran around their feet. Flies gathered everywhere and, more than once, Mary Jane had to pull them from her mouth and nose. Dogs, skeletal and drooling, roamed in-between stationary and slow-moving cartwheels. One had recently whelped and her teats dragged on the dried mud. A boy, probably less than ten years old, cried out: 'Rat poison, best ever, only a penny, guaranteed, strong as a dog's bite. Rat poison, best you'll find …' A young girl sat on a wooden box behind a table covered in two mismatched pieces of threadbare carpet on which all manner of bric-a-brac was displayed. Her voice rose plaintively above the noise of the street. Behind her stood an elderly woman who looked expectantly into every face that passed, as if she were offering the child herself for sale. Her mouth was frozen in the shape of a ceramic grin that revealed four yellowing, misshapen teeth planted in her upper gum like piano keys. A scarecrow in men's clothes lay on a bed of rotting vegetables near a wall. The buttons in his trousers were bedded in a large pool of piss.

Mary Jane tried to keep to the footpath which at one point led her beside a milk-cart horse. Its head was lowered nonchantly to a bucket which was of more interest to a giant rat running around its legs. Rats still frightened Mary Jane, especially when she tried to sleep in her rooms on her own. She patted the horse's curved, scrawny neck. The flies which she brushed away with her bonnet joined those crawling and zooming around its ears and eyes. Others were distracted by the discharge from its nostrils.

A gentleman in a tall hat and ankle-length coat pulled her gently away.

'I would not loiter here, Miss,' he advised. 'Glanders.'

One word. That's all he had to say. Mary Jane allowed herself to be moved.

'Glanders? Do you think?' she checked with him.

'I am sure,' he insisted. 'That critter needs to be in the knacker's yard.'

Together they hurried on. Mary Jane had to keep raising the hem of her skirt and her shoes were already becoming discoloured and slippery. The stranger had an eye for details when it came to women. He noticed a hole in her stockings and the way her hair curled from under her bonnet. She gave him the impression she was approachable. No, she wore a maid's uniform under her coat, she was accessible. She strode like someone confident that this walk to menial work would not be part of her life for ever. They rushed for a while without speaking and not always beside each other because slurry, dung and other waste came between them. To her, he looked like he was significant. She wanted the people she passed every day to see them together. Just by the way he held himself and expressed an awareness of her, he made her feel like a lady. There was something about him she found magnetic. He dressed like her father and smelt of his scented soap. She wished this man were her father instead of her own.

That evening, when she was telling Meic about her stranger, as she called him, she remembered he had said something about having to make arrangements for a visitor. Meic thought she was implying that within a few seconds of them meeting he was confiding in her. It made him smile. Excitedly, she went on to say that her gentleman's tone of voice suggested he was disgruntled at having to do so. Some of this she had gleaned from staff gossip in the hotel. Mary Jane had wanted to talk with him herself and she convinced herself that he wanted to speak with her. But why would he need to talk with a hotel maid if he were that important, Meic asked himself.

Mary Jane's sense of her own importance had once again become a taut thread. In truth, Mary Jane and her gentleman friend did not enter the hotel together. She took the narrow shortcut that she followed every morning to the side entrance of the Stepney Arms. It led eventually to the slaughterhouse but Mary Jane never walked that far. The screams of slaughter made her think of the manic crying from the madhouse near Carmarthen. In the evening, the passageway was full of the smell of malt, shellfish and urine. Toward the end of the week, after dark, it was one of the most raucous rats runs in Llanelli. Dozens of people crammed into it. There were brawls, even knife fights. It was not unusual to see a nose bloodied or even a face sliced in a skirmish over a knee trembler. Even of an afternoon, there were women trying to hit on passing men and men looking for invitations into smelly rooms or back alleys.

Usually, after she had turned into this narrow passageway of a morning, the clatter of horse traffic and the cacophony of people shouting each other in Market Street faded, but today, they stayed with her, almost drowning the shrill screeching of caged birds hanging from the ramshackle windows above her. As she extended the gloved hand over her nose, she marvelled that those who lived here could keep their windows open. The smell from human waste and left-overs in the drains slumped into her stomach.

Mary Jane realised that she was late. Entering through the side door, she had to slope through the lobby, something which staff were not allowed to do. They had their own corridors and stairs to make their way through the hotel and only in uniform could they step among the guests. She stayed close to the walls like some kind of rodent from the street. As she did so, she saw him at the reception. The manager was talking with him which was something she only did to flatter high profile guests. His visitor must be important she thought. But she also felt ashamed, not wanting him to see her and especially to see her called out in public for being where she should not have been and still in her outside clothes. The hotel owner had joined them and the three of them were so otherwise engaged that she was able to sidle through another door, hidden in a group of fellow maids.

Awst | August 1879

But she wasn't just a maid. She was Mary Jane. Marie Jeanette. The tea room where she had chosen for them to meet said a lot about how she perceived herself. Megan had not visited anywhere so grand even in London. She had to pinch herself to remember that Mary Jane was a maid in a hotel and her brother a miner. A waiter led her beneath the high vaulted ceiling and between tables with carefully-ironed tablecloths to where Mary Jane was waiting. She had been looking fairly serious as Megan crossed the room but her face lifted into a wonderfully warm smile as soon as she spotted her. As Megan's chair was drawn out for her and the waiter hovered until he was sure she was comfortable, Mary Jane made a point of thanking him, kindly but with a brevity she clearly felt appropriate to the situation.

This was a meeting which Mary Jane told her friends about, long after she had left Carmarthenshire, sometimes crudely summarising it, or, as some felt, weaving it into something of a fairy-tale, the loving wife outwitting her husband's wicked sister from the icy north. Megan had brought a handful of recipes with her. Most of them were written in her mother's handwriting but a few of them were in her own. She had selected them carefully and when she handed them over to Mary Jane, she noticed how slowly and carefully she read them, perhaps moving a little more swiftly over those written in Welsh. She could not decide whether Mary Jane's Welsh was better than her English or because, as traditional Welsh recipes, she was more familiar with them.

As Mary Jane read, Megan asked her when it was that she had left Ireland.

'I do not remember Ireland,' she responded, not quite answering the question she was asked, as if she were regarding it as some kind of trap. Then she added, 'The family moved to Wales shortly after I was born.' Then she contradicted herself. 'Yes, I do remember Ireland, through the stories and songs of my older brothers and sisters.' Becoming more reflective, she suggested, 'memories are not just our own. You must know that, being more Welsh than I am.'

A log dropped into the hollow of the fire creating a shower of sparks.

Although they were only a short way into their first conversation, Megan was already beginning to think of Mary Jane as a deeper character than she had expected, who reminded her a little of herself. She could see why her brother had become involved with her. She looked around at the other customers, especially the women, who were mostly sat in a straight-backed, commercial class kind of way. Then, she bowled Mary Jane the kind of question that landed her in trouble in her schooldays at Llanrwst, especially with one particular teacher.

'Do you see yourself as Irish or Welsh?' she asked.

Mary Jane swiped back swifter than a cat.

'Neither,' she said. Then, like a cat, she waited for further movement with a sly look from the corner of her eyes.

It made Megan suspect that this was a question she had been asked a few times in the past. Mary Jane placed the small stack of recipes on the edge of their table and looked up at the ceiling. It was a gesture which made Megan remember her own habit of doing this which caused one teacher in school to remind her sarcastically that the answer to a problem she had set her was not written above her head. When Mary Jane continued, she was even more cryptic.

'I see myself as I want to see myself and not as others want me to see myself,' she said. Megan could not make out whether she was trying to be profound or deliberately obtuse and unhelpful. She stared at Megan as if they were playing poker and she was weighing which card to play. She did not wait long before asking Megan whether she saw herself as others saw her or as someone that others did not always see. To Megan's mind, thinking of her own childhood, Mary Jane could have added, because of their own failings and opinions. Mary Jane smiled again, as if to tell her that she did not have to say what she thought because Mary Jane had already seen how alike the two were.

Megan noticed that Mary Jane had aligned the edges of her recipes as best she could, even though the papers were of different sizes. It was not easy for her because two of her fingers on one hand, Megan noticed, were stiff and did not easily bend toward, or close neatly into, her palm. She placed one recipe which she had read once, and then a second time, on top of the pile. Every now and again, she would return to straightening and tidying the papers before moving across the table to adjust and readjust her cutlery often replacing them in exactly the same position.

Occasionally, she would stare out of the window as if something had irritated her. When she looked back, she was friendly again as if there were more than one conversation happening in her head, one with Megan and several others with different people. It was a strange experience and not one that Megan had ever had with anyone else.

Among the recipes, Megan had strategically inserted a few that were more expensive than the others, needing pricier or rarer ingredients, and which required better culinary skills than the others. She had done this in order to assess Mary Jane's reactions and glean insight into how well off they were as both worked in relatively low paid manual jobs. Mary Jane did not mention any recipe in terms of its cost or the skills it needed. If that were in her mind, she kept it to herself. Now that she had seen what sort of a person Mary Jane was and how alike they were, Megan felt guilty that she had tried to trick her in this way. She hoped that Mary Jane had not noticed how the recipes had been arranged and had not put on a poker player's face to fool her. She wanted Mary Jane to like her. She wanted to stay close to her brother.

At one point, Mary Jane flicked through the recipes and collated a number of traditional Welsh recipes as if she were really interested in them. Then assuming a slight French accent, as if she suddenly wanted to inject a sense of fun into their conversation, she admitted that Meic was becoming slightly tired of her French cooking especially her service à la russe.

'Personally,' she said, 'I love putting a course at a time on our table.' Then she added, perhaps a little pointedly, 'but a lot of what we now think of as expensive were once peasant dishes: Soupe à l'oignon, rillettes de porc, rabbit cassoulet which was a French farmer's dish and Meic's favourite, lamb à la Bourguignone.'

When Megan asked her where she obtained her knowledge of French cuisine, she confided that she had spent some time in Paris with her eldest sister in a tone of voice that underscored how privileged she felt herself to be. Then, in fluent Welsh, she recited the names of the Welsh dishes Megan had handed her. But she also introduced some of her own such as broth traed lloi, which she said Meic especially enjoyed, as if he were a stranger to Megan, and pen buwch (ox cheek) when they were short of money.

A lady on the next table started violently twitching her nose, all the world like a rabbit, as she tried to stifle a sneeze. Megan suddenly felt that she was sitting in a scene in a taxidermist's shop window. When the waiter returned to their table, and without ascertaining whether he even spoke French, Mary Jane ordered the Ivy Hotel's best pastries and a range of cakes to accompany their tea as if they were sat in a café in Paris. Her voice had a lovely low lilt that carried to every corner of the tea room. The hotel was long used to catering for continental visitors and overseas dignitaries and the waiter was not thrown by her French. Megan saw him as the only male mouse in the room, and after he had taken their order, she watched him snatch up the menus in his little pick paws with the aplomb of an omnibus conductor tearing off tickets.

As Mary Jane shuffled the recipes again, she commented here and there, highlighting in Welsh what Meic would like among the traditional recipes. Megan was not sure what was happening. It was almost as if she were telling Megan that she knew her brother better than she did. But what especially worried Megan was why she felt it necessary to do so. Had she detected a closeness between brother and sister that somehow threatened her? Was this something that she had picked up from Megan, even in such a short space of time or from only a few letters between them, or had she felt this from things which Meic had said to her. Just as Mary Jane had led Megan to a place where she was forced to wonder how much she knew of her, Mary Jane launched into how she saw Meic and why she loved him.

'Meic is not like most men. Men can be cruel.'

Megan wondered about Mary Jane's experience of men. She knew farmers and she knew that they could be cruel. As if reading her mind, Mary Jane asked whether she liked farming. Megan had to admit that for her farming was too much about ... but she was not allowed to finish for Mary Jane suggested the word for which she was perhaps searching, 'slaughter'. One hundred and fifty years into the future, her descendant would read a novelist who describes the heart of the country as mean and spiteful.

Megan paused, conjecturing whether her companion was talking about her experience of the countryside, commenting upon the nature of the recipes which she had given her to read and the butchery which underlay them or speaking from her own knowledge of how violent men could be.

'Isn't this a bit contradictory,' Megan challenged her. 'Eating meat and finding the slaughter of animals distasteful?'

'Love and slaughter in the countryside. Who wants to be an animal, eh? Not every animal has to be killed and no animal deserves,' she thought for a while, 'to live without experiencing love. Fy ffrind, mon ami,' she said, stretching across the table, holding one of Megan's wrists in her hands and looking into her eyes, 'an animal can look you in the eye and that shows it has intelligence and a level of awareness which is a measure of that intelligence. Your brother taught me that.'

She let go of Megan's hands and sat back into her chair. 'Your brother taught me that.' The words ricocheted around Megan's head. Once again, she felt that she was being manipulated, outwitted, as if Mary Jane had set out to touch her and make contact with her, before pouncing on her as a predator on its prey.

When Mary Jane talked for more than a few sentences, ideas tumbled around like objects in a hastily searched cwtch bag. It was a characteristic everyone in the Stepney Arms observed and those who gathered around her in the Llanelli pubs found entertaining. Megan admired how she quickly seized on their conversation, taking it in different directions according to her whims.

'Sometimes the world does not feel like home, don't you think?'

'And how do you manage that?' Megan asked.

'I have always been able to look into what for me is my little heaven, that silence that is beyond everything.'

She then sat silently as if to emphasise the point. Some of her sentences, Megan noticed, had such haste that it seemed she was rushing to make a point in a riposte. Others loitered in the air, as if looking for a place to rest.

'Mary Jane,' she said, suddenly speaking of herself in the third person, loosening her grip on Megan but not completely letting go, 'does not want to be a farmer either.'

Then she burst into laughter as if she had successfully read Megan's mind, and raised her hands above her head, oblivious of, or perhaps even enjoying, the attention she was receiving from the other tables. Megan wondered how many others in the Ivy Hotel tearoom were farmers or from agricultural families.

'She wants to own a hotel,' Mary Jane continued in the third person before suddenly halting, to allow a train of thought that was new even to herself. 'Or a fashion boutique.'

Megan observed at least one couple looking away to one side and smirking as Mary Jane announced this.

Megan was encouraged to look again at Mary Jane's clothes. She had to admit that she was better dressed than herself and that her clothes competed well with what others in the room were wearing. Clearly, Mary Jane was a person who adored fashion and she wanted to be seen as such. Megan pondered once again where the money came from for Mary Jane to dress as expensively as she did and to host teas like this.

Then, as her brother was later to tell her in a letter was characteristic of her, Mary Jane became quiet and very gradually her face darkened as happens when a cloud begins to dim the daylight. She sat back in her chair, like a medium suddenly possessed of insight from outside of herself. Her previously laughing eyes lost their perfect circle and narrowed as if she were trying to focus on something really close to her. Sighing, she brought her face forward without glancing away from Megan.

'Dych chi a minnau, rwy'n credo, wedi profi creulondeb. Ydw i'n gywir?'

(You and I, I think, have experienced cruelty. Right?)

At first, it was the accuracy of what Mary Jane had said that shook Megan. She had no knowledge of what had happened to Mary Jane in her life but clearly, she had experienced brutality as she had done. But, although the crowded tearoom was hot and stuffy, Megan felt cold and shivery beneath Mary Jane's stare. It was like a spirit were speaking through her and was looking out of Mary Jane's eyes. Her eyes were like molluscs sucked out of their shells. Megan felt relieved when Mary Jane sat back again but as she did so, Megan felt that there was someone else there easing her shoulders, as if to say, Mary Jane that is enough.

Mehefin | June 2016

Above them is a painting of a fish that no local person has ever seen. Some of the characteristic features of fish from the Dee are identifiable but so much is baffling. Some people say they can see a cobra in it, others a bloated eel, and some think it is a giant cod that has been squashed. There is something dog-like about its jaws which hold rows of large, strong-looking teeth capable of tearing the toughest flesh.

A chorus of the Welsh rugby anthem, 'Hymns and Arias', from the bar next door dies down. The landlord can be heard urging caution as someone orders another whisky double.

'This can be lethal stuff,' he says, 'after the number of pints you have had.'

Mary-Jane's uncle is concentrating on a wall of beer mats he is building around a bowl of salted peanuts. One of his companions is arguing his case, intently but in whispers, while the other is staring at Ned's balding crown. When he finishes, the three sit in silence, pondering the picture of the fish. Ned places a pub menu over the beer mats he has organised. Immediately, the construction reminds him of the massive capstone of the Kilcooney Dolmen, in Co. Donegal, one of the largest and most famous tombs of its type in Europe. The Kilcooney capstone appears different from every angle from which it is viewed, rather like the fish in the picture, and Ned tries to see whether this is true of his own replica of it. Some say that the Kilcooney capstone resembles a whale, others see it as a bird in flight. His own model looks flat and rectangular no matter from what angle it is viewed. The others want a response, but he squints and holds his face close to his table-mounted Kilcooney

Dolmen, persisting in different perspectives from different angles.

'Look, at that,' his companion says in a strong Dublin accent, pointing to the menu, fish pie. You always see fish pie, not cod pie.'

Ned gathers his unused beer mats as if they were chips in a poker game. His pint has turned into a stocky glass of smoky whisky. While he has been concentrating on his sculpture, one of the others has been to the bar. Ned imagines himself seated on a stool at the end of a long skittle alley of a counter with the glass of whisky, propelled with a gunslinger's velocity, hurtling toward him. He wants to say that you see 'cod and chips' everywhere. But he doesn't quite have the courage.

Ned can hear a persistently slurry voice and he looks up to see ten-pound notes being stuffed ostentatiously into the landlord's breast pocket. He knows that this man and his friends will end up heaving all their drink down a toilet or a gutter somewhere but they are happy for now. He tries to study the fish above them as if he were seeing it for the first time. He thinks of it with the head and tail cut off, the thick body weighed and priced, and the rest sold to make the pub's favourite lunch, cawl pysgod (fish soup). The thick fillets of fish would turn easily into cash. Each succulent piece could be sliced and counted for. But all he sees is something no one would want to eat even if they knew how to prepare it unless it were hidden with haddock, salmon and prawns in a curry. When meat is done with, he wonders, will fish still be caught?

'No one asks what the fish is, do they?' his friend insists. 'It might be Vietnamese river cobbler.'

'What the feck's that?' his companion interjects.

But his friend continues, 'cod, haddock or any white fish. They do not care.'

'Do you really think so?' whispers Ned.

The beer mats are too small to support the menu card.

Eventually, the whole structure collapses.

'Ok. Forget fish,' his companion retorts in response to Ned's sceptical face.

'Meat pie,' the other companion suggests. 'There you are, meat pie. No one asks what the meat is in the meat pie.'

'Our customers order lamb, pork, beef, chicken,' Ned says.

'What do you slaughter most?'

'Around here, sheep. Some beef.'

'And what do people taste in their meat pies? The gravy, the bourguignon, the tikka curry.'

Ned nodded. 'But not horse,' he says, causing the other two to look around and shush him.

They bring their heads together as one of the men from Dublin whispers, 'They would eat it if they did not know it was mixed with their beef. It is just the idea that puts them off. Australians eat kangaroo and crocodile.'

He stares knowingly at Ned, as if to rest his case.

Ned looks again at the fish.

'This is not Australia,' he says.

The gunslinger at the end of the bar whom Ned can see in his mind's eye finishes his whisky and slowly takes off his gloves. He pulls his long coat aside so that everyone can see the long gun strapped to his thigh.

The other man at Ned's table presses the point home.

'I bet there are people in this town who have eaten,' he says returning to a whisper, 'horse meat in France, Belgium, Asia or South America without even realising it.'

'You have a deal, stranger,' says Ned's gunman. 'But know this,

I charge a high price for my killing.'

'You clearly need my slaughterhouse and my distribution,' Ned says. Then adds, as if his gunslinger has taken his place, 'I need plenty of cash to pay the butchers after dark. This will have to be done at night. This is a risk.'

There is silence. They both know that Ned needs a deal. The tally of animals coming for slaughter has fallen. In some areas, there are restrictions on animal movement because of outbreaks of tuberculosis. Ned stands where his gunslinger is standing and studies their faces from the far end of the saloon.

He repeated, because in his head he could hear his gunslinger repeating what he had said. 'A big risk ... but if we can agree a price,' he suggests, gulping the whisky, 'we may have a deal. Remember, we do not have a licence to slaughter horses.'

'You will be paid handsomely for the risk. You are not the only slaughter and meat distributor on our list. But you are a small company. Less noticeable. Up here in the hills. Understand?'

Ned nods.

'We ship the horses in. It will all be done at night, long after you have closed. Everything done quickly. Everything cleaned up. No one will see anything. But if they do ... The following day it will all seem as a dream. Do you have people you can trust?'

Ned nods again. He knows he has experienced slaughter people he can trust because they need the money. Ned and trust are indivisible he thinks to himself.

'They need their jobs, right?' says the Irishman.

Ned nods a third time.

'We are known for what we sell,' Ned says. 'Everybody in the chain knows they can rely on us. That is why they buy from us. So, all this has to be handled carefully.'

The other two men raise their glasses. Ned raises his. Their ambitions ching, ring and chime.

A barman collects the menu. Lunch is finished. From now on until the evening, it is drinks and bar snacks only.

One of the Irishmen, Ned isn't sure which one, gives his thighs a reassuring squeeze. 'Hymns and Arias' begins again but this time lines are hurried or skipped to get to the chorus.

Ned makes his way through a jostling crowd of singing voices. The next moment, he is being asked if he is alright. He finds himself backed up against what he thinks is a wall. Someone tugs at his lapel to reach inside his jacket. His eyes close and he rolls to one side, snorting hard and wanting to spit. What is going on here, he hears his own voice asking. He is barely able to decipher what he is saying as if his mouth is stuffed with marshmallows. He collapses between two shoulders much heavier and sturdier than his own.

Awst | August 1879

The arrival of cakes, pastries, preserves and neat triangles of crustless sandwiches interrupted the solemn mood into which Mary Jane had lapsed. As a waiter and waitress made space by moving cups and plates, Mary Jane started singing a Welsh lullaby with an Irish lilt and she did so as if she were not simply singing but tasting each of the words.

Ni fydd unrhywbeth yn tarfu ar eich slumber

Ni fydd unrhyw un yn gwneud niwed i chi

(Nothing shall disturb your slumber

Nobody will do you harm)

She sang very quietly but very beautifully. Megan questioned why she had suddenly chosen to sing in the middle of their tea and for whom was she singing, Megan or herself. What was in her mind as she sang of nothing disturbing slumber and nobody doing harm? Was she trying to undo what she said when she suggested to Megan that they had both experienced cruelty?

Megan had ordered coffee, a taste for which she had picked up in London, and Mary Jane tea. A steady stream of pitch-black coffee, with a distinct aroma, poured from the narrow spout of the china coffee cup. Coffee should be taken hot. Megan knew that but the cup was too hot to her finger tips and she couldn't bear the thought of bringing it to her lips. She waited while Mary Jane took one of the silver spoons and stirred the tea pot. As she glanced again into the room, she saw a myriad of reflections in the silver pots and bowls on all the different tables and the shine cast by all the glasses. The blues in the plates spoke to her of summer skies.

When all the cakes and pastries had been plated and placed, the laughing and warm Mary Jane returned. She had included the café's special cake in her order. Excitedly, she watched Megan lift a small cube of it to her lips. It was moist, almost black. The fork was cold on Megan's lips and she winced slightly. Mary Jane continued to watch, waiting, expectant. The intense sweetness came as more of a shock than the coldness of the silver. After the initial sugary onslaught, Megan experienced the taste of early autumn apples and the sharp tang of fresh blackberries. She smiled at Mary Jane. The apple and blackberry, falling together on the back of her tongue and then rolling lovingly into her throat, recreated for her the pure innocence of childhood. Mary Jane understood and was not disappointed by the effect she read in Megan's pursed lips. She was satisfied. But still she waited. It was not long before the sweet apple and bitter-sweet blackberry were overtaken by the much more adult taste which Mary Jane knew was coming, of cracked almond, like the first hint of death entering childhood, or the first experience of injustice.

Small talk tumbled from Mary Jane's lips with crumbs from the scones as she spoke of the strain of being a maid and what unbelievable horrors she had found in the rooms of the most respectable guests and how women were no better than the men. She made Megan gasp and giggle with ease. She led her from the hotel into different parts of Llanelli and Carmarthen but became most interested in Megan's life in London as if that were a journey which she certainly intended to take herself one day.

Each of the young women had something they would like to forget. Mary Jane would like not to remember why some of her fingers were stiff as if arthritis had crawled into her bones and rested there, anticipating the older woman she believed she would one day become. There were tiny scars on the back of Megan's legs, one of them especially, that turned a shade of blue when her legs were bare in winter. She would like not to remember the farm, the life her father had sold. When her eyes rested on Mary Jane's expensive velvet coat, she remembered the long deep, surprisingly soft hair into which she had sank her fingers and a bull that had long gone.

As the evening came on, Mary Jane made her excuses to Megan and said that it was time she made her way back to Llanelli. Megan rose, thanking her for the afternoon and the tea which had been so enjoyable and interesting. As they reached the door, one of the last things she said to Mary Jane was how she had wished they had met earlier. Mary Jane reciprocated then hurried into the Carmarthen traffic of horses and hansoms. Megan watched her in the street, half expecting her to look back and wave or something. The early evening light seemed ghostly, monochrome, as if Mary Jane were in a black and white illustration from the Carmarthen Weekly Reporter.

The following day, Megan had arranged to meet her brother, the ghost throughout her lavish conversation with Mary Jane. They did not meet, as she had met Mary Jane, in an expensive tea room but on a bench in a park at the centre of Llanelli. He was late and somehow she had the impression that he and Mary Jane had talked about her conversation with Megan the day before. Mary Jane had started her shift in the Stepney Arms. The meeting with her brother was less enthusiastic than Megan had expected and he had promised. She had been working up to this for several months. She expected to see her brother as she had known him at Hill House. But the young man who searched her out was very different. He was very tired, having worked extra hours while she and Mary Jane were in Carmarthen, and very evidently unrelaxed. His face was much more lined than it was less than a year ago and marked by blue veins of coal dust. He suddenly seemed to her older than their father whereas Mary Jane seemed younger than both of them. Whereas Mary Jane had been chatty, interested, even interrogative, he seemed to have nothing to say. Whatever spark had once been between them had disappeared. The conversation was awkward and reminded her of her relationship with her father. She reminded him, although he never said so, of their mother. Their embrace lasted less time than the hugs they gave each other when he returned from a day in the hills back home. It ended with them sliding awkwardly out of each other's grasp.

The two of them sat and asked each other questions. At first, they spoke kindly but it was not long before everything became stilted. There were times when the silences between them lasted longer than what they said to each other. They talked about her experience of London, that was when he nodded the most and spent most time looking into her face. When she asked about the colliery, he whipped his sentences together and rushed to the end of what he had to say which was not very much. The only time the younger, more thoughtful Meic returned was when he told her about Mary Jane, the recipes she had brought her and the different dishes they looked forward to eating.

'Now, then,' Megan retorted, conveniently forgetting the English food her mother usually served, 'you will feel you are back home, in Hill House, and we are all around the table again, when she serves you our dishes from north Wales.'

'I am sure,' he said, disbelievingly.

She was uncertain whether this were something he wanted or the last thing in his mind.

She tried to speak Welsh, as they used to on their country walks, but when she did, he brushed her away. Bringing to mind what they saw and discovered in those days, things that meant so much to her now, sounded in his ear like a jangling cowbell.

Her words felt cold and dry even to herself.

It wasn't long before their meeting lost even the little momentum with which it started. He rose, offered her his hand, and suggested he walk her to the station. He asked her the time of her train which made him shake his head, lamenting that they ran so infrequently. Her train was farther away than he thought, perhaps hoped, but he suddenly livened up, inviting her to join him on a tour of the town.

For a while, as they walked through the crowded streets, where some of the buildings were so close together that they shut out the light, Megan felt she was back in London. They talked about how different it all was from Llanrwst and Denbigh. They recalled these towns in pieces like the lumps of toffee he stopped and bought her from a street vendor. Slowly, at long last, it seemed as if they were coming together again. But nearer the station, he returned to the stranger who had sat awkwardly with her on the bench.

On her way back to London, she day-dreamed about Meic less than she thought she would. Instead, she found herself reviewing her meeting with Mary Jane over and over in her head. At one point, she saw themselves as two cats taking up positions, trying to work out whether the other might be some kind of adversary. Innocent lines re-entered her head with a different overcoat of insinuation: 'Meic has said a great deal about you', 'You seem to have been the only young woman he has really known' (this time without Mary Jane's laugh), 'I gather that you are very fond of each other.'

Mehefin | *June 2016*

The day after, Ned is bad. His head feels as if it has been crowbarred. The events of the previous afternoon dribble into his brain. He is on his knees in the bathroom. The toilet seat is raised in front of his face like a shaving mirror. It is covered in unidentifiable splashes. He swallows hard, realising that the swirling has slowed but has not quite stopped. He has no trousers on and his shirt and tie mock him from a muddle beside the shower. He rises gradually, spreading his palms around his head and wishing they were icepacks. His forehead is oven hot. Struggling into his bedroom, he tries to stich his memories together. A beige envelope hovers in the middle of his duvet and he tries to catch it. It has split open and as soon as he grabs it, twenty and fifty-pound notes spew out in front of him.

A tractor splutters in the yard below his flat and drills into his head. He cannot remember having been this drunk since he was a youngster. A queue of cows stretches out from the milking shed in the distance. He can just see them as he sits upright and begins to count the notes, but it is an activity that requires more careful attention than he can muster. He discovers tablets in his bedside table drawer and swallows them without water. One sticks at the back of his tongue, dissolving in his spittle. The money is spread before him like a magician's fan. He doses for a while and when he awakes, he manages to satisfy himself that there is nine thousand and eight hundred pounds in various denominations and there is not a crispy fresh note among them. He calls himself a bollox. They couldn't even make it a perfect ten, he says to himself.

Chapter Thirteen
The Maid and the Princess

Tachwedd | November 1888

She never ceased to amaze us. You never knew what she would say next. She was a story teller and a story in herself. I see you are writing that down. You like that, don't you? Was it all a fabrication? Sometimes. In the Queens. When she was drunk. When she wanted. No ... when she needed ... That is, it. When she needed to impress. When she spoke upper class, like. Did any of you hear her speak? She was like an actress ... There is a word for it. Isn't there? To be able to speak that way. Like glass. Do you know what I mean? If a man come in who was well-dressed ... like a doctor or something ... She would change ... start putting on airs and graces, as if she were somebody ... I mean really something ... And she would say the most outrageous things, in a loud voice so as they would hear, like. Then she would begin, honest now, I am not making this up, to talk in other languages. Some said she was speaking French. I didn't know, I don't even speak English proper. But some of these gentlemen, they were right impressed. A couple of times, they took her up and spoke back to her in the French or whatever it was. Of course, I was drunk, too, and showing them my legs. I am in there looking for a man to take outside ... at least one ... she would only take some of 'em ... only the gentlemen ... those who spoke whatever language it was that she was speaking, back to her room. She was lucky she had one close by. She shared it, like. But it didn't turn out lucky for her in the end. Poor girl. Look at it this way. We were with her when she wasn't ginned up. Middle of the afternoon, several of us, gathered in her room, with her friend, he was there very often, and she would speak in that language or some other language. She knew we didn't understand her but she did it just so as to impress us. She would retell the stories we heard nights before. OK they weren't the same. They were changed like. Each time she told a story, it was different. But bits of it were the same. Like I said, she was a story herself. I remember one night, before we all went out. Because of what was happening, we tried to keep together. Nobody wanted to be alone. But, of course, that is how you often ended up. Anyway, that one night she told us she had a child, a three-year old. It wasn't with her. She never said where it was. But Christ. She never seemed the type to have a child. Always too careful. Of course, a lot of us have been bunked up. We have had to get rid. But she was more upper class. They do not have to get rid. Not like the rest of us.

Chwefror | February 1879

Mary Jane defiantly returned the wine bottle across the table. There were times when she destabilised him. This was one of them.

'I couldn't sleep last night,' she said.

Meic waited for her to continue rather than ask the obvious question.

'My head was full of the terribles, you see.'

'The terribles?' he questioned.

Mary-Jane turned to her adopted tongue. 'Roedd gen i lais yn fy mhen yn dweud nad oeddwn yn ddigon da' (There was a voice in my head, telling me that I wasn't good enough).

Meic found it difficult to think of Mary Jane ever imagining that she was not good enough. She had so much more confidence and ability than he believed he had. But the voice inside her head. That really worried him. It was beyond him.

She could see how confused and worried he was. She didn't know what to say to him.

'That's how it gets at times, love,' she said. 'I do bad things.'

She had become more and more reluctant to talk about her past, as if she had enough difficulty coping with her present. That is what her friends would say to journalists, whoever was interested, years later: she found it hard to live in the present. For her, there seemed to be no pure present. The past kept crowding in. Or maybe it was the future that was intruding. Sometimes she seemed to suggest that she had already lived her future.

'What kind of bad things?' Meic asked.

'I cannot talk about them now. Only, understand that I do bad things and I am not sure why. Sometimes I think it is because I am mad. Do you think I am mad?'

Each word fell with the thump of a butcher's cleaver.

'I am afraid I am going to lose control,' she added.

His attention kept slipping from her words, dragged down into the seeping grey beneath them. She frightened him more the more she continued.

'You are clearly worried about something. What are you worried about?' he asked, trying to calm and reassure her. He didn't understand why she was like this sometimes. All the boundaries she constructed around herself seemed to collapse, piece by piece, in front of him.

'There was a time, maybe … two years ago … when I lost it,' she said. 'Really lost it. You didn't know me then. A night when my head was packed with the terribles. That night I had a terrifying nightmare … well it might not have been a nightmare … I experienced something that really frightened me ... I never want to be that frightened again. The devil was in my room ... undressing me.'

'You dreamt about the devil undressing you?' She had never even hinted at this story before.

'I said the catechism over and over again. He was standing beside my bed. I do not know even now whether it was a dream. Or some kind of ... I was outside it all ... watching ... I could see myself just lying there ... as if I were looking at my own corpse ... I had been drinking and thinking about my father. I never want to lose that much control again.'

Mary Jane paused and looked at Meic for a response. He remained focused as if he were studying one of his sheep back home. She seemed so frightened by it even now. She thought that Meic and that man in her nightmare had the same expressionless stare. The man in her dream had a scarf around his face but when she remembered his face from the dream, he did not have a mask.

'What did you think he was going to do?'

Again, she paused as if she was not sure how much she wanted to remember.

'I thought he was going to make me do something.'

Meic had never had a conversation of this kind with her before. He was a man who worked and drank with men. He continued to feel out of his depth. We can be sure that this evening, she said much more than this. She wanted to communicate the terror which she lived with. He asked her what the terribles were like and whether they always involved dreams. She said that sometimes they were like really awful headaches. As if someone were marching around inside her head in a temper, slamming door and after door as hard as they could. He, like all lovers, would have willingly sat and absorbed her pain as if it were his own if he could. The words I write are probably not the ones that actually passed between them. But given what we know of her, and the times in which they lived, this was very likely the conversation which they had.

'Make you do something?' he queried.

'I thought he was going to make me kill myself after he raped me.'

'Megan ...' then he stopped. She didn't hear 'Megan', and he immediately garbled 'Mary Jane'. He could be forgiven, he was drunk. Perhaps. 'Is suicide something you think about often?' he asked.

He was really shocked and thinking that he had really only thought he knew her. He cursed himself for calling her Megan.

'Sometimes. All my life I have been locked in my body, trying to break free, as if I am the subject in a story that has already been written. That makes no sense, does it?'

He couldn't think of anything to say. Megan had once said something similar to him after she was beaten and humiliated in school.

Eventually, he asked, 'How did the dream end?'

'You call it a dream,' she said aggressively. 'It was a nightmare. But not even that. I woke at some point during the night ... I had not been raped ... but I was naked.'

They sat without saying anything. Each drank without looking at the other.

'There was something else,' she said.

Meic suspected as much. He gulped down his drink as if to show solidarity with her.

***

That night, as she lay beside Meic, she dreamt of the stoked-up furnaces in the foundries, the coal waiting in trucks to be cremated in the ovens like slaughtered, sick cattle. The red heat rose and rose, as if desperate for release. A monstrous hunger that would leap into the world and burn everything.

When she awoke, the room was cold and a damp air that smelled of death slid through a crack in the window pane and circled endlessly around their bed like a stray dog waiting to bite. The window itself was coated on the outside in grime and the consolidated remnants of smog. It was difficult to see through them and if you could, there was not much to see, only another grey building like the one in which they lived. Then Meic, too, woke. She looked into his face, furrowed, trying to make sense of who they were and why they were together. He was a quiet man, powerful but pacific, so unlike her father. She could not speak, or as now even think, about her father except in Welsh, a habit from childhood, for fear he was listening. Meic did not have a fiery temper, he always seemed in control of himself, he was a sheep not a bull. She was grateful for that.

Despite having bathed, there was a shading of coal dirt around one of Meic's eyes, like a fading bruise, which made the white of his eye milkier than usual. When she put her small white hand, surprisingly soft given the amount of cleaning and scrubbing that she did, to his chin, she saw a smear of blood beneath one of her finger nails from the rabbit and a grain of coal dust from washing Meic's back under another. So many times, their hands, hers with a few stiffened fingers and his with calluses from the colliery, traced familiar tracks along each other's torso and limbs.

'Who do you see?' she asks him, not aloud. 'Who is it that you make love with?'

For a moment, she sought the signs that he was readying himself to have sex with her. She waited for those first moves, the ritual of an early morning, comforting affection. But there were none. She turned onto her back. When she came to think about it, neither of them had ever freely communicated, even with their bodies. He tended to use his body to silence her and try to smother her needs with what he wanted. But she knew how to use her body to manipulate him in the directions she wanted. Not that that was easy.

She loved being with Meic but she couldn't help thinking they were together in the hollow of a wave which would soon crash. She could not help but count slithers of old wood in the water like strands of sea-weed. The terribles were stirring. She lay there in her own space beside him, her arms sentinelled beside her body. Not for the first time, she agonized for her absent sister. Not for the last time, he ached for his.

Ebrill | April 1879

It was impossible to tell whether he was surprised, pleased or both. But he recognised Mary Jane immediately, even though they had only walked a few hundred yards together the previous month. He was seated in a far corner of one of the larger rooms in the Arms, next to a table on which his papers were carefully arranged.

Mary Jane noticed his documents. Their organization pleased her. She knew not to enter the centre of the room when the guests were present. She stood carefully, with her hands behind her back, near the door, as maids did while waiting their instructions.

His stare grasped her and held her firmly. 'You are the maid in charge of this floor?' he said, leaving Mary-Jane uncertain as to whether he was seeking confirmation of what he already knew or expressing surprise.

She was about to correct him. She cleaned and tidied the rooms, she was not in charge of anything. Then she decided she liked him thinking of her as some kind of supervisor.

'Yes, sir,' she confirmed.

He closed his newspaper and folded it carefully, positioning it next to a side plate as if it were an additional knife. As she observed this, approving each deliberate movement, she noticed that his hands were very white, unmarked, unlike Meic's, and his nails were carefully manicured. His cuffs fell neatly over his wrists. His shoulders were rounded and she wasn't certain whether this was from his height or half a lifetime bent over a desk. She wondered if he were some kind of doctor.

His voice was very English and well-modulated. 'We have .... a special guest in this hotel ... from tomorrow evening .... special.'

Again, she simply indicated that she was listening intently, as she would have done with any guest on this floor.

'The Princess wants one maid from the hotel to be her maid while she is here.' He paused. The word Princess shocked her. While she waited, she studied the slender, firm mouth beneath his handle-bar moustache which, like his well-trimmed eyebrows, was perfectly black. There was a sheen to his face, especially his cheeks, which she could not remember seeing on a man before. 'She hasn't met you, so this is not an indication of any esteem in which the royal party holds you.'

She wondered why he had said this. There was something oddly feminine about him she thought but she decided he was also bitchy. He went on to say that he had talked with Mrs Llewellyn and she had recommended her.

'I have come to know her well and I believe I can trust her judgement.'

Mary Jane was surprised to hear that Mrs Llewellyn knew of her, even knew her name, but she felt proud. She allowed herself a short, quick smile before returning her face to the mask she normally wore as a maid. In response to her pleasure, which he quickly noticed, he became softer.

'I believe you to be reliable.'

'I do my best,' she said, modestly but reassuringly. It was like she had made a promise to him.

'Good,' he responded, a little brusquely, as if some kind of distraction had passed between them, and he wanted to get on. He took his watch from his waistcoat pocket, opened it, then closed it sharply, without even looking at its dial. It reminded her of her father.

'There are some rules,' he pursued as if he were a teacher inducting her into his class. 'You should not speak unless the Princess of Wales addresses you. If she does so, you must say no more than is absolutely necessary. If you have a need to ask her anything, she is Your Royal Highness and thereafter Madam or Ma'am. Remember she is your … our … future queen.' The pocket watch still in his hand was flicked open. This time, he studied its face as if it were some kind of alternative to looking into Mary Jane's eyes. Then he snapped the watch shut again and this time returned it to his pocket. 'You do what she asks you. And you never look at her. You keep your eyes averted. Understand?'

Mary Jane looked down at the floor as if to show him that she knew how to avert her eyes.

'Yes.' Then she remembered. 'Yes, sir. I understand.'

'But, appreciate this, also,' he said, rising at last from his chair and correspondingly raising his voice which made Mary Jane fear that she had upset him in some way, 'the Princess is not from … an English family. She is …'

'Danish,' Mary Jane interrupted, immediately regretting that she had done so. He stopped speaking and stared. Although she was tall, he towered over her, as if he had been, she thought, a guardsman. There was an awkward silence between them in which she feared that she had inadvertently suggested that she would volunteer conversation to the Princess.

'It was in the paper,' she explained, clearly flustered.

He seemed reassured by her embarrassment. She clearly knew the error of her ways, he thought.

'She is … Danish, as you say. Their Royal Family is … closer to the people. I mean, they allow their subjects to become more familiar with them. The Princess is not used to our formalities, to our sense of etiquette. She is inclined,' again, he hesitated, as if unsure that he should really be saying this. 'She has a tendency to forget who she is, our future queen, and become overfamiliar with her staff. That might be well and good in Denmark, in keeping with how they do things in those northern countries.'

He let himself drift into silence. Mary Jane nodded. She wasn't sure whether she should express gratitude for the inside information he was providing, clearly at some risk to himself, or confirm in some way that she agreed with him. She felt a new confidence had developed between them. A sense of trust albeit one that was little more than skin deep. Perhaps she was being naïve.

'I expect you, Mary … Mary Jane … to be careful. You strike me as the sort of young woman who knows how to be careful.'

She was used to men, especially those from a higher position in society, asking her, saying that they expected her, to be careful. When they did so, they usually touched the side of her face, tenderly, threateningly. It surprised her that so many men, in touching a woman, ever so slightly, deftly combined the two. He remained apart from her with one hand in a trouser pocket and the other held loosely by his side. Then he moved nearer her.

'You might see things or overhear what you are not meant to. You will forget everything. Immediately. You understand?'

The gentle man who had guided her through a thoroughfare the previous month had stepped aside. He now seemed like most men she knew, like many of the commercial travellers who stayed at the Arms, but with a greater aura of power about him.

'And you must never tell anyone, not your colleagues, not your friends nor even your own family anything you observe or hear. Once she has left, the Princess Alexandra was never here.'

But then, almost apologetically, he stepped back. He became kinder once more.

'If there are problems, come and tell me. For the duration of Her Royal Highness's visit, I shall be here in this room. Think of me as ... as ... as your father.'

'Thank you,' she responded before remembering to add, 'sir'.

He spoke more advisedly than he had up until then. He addressed her as a father might, but not her father.

'This is an important responsibility for you,' he counselled in a much quieter voice than when he had laid out his instructions. She was used to men shifting to a low, seductive register. Reassuring her. Confirming how they would always be there for whomever it was they wanted at that particular moment. Usually, it was before they started touching, a signal that everything was about to become intimate. She wondered if this were something sons learned from their fathers. This was usually the moment when promises were made. Never to be kept, of course.

He stared out of the window as if he were listening for something from the street below.

'You might find this a step up,' he advised, as if he had been reminded by all the people bustling beneath him. 'It might lead to you coming to London ...' He hesitated again. For the first time, she saw the depth of his awkwardness with her. 'It might result in ... it might provide you with ... invitations.'

'Invitations.' That word stung her. So many men told her they could open doors for her. As if they alone recognised something in her other than a lowly, available maid. She wasn't sure what her 'father' meant. For a few seconds, she thought about asking him to explain. But then she realised that perhaps she was not meant to. She decided against pursuing the matter.

Just as he turned the word over in the silence between them, he repeated it, adding 'You understand, don't you? I realise how you must live. But there are opportunities elsewhere. Opportunities that may advance you.'

She didn't. For the moment. But eventually she might. She kept with her decision to say nothing.

'Do you know what my position is?' he asked. She didn't and he knew that. 'I do not work for the Princess. I am one of the Prince of Wales's men. That is how we see ourselves.' He walked softly forward again. 'That is how we see ourselves. The Prince's men. Our future king. The Princess travels. She likes to get away ... away from the palace. You are a woman, you can appreciate that, I am sure. Our role is to protect her. To hide her from herself ... until she learns our ways ... our view of things.'

Mawrth | March 2016

'Beth yw'r peth mwyaf anarferol rywt ti wedi 'i fwyta erioed?' (What is the most unusual thing you have eaten) Mary-Jane's friend asks her.

They are sitting on a wall outside a fish and chip shop. Mary-Jane has not seen this question coming. She is holding a piece of fish between her fingers and wonders whether it was this which prompted an enquiry into the extraordinary things she had eaten. A problem she is finding in her relationship with Amelia is that she has a tendency to march around as if she is trying to find where all her corpses are buried. It is difficult for Mary-Jane to remember what things she has eaten that could be classed as extraordinary because, like all students following a long course, she travelled so much when she was younger. She buys herself time, observing 'Mae fy arferion bwyta wedi newid dros y blynyddoedd.'(My eating habits have changed over the years)

It is true, her eating habits have changed over the years, especially over the last year. She wonders whether this is attributable to getting older. She has found that she eats less meat, more vegetarian meals, partly because of her changing relationship with nature and partly from working so closely with animals. Now, of course, there was the influence of Amelia and her reaction against her uncle and the way in which he saw things and conducted himself.

Food that was extraordinary when Mary-Jane first tried it, often on overseas trips, like crocodile meat, was now readily available even in the most ordinary supermarkets. Her mind wanders through Asia and Africa. Maybe, she thinks, it is there that she has had the most extraordinary food by Welsh standards. She remembers a meal in China on an exchange visit which has revolted her every time she remembers it.

'Minion hwyaid,' she says at last.

'Ducks' lips,' Amelia spits back in translation.

Immediately, Mary-Jane realises that she has disgusted her friend as much as she had been disgusted at the time. She explains that it was a banquet that her hosts had given and that duck lips were, she struggles for the word, 'danteithfwyd'.

'Some delicacy,' Amelia scoffs.

Mary-Jane notices that she has closed the lid over her chips and is crunching the box in her hands.

'If you're offered something like that, it is regarded as a great insult to refuse it,' she explains.

'Ryw'n credu y dylet fod wedi ei wrthod o leiaf,' (I think that you should have refused it at least) Amelia says.

'Leiaf' Mary-Jane says to herself. 'At least' had a sting in the tail.

In Amelia's book, she had committed an unpardonable sin.

'What is it,' Amelia asks, 'that allows the human race to mass-produce animals for consumption while eating each other is taboo?'

She pulls each sentence as taut as she can before releasing it. A line appears to have been crossed.

They do not speak for a while. Mary-Jane watches Amelia put on her walking boots. She hears Amelia muttering something to herself, evidently in disgust.

Things have not been good between them recently. Maybe Amelia, she thinks, is having doubts about her. She hopes not.

They rise almost together, Mary-Jane as usual carrying her boots with her socks stuffed inside them. A stile in a stone wall leads to a thickened tangle of grass, brambles and crushed leaves. Amelia wonders how Mary-Jane will cope in her bare feet but she manages. The path narrows suddenly and dips toward a stagnant stream. Indistinguishable smells criss-cross each other. Unidentifiable flies waltz over the water. The light plays picky-boo inside clusters of thistles. Mary-Jane thinks about MJ for a while and how she is beginning to feel that her family history is playing games with her.

There are distractions for which Mary-Jane, and perhaps Amelia too, is grateful. Discarded sticks, half a page of classified ads from the free newspaper and an empty can that rolls over with the ease of a river vole. The smells become most intense where the stream is deepest. Tiny fish, no bigger than nail parings, emerge near mossy stones then disappear into their muddy holes. The flies become fatter. Their wings catch sunlight, magnifying their bodies, and glint in patches of sunlight. A long, string thread with no body or wings appears. It floats freely above the stream and puzzles both of them. One micro-second it is distant from them, almost vanishing, and then close-up to them again. Amelia shouts back from her place in the lead that it is something alien.

They have no idea where they are going. Amelia is getting

farther and farther ahead. Mary-Jane is content to let her. She is not entirely comfortable walking with others beside her, even Amelia. She has spent much of her life alone, snatching moments of solitary pleasure where she can, usually strolling, reading or practising her surgery. Then the narrow path turns quickly from the stream and ascends into open fields.

Mary-Jane experiences a wonderful sense of emerging. Everything makes sense again like a concealed hand of cards has been revealed. All the fresh detail comes so suddenly that she feels her mind expand with the light.

Again, they join up with each other. When they turn back, they cannot see the exit from the path that had followed the stream. The silence between them is unbroken.

Ebrill | April 1878

Now there was silence. Everything stopped. He withdrew from her. She remained over the back of the chair and he could see that he had hurt her. That gave him pleasure. He left her and went to wash in the basin in the corner of the room.

As the water turned the colour of fading fence paint, Mary-Jane slowly straightened herself, trying not to grimace as she did so. She used a cloth to wipe her thighs so that her undergarments would not be too stained. She could see that there were spots of blood around the edge of the basin. She knew that it was hers. He didn't know what to do with the water and went to the head of the bed to dress.

'I can rely on your discretion, can't I Martha?' he said.

She had not given him her real name, as if it would shame her if she did so. 'I'm a maid,' she replied coldly. 'We see a lot that we are not supposed to.'

'And you can rely on me to help you, if you need assistance,' he said warmly.

She smiled automatically. Did he really not understand how much women like herself despised him?

'Rwyt ti'n ferch dda, Martha', (You are a good girl, Martha) he said patronisingly, looking at the wall toward which he had thrust her face. He fastened his collar and searched among the ruffled bed sheets for his neck scarf. They were both fully dressed again although Mary-Jane felt untidy and in need of a bath. He left her and she listened to him descend the stairs. She covered the basin with a cloth and carried it to the washroom that she and the other maids shared. Through its one small window, she watched him make his way along the High Street raising his hat to a woman with children who greeted him.

She closed the washroom door and stripped, pulling her blouse over her head and dropping her skirt and pants in rings around her feet. Wanting a cleansing storm of soapy water, all she could muster was a mocking drizzle from a sponge. If she could, she would have stripped herself of her skin to scrub the sin out of the innermost sinews of her body. She plunged her arms deep into the bowl of water, needing it to be hotter so that she might take comfort in the pain, find a kind of absolution in the hurt.

Ebrill | April 1878

In the foyer, The London Illustrated clashed with the Llanelli News. It was as if they were in a boxing ring together.

The Princess's silhouette crossed a third of two columns in the centre pages of both. Everyone who picked them up commented on how beautiful she was. For many of them, this was the closest they would ever come to her. Her skirts were luxuriously long and she carried herself like a dancer or a gymnast. Her arms were carefully folded so as to emphasise her long, silk gloves. Her combed-up hair, twisted into a bun behind her head, stressed the curvature of her face and it was obvious now how much her dark lively eyes and her high cheek-bones contributed to the regal aura that surrounded her.

In her eyes, there was something undefinable, risky, deep and not yet fulfilled. As the women in the hotel foyer studied her, she stared right back at them. Her eyes were piercing, but not in an aggressive way. It was as if she were seeing into their souls, as women, looking deeper than anyone else had ever done. The rich clothes, the beautiful jewellery and her regal gaze defined her and distanced her. But her face said so much more. It had a truer beauty than all her clothes. It was her face which made her interesting and suggested that she had something to share with them.

The women talked about how she took them by surprise. How she made them feel that they wanted to spend time with her, with no one else apart from her. They followed her toward the hotel lounge and the dining room as far as they were allowed. She was so relaxed she looked as if she would have allowed them all in if it were up to her. She made them want to walk together, separate from the men, and talk about what they had seen in her picture. She made them feel differently about themselves.

One of the upstairs maids brought a copy of the Illustrated News downstairs and all the female staff gathered around it. As they excitedly passed the Princess's picture around, they all began to fall silent. No one was able to talk about the impression she made on them.

'Just think,' said one of them at last, 'she is here, under this very roof.'

A few of them plotted. How might they get up to her room? How might they speak with her? Where would be the best place to stand as she comes down for breakfast? Will there be reporters from London?

One of the maids was the last to be given a chance to see the picture because she was the most envied. The Princess was staying in a room which was her responsibility. The Princess had made it clear that she had wanted the floor to herself and that only one of the maids would attend her.

Mary Jane found herself mocked as 'the maid by royal appointment'. She began to see something of herself in the Princess. It was as if the Princess was a long-lost sister.

Mai | *May 1878*

Mary Jane had begun boiling the water for their evening baths when she remembered the money that she had stuffed into her bag. She had taken her purse into their bedroom, counting up the coins as she went. Getting down on her knees, she had removed a loose brick from the bedroom fireplace which they never used. Reaching into the hole had been difficult and she had found that she had had to lie on the floor to ease the pain ripping between her buttocks. The size of the collection of coins that she was acquiring inspired her, offered her relief, and now she had added a new handful to them, all the time listening for Meic's footsteps on the stairs. Replacing the brick, carefully, she had made sure there were no signs that it had ever been removed. This was becoming more and more difficult each time she went there. Brick dust left a smear on the edges of her apron and she had put it into her mouth to wet it before trying to rub it off, but her saliva had only made matters worse. She had returned to their metal bath before she had remembered her purse on the bed. Slowly, having to put a hand on the small of her back, she went and retrieved it, hiding it, like she hid many of her things, this time beneath her ironing pile. Meic was a kind and gentle person. But she knew that if he discovered what she had been doing and had been hoarding her money this way she would cop it.

Later that evening, she fried some fillets of salmon trout that Meic had caught with his friends. Most of the salmon fishing occurred at night with the help of a dazzling lantern. But for a few days each year, the salmon could be taken in broad daylight when the spoils would be shared before dusk. She admired the women, of all ages, who were prepared to wade waist deep into the river and throw a fine fish onto the bank and remembered how adept her brothers were at catching fish with pitchforks. She had always been put off going into the water herself by the prospect of water rats lurking in the blackness. But there was a time when she landed a trout with a worm on a hook and another when her squeamishness cost them all a wriggling, thrashing eel she had half lifted from the water. One of her earliest memories was of her father following a salmon from pool to pool until, at last, he seized it. She remembered how, carrying it back to where the family had gathered to watch, his pride beamed like a lantern.

As Meic bathed, the fried pieces of fish seemed to dance in the fat to the rhythm of his splashing. Mary Jane, unbeknown to him, turned to watch him for a while. She noticed a large cut, a blue-black whip like stripe, across his shoulders and running into the centre of his back. There was congealed blood where the cut seemed deepest just below his shoulder blades. He stopped washing himself as her fingers gently traced the wound. She breathed in his special scent of coal, sweat and soap. That afternoon, he explained, he had had to crawl into a small clearing in a new seam and a sharp edge of coal above him had ripped his bare back.

'Did you not feel it?' she asked, unscrewing the top on a jar of jelly.

'A little but everything else was hurting even more,' he laughed.

The soothing coolness of Mary Jane's compound slithered into the deep recesses of his body.

'That is good stuff,' he said.

It was a jar for which she had asked him for extra money when she brought it home a few months previously. She had made out that she had bought it when in fact it had been left in a room at the hotel after the doctor had visited a guest.

Meic's back was becoming as veined as a leaf. She rubbed some more jelly into it as he bent forward in the blackened water. The maid and the iron man, she thought as she straightened herself once more, screwing the top as tightly as she could so that the ointment would last.

The fillets were lying in a shallow, still pool of fat which had lost much of its vitality. The water around the potatoes and carrots still seemed angry. She always boiled them vigorously because Meic liked his vegetables soft, not *al dente* like she said they served them in Paris.

A few minutes later, from the kitchen, she heard the heavy crash of water as he stood up in the bath. He dried himself rigorously. She avoided looking at him and having drained their potatoes, she mashed them viciously.

Tachwedd | November 1878

When Mary Jane went into the guest's room to turn down the bed, as she did for all the VIPs, the Princess was seated at a small table overlooked by her lady-in-waiting who travelled everywhere with her and with whom she was very close. They were discussing what appeared to be the outline of a dress to which Princess Alexandra was making alterations. Forgetting all the tuition she had received from her managers on how to behave and what to say, Mary Jane found herself stammering. Unexpectedly, Alexandra rose from her chair and approached her.

'Please,' implored the Princess, 'call me ... Alix.'

Even relaxing in her room, she wore clothes that Mary Jane envied. Then she realised that she must have been staring at the row of garments on a mobile wardrobe rail for the Princess observed, 'You like clothes do you, Mary Jane?'

They both found themselves looking at the clothes which had been returned to their hangers. All Mary Jane could think of saying was 'Do not all women?'

'Tu dis la verité' (you speak the truth), the Princess responded, with such ease that it made Mary Jane certain that she must have been misled by the Arms into thinking that her maid was fluent in French. But she continued in English.

'I do not like the way the press sometimes describes my clothes as ... sexual. That takes all the beauty out of them. Don't you think? I like them all for their beauty. But the Prince of Wales chides me for spending too much.'

'Meic ... my husband ... is the same,' Mary Jane stammered once more, noticing the enthusiasm in the Princess's face, as if she were pleased to find common ground between them so quickly.

Mary Jane found herself cooing at the French label in one of the dresses.

'I love Paris,' said the Princess. 'It is my escape, especially when I have my children with me. Do you have children, Mary Jane?'

She shook her head, slowly and sadly. That would have surprised Meic if he had seen it.

'But Paris is my escape, too,' she said, not wishing the spirited conversation between them to fall flat.

The Princess hesitated, trying to hide her surprise to find a French-speaking Irish-Welsh maid in Llanelli who knew Paris.

Risking becoming too personal, Mary Jane observed, 'I would have thought a princess at court could spend up to her neck.'

This silenced the Princess for a while but her face eventually broke into a sly smile.

'All the money allowed to me is tightly controlled by the men. I have to beg for everything. My people do not know what it is really like to be a princess. How I hate men sometimes, Mary Jane. Do you know, when I first married the Prince of Wales, it was a struggle even to dress myself? I was like a puppet. They dressed me, controlled what I ate, decided when I went out and when I stayed behind the palace walls, when I played my music and what I played. Mary Jane, you would not believe it.'

She ran her fingers over the dress which Mary Jane's eyes had quickly picked out, admiring the needle work as if, like her maid, she had never seen it before. Then she allowed her finger tips to acknowledge all her dresses. Each of them seemed cut to accentuate the Princess's silhouette which, compared with the girth of her lady-in-waiting who stood close by, was one of control and restraint. Mary Jane marvelled at the variety: reception dresses, home dinner toilette and concert toilette each distinguished by different sleeve lengths, necklines and ornamentation. At the end of the wardrobe, there were a few coats, some for train travel, robust enough to withstand the rigours and grime of the railway, and others for street wear of the kind which Mary Jane had only seen in frivolous, women's magazines. They were made from pale, unadorned cotton, with deep collars and cuffs and centre-front buttons. There was also a cloak which the Princess could wear over her gowns and fling off quickly.

Mary Jane loved the way in which the Princess spoke to each of her outfits in turn as if they each had their own identity. It seemed to her that she had been invited to witness the Princess's own personal ritual and she felt very privileged. She wondered whether in spite of her wealth and the entourage at her every beck and call, the Princess was actually very lonely.

There were several pairs of shoes beneath the dresses and skirts. As Mary Jane followed the Princess's ritual, she was arrested by the strong smell of ammonia. So, she surmised to herself, both princesses and chamber maids deploy ammonia to disguise the smell of feet in their shoes.

'Mary Jane, I must rest a little while,' the Princess said, 'but I should like you to return later this evening ... so we can talk some more. You are a very interesting person and I would like to learn more about you. Tu as de l 'esprit. Je peux le sentir.'

That the Princess found her interesting and felt that she had spirit was beyond her dreams.

'I do not have anyone here with whom I can really talk. I believe you and I ... should talk ... really talk ... as two women.'

'Of course, your Royal Highness,' Mary Jane replied enthusiastically.

'Please, Alix. Do remember,' the Princess corrected her.

She handed Mary Jane the dress which she had been wearing when she and her fellow maids had watched her enter the hotel. It had been raining and slush had coagulated around the hem. She mimed a vigorous brushing motion as soon as her hands were free. Mary Jane felt her arms straining under the stress of the surprisingly heavy garment. Over the top, the Princess's lady-in-waiting placed one of the straight-lined jackets with which the public associated Alexandra, pointing out that it needed spot cleaning.

As she closed the door, Mary Jane felt there were two people staying in the hotel. The Princess and Alix. She felt that she understood the Princess but she was uncertain about Alix.

Hydref / October 1881

Megan and her new colleagues had arranged to gather in a vegetarian café for supper. She had never eaten in a London café before and immediately compared it with the tea room in which she had first met Mary Jane. On her way there, the perpetual redbrick walls, lined with soot and dirt and the urinary smells that clung to every passageway in this part of London, depressed her more than ever. The little café near the seed shop which her colleagues had told her to look out for was thriving. Its window glistened in reds, yellows, greens and blacks like minerals in pieces of rock. They reminded her of the festival of colour in their small summer garden back home. Then she remembered that Hill House farm was not her home anymore. From the café kitchen, the rattle of pots and pans reached the pavement. She was slow to go in. This was all too new, too scary.

Inside, she could hardly see anybody through the weak, early evening light. No waiter came forward to fetch her, as in Carmarthen, and there was no vast chandelier overhead. Eventually, she found her colleagues, and some of their friends of whom she had heard much about but had never met, huddled around a table that seemed too small for them all. Everyone was dressed in winter colours even though the summer had only just turned. Dark brown, blue or black wool jackets and bonnets that fitted perfectly. Smart clothes, not too tight, too short or too big, and without the patches which she always saw in everything people wore in her home village whatever the occasion. All of their gazes seemed to be fixed intently on her as if they knew that she did not go out much. She felt uncomfortable, sick almost, until one of them, the member of the team to whom she felt the closest, rose and everyone else did the same. A young man whom she had never met before pulled out a chair for her. She had to sit much closer to people than she normally did, her shoulders hunched within a space too tight for her. Arms and legs pressed against her.

She had not realised that she was late until it was pointed out to her. They were all ready to order which put more pressure on her, a young woman who had never been to a London eatery before, let alone a vegetarian one. She quickly scanned the menu hoping for something Welsh and familiar. The English language and the city dishes conspired to make things difficult for her. Purposely, she believed. There was nothing like her mother put on their table of an evening.

'Is there anything you would recommend?' she asked. 'I am

afraid ....'

'Most of us have chosen the pie,' someone said.

Then they all realised that there were people pressed around the table that she had never met and a rapid round of introductions followed. A cacophony of enthusiastic young voices. Her legs trembled slightly beneath the table. They all seemed excited to be able to gather like this.

Megan had never known until she came to St Johns that there were so many people who were vegetarians in Victoria's England. She wanted to know more about vegetarianism, why they were vegetarians and where it had all come from. But she was unable, and a little afraid, to interrupt the conversation that had already begun. The café served their meals, browned crusty pies served with heaped green vegetables that shone in the lantern light and the steam that rose from them against the large, white plates. Even at home, their meals had never been served from the oven as quickly as this. When she cut into her pie, the pastry cracked and fell into a dark hole where at home she would have found chunks of meat, nestled against root vegetables, in a rich, beefy gravy. Her fork descended into air, eventually reaching a shallow bed of succulent mushrooms, tiny bits of chopped carrot and slices of red onion. It was hard for her to back the filling up against her fork, especially with the way in which her arms were pinioned to her side by the crush of people around her. As she tried to decipher the taste in the ingredients, the others asked her where she had come from. None of them knew north Wales but one of them had been to Swansea, once. They found her English difficult, like a stream coming up against hard rocks. The conversation became more intense than she had expected and wanted. They quizzed her on farm life, what it was like to 'birth lambs', as one of them put it, only to butcher them six weeks later. In her mind's eye, Megan saw herself as a lone shepherdess on the Welsh hills. Eventually, one or two of them realised that they were interrogating her as if she were the representative of the wider animal-eating society. One of them said that, in a few days' time, she would meet a new colleague, an etymologist with a passion for insects and moths.

'Why do you think that because I am from a farming family that such a person would have the remotest interest for me?' she was ready to protest. But she didn't. She simply thought it.

Toward the end of the meal, they talked through the plan for the year. There was no mention of the seasons which had divided Megan's year, bringing rams to the ewes, lambing, sheering, selecting the fattest lambs for slaughter.

Tachwedd | November 1878

The evening before the Princess left the hotel and Mary Jane's assignment came to an end, she found her father, as she had been asked to think of him, in the corridor that led to her room. Beside the row of dark, solid doors, he seemed a little shorter than she had thought. She instinctively looked down at the shoes he was wearing and wondered whether he had worn higher heeled boots that other morning. He seemed a little nervous and spoke quietly as if he didn't want to be heard talking with her. He didn't so much as stop to speak with her as paused to do so. She noticed that he was holding his pocket watch and its chain was straining his silk waistcoat.

'You have done well. The Princess is very pleased with you.' Again, his phrases were as clipped as his moustache. Then as he passed her, she observed that the case of the pocket watch half-closed, as if it were some kind of wink.

He snapped it shut as soon as he realised and the metallic click seemed a signal for him to turn around and take a few steps back. Her eyes were still on him, maids did not walk away from prestigious guests until they were sure that they had been dismissed.

He turned to face her before he had taken more than a few

steps.

'Just before you leave, the Princess will hand you a note in a sealed envelope.'

Then followed the pause which Mary Jane had come to expect.

'She doesn't know what is in it. She will pretend she does. Do not open it in front of her. Just thank her and leave. Being handed the note is your ... signal ... to leave. You will not see her again.'

Then there was a much longer hesitation in which she expected him to play once again with his watch. 'It is I who wrote it. It is an ... invitation ... like I spoke of.'

He then turned smartly on his heels, which again made her think that in a former life he had been a guardsman, and strode away, indicating that the maid might carry on with her schedule. When Mary Jane reached the door of the Princess's suite, she went through the usual procedure of knocking without too much force and waiting at a respectable distance into the corridor. One of the Princess's personal staff invited her to join the last-minute packing and organising, handing her one or two gowns and cloaks that needed cleaning and pressing before breakfast and asking her to wait.

The Princess herself emerged from an adjoining room and called her inside where she was in the middle of sorting papers and telegrams. Mary Jane stood just inside the room with her arms taken up with the clothes which she had been given, their weight already causing the muscles in her lower back and above her buttocks to ache. As she had been advised, she waited for the Princess to speak and kept her eyes cast downward.

'I was thinking about you yesterday and your interest in drawing. Tell me about that.'

'Well, your Royal Highness ...' She waited for the Princess to correct her again and remind her that she might refer to her as Alix but she didn't. Slowly and uncertainly, she continued, 'they sent myself and my sister to stay with my aunt in Paris. I was,' she hesitated, 'fourteen years of age and having difficulty with my parents, especially fy nhad ... my father ... and I had what they called the 'troubles' or ... the ...'

The Princess interrupted, repeating the word and questioning what she meant. Mary Jane explained that it was difficult for her to describe but it was like 'mae pobl yn cerdded yn fy mhen' ... people walking around inside my head ... and terrible darkness ...' Alexandra appeared suddenly interested in her account, more so than anyone Mary Jane could remember, apart from her eldest sister. She looked into Mary Jane's appealing eyes, born of a strange sadness, she thought, as though a little girl was reaching out to her through a misty window.

Once again, Mary Jane lowered her gaze. No sooner had she done so, than the Princess reached forward and raised Mary Jane's chin so that she could see into her eyes again. Such sadness she said to herself. A sadness she couldn't fathom. She asked whether the drawing helped with, she hesitated trying to remember what Mary Jane had called them, the 'troubles'.

'Yes,' she said. 'You touch the lead and the paper. They are so firm. There is no barrier between you and what is beyond you.' For a moment, she imagined herself trying to explain this to Meic. She could see his eyes glazing over. But the Princess continued to be interested. Almost apologetically, the maids had been trained to apologise whenever misunderstanding came between them and their prestigious clients, she laughed quietly, 'anyway that is what I have found.'

Alexandra twisted away from her, but instead of following the protocol of being in a royal presence, Mary Jane volunteered further thoughts about how it had helped her with her own personal development. The Princess turned toward her once more, and so quickly that she was expecting a reprimand. Instead, the Princess stood, very tall, very erect and very thoughtful.

'I appreciate what you have said. I have a boy a few years younger than yourself. Yes, he too - how did you express it? – has people inside his head. His father is not interested in his problems – what passed between you and your father, I wonder? (Mary Jane knew better than to answer) – and I have been looking for a way to help him. Maybe you have given me a clue. We will see.'

In silence, Princess and maid looked at each other. Something of an intimacy between them which Mary Jane had sensed a few evenings previously returned.

But, it was broken sharply. 'Well, take these clothes and make sure they are returned here, to my dressers, before breakfast.'

The Princess began to focus once again on her papers. Mary Jane knew that she had been given the signal to leave and she was almost in the corridor when the Princess called her, and placed in the one hand that protruded from beneath the armful of clothes, a small envelope.

Mary Jane did not open it for several days. She did not know why. Somehow it was a thread that connected her with the Princess, a material expression of the bond that she felt was between them. When she did slit the envelope, somehow only a clean cut with a small paperknife seemed appropriate, she was disappointed that it was not written in the Princess's hand even though her 'father' had told her that he had written it. She studied its large vertical strokes and impressive loops wondering why she had expected anything else. The ostentatious calligraphy and the terse content betrayed much about the men around her of whom the Princess had spoken. Mary Jane wasn't sure what she had expected to read in the note. Whatever that was, it was not this. A reference to her interest in clothes (that she thought must have come from the Princess, her presence in the note which no one else might recognise but which she herself would cherish) and a woman's name, a French name, and the name and address of a boutique in Oxford Street in London. The Princess had long since left south Wales and was, she had read in the London pages of the local newspaper, reunited with the Prince. She pondered what Alexandra had told her about her son, how they were probably together too, and how she might be talking to him about drawing. It was like Alexandra's presence in the note. Mary Jane felt she would be there as they discussed the value of art for him but no one else would know that. These were secrets between a Princess and her maid which bound them in a way only they understood. She folded the note, making a crease across the page which separated Oxford Street in the address from London.

Awst | August 1914

'I am going to be one of the first,' he tells me. He makes me proud when he talks like this. I am scared for him, but also resentful.

'It will just be for a few months. It will be over by Christmas they say. I will be back before you know it.' I love him for saying this. But I do not believe what he is saying. I will be lonely with just Branwen Siân and mam-gu. More than ever, I am glad to have her.

I search for our camera. I want to preserve this moment.

PART FOUR

DARKER

*Hold a snowflake in your hands.
As you study it, it melts between your fingers and vanishes.*

Carlo Rovelli

Chapter Fourteen
The Widow and the Spinster

Ionawr | January 1881

As she held his face between her palms like two prayer books, she noticed something trapped behind his tongue. She made tweezers of her fingers and eased it forward. Air erupted from his dead throat as if it were trying to form the last word that he had wanted to speak. In her hand, she held a small, sharp splinter of anthracite that must have got lodged in his mouth in the fall. She closed her hand over it, a token of the life, matter and spirit on which she had relied. There were bristles on his chin. He had not shaved that morning, maybe because of the argument between them when he left.

That morning he had turned on her, they had twisted into each other, mercilessly as only a couple can. Her face stern as a statue, her words cold like a statute, demanding and crushing, and he pronouncing her name in full, with a sharpness she had never heard from him before. He had begun to talk of following his instincts and returning home, even though, as she had yelled at him, there was no home anymore except here in Llanelli with her. No Hill House, no father, no mother and no bloody sister. Neither had bid the other goodbye or expressed their love for each other as they did most days. The simple lines of the piece of coal dug into her flesh and reminded her of his fingernails when they made love together.

Someone who smelt of fire, soot and coal was pulling her up

and another in a sweaty suit that smelt of cabbage and fried onions was telling her to come out of the way. But she didn't want to because all their life together she had got out of his way and now she wished that she hadn't.

He had been underground since mid-morning and his body was very cold and grey. She felt resentment for what they both had had to endure. His face looked different. Already what was human was departing. The nothingness beneath everything was taking him. She had no sense of a spirit achieving freedom. Only a body, she had once loved, now lifeless, a corpse and, after everything, this was all there was. Grief is always as deep as the love it supplants. Something had been sucked from the earth, from her life. She pressed the splinter as hard as some of her cardboard fingers would allow until her palms started to bleed. She wanted to remember. Everything. That would keep him alive inside her. After her time, maybe there would be someone else who would remember him. Them. She wanted to think of them going forward to the point where maybe things would make sense.

She squeezed everything she could see around her for answers. No, for consolation. But in the coke-shrouded yard with mounds of coal looking as if they were about to move in like storm clouds, wagons with the appearance of warty sea-monsters and towering shaft-heads like ancient, helmeted gods, there was only threat, violence and death.

One of the men nearby, who had watched her roll Meic's tongue forward, said that a survivor had heard Meic trying to cry out. He was trying to say 'M …'

'Maybe it was "Mam",' another suggested.

'Or "Mary Jane", that is my name,' she responded. After the argument between them, there was consolation in thinking his last thoughts were of her.

'More "Me …",' he said, somewhat callously, he had been told.

'Maybe "Mercy",' which made sense to his ears because most of the men who worked the pit were very religious which was how they coped with disaster and death.

No. Not Megan, Mary Jane said to herself as the forbidding thought passed in front of her. 'Mary Jane,' she said outloud. As she looked down at him, he looked so small beside the mounds of rock, the tools, the wood and the winding wheels, now so close.

She could not stop weeping.

***

He did not weep. But when he heard of Meic's death, he felt kindness toward him, toward both of them. That would have surprised her. Not love. Love did not come into it. But warmth.

He was getting older now. He had begun regretting what he hadn't done as much as what he had. Much of what he had done had hurt him and others, too many others, even his own flesh and blood. There were times now when he sought the priest as urgently as if he had been told he was at the point of death. He needed absolution. He wanted to confess, as the memories returned. He wanted to speak his sins aloud, he needed everyone to hear them. But there was nothing in the holy water, the prayers and the blessings that helped him. He cursed endlessly the possessiveness of envy, hate and cruelty. How much stronger they had been in his life than love. In his corduroy suit and sharp reflection, he was hiding, hiding from the fact that he had long since died.

Gorfennaf | July 2016

Mary-Jane waits for the receptionists to complete counting the day's takings. She is anxious to know whether the down turn in their income is continuing. A new surgery has opened recently as part of a pet store in the next street and already it is having an impact on their business. But she knows that a number of her clients who deserted her for the new practice because it was cheaper have returned. What they have told her has made her anxious about the quality of the treatment their pets have received.

Amelia eventually arrives, hidden, as she often is, by the hood of her anorak, her face covered by a scarf. She carries her motor bike helmet and her boots are muddy. Angharad is on her way home and stops to greet her. Amelia and Angharad like each other, they have the same instinctual feeling for animals. Amelia has a toughness which Angharad is trying to acquire. That Amelia is a biker enhances her appeal for the young nurse. She has never had a close female friend who smelt of leather and oil.

This time, Amelia, who is limping, brushes Angharad aside, gesturing to Mary-Jane to leave the waiting area and they make their way to her consulting room. Her name is on the door, Dr Mary-Jane Sullivan. Inside, Amelia removes her coat and undoes the scarf. Her face is wet with tears and Mary-Jane can see that she has been beaten. She asks Amelia who has done this to her but she shakes her head. As Mary-Jane applies antiseptic and iodine, she notices that Amelia holds her ribs. She says very little, but when she does, she refers only to 'they' and says that they punched her in the abdomen and kicked her a few times.

The receptionist arrives with a summary of the day's takings but is shooed away. Everyone in the practice knows about Amelia and the campaigns in which she is involved and has feared that something like this would happen. As Mary-Jane tries to dab antiseptic around Amelia's mouth, she pauses to observe the damage to her face more closely. Her upper lip is curling around a large bruise that closes the gap between her mouth and her nose. One of her teeth is chipped and there is blood drying in her nostrils. Mary-Jane offers to drive her to the hospital but again Amelia shakes her head. Her nose is swollen but does not appear to be broken.

That evening, Mary-Jane settles Amelia on the sofa and heaps cushions behind her head. Later, she fetches pillows from the beds upstairs. Amelia insists all the time that she will be alright and doesn't need to be mothered as she puts it. But Mary-Jane observes that she clasps and holds her stomach every time she tries to move. Her ankle now is swollen and a blue-black bruise is spreading and darkening from her Achilles tendon as if Hector had scored a direct hit.

As the days pass and Amelia prepares to return to her work on the vegetable farm, Mary-Jane is told more details about the attack. She had been with her friends, distributing leaflets against the meat trade when they were chased by a gang who suddenly appeared from the outer reaches of the car park. Several of them had sawn-off fence posts and they attacked Amelia's friends while she was punched and kicked. She feels that she has got off lightly.

'At least I have something of a face left,' she sighs 'and I can still put one-foot in front of the other, even if very painfully.'

When Mary-Jane sees her friend naked, the whole of one side of her is a dark blue and red bruise

Ebrill | April 1881

His parents and his sister. They stood around him, their faces stiff with grief and the cold, as if he had never left home, as if the family had not fallen apart, and they had all remained at Hill House. They seemed unaware of the minister waiting opposite them, his Bible tightly closed. The aspirin sun was hardly able to assert itself from behind the darkening clouds. The light was dropping on all fours. Megan stood between her mother and father, the taller of the three, seeking the support she received only from Meic when they all lived under the same roof. She tried not to think too much about her last meeting with her brother. How they seemed unable to talk with each other, how little he had to say to her, how much she was hoping to say, how much she had wanted to confide in him, but could not. Her eyes passed up and down the steep sides of earth. They changed from rich brown to deep black, embracing long straggly roots of grass and bits of stone that glinted when the sun shone, then fell away to the flimsy wooded coffin. His narrow cell. That was all she could think of. There was no consolation.

Mary Jane watched from a long way off, hardly distinguishable in her thin figure, black bonnet and widow's weeds, from the clump of wintry trees which hid her. Elm and birch, a patch of darkness in the gathering gloom that never moved.

The three mourners, with their priest, guided each other away from the grave, none of them looking in any direction other than down, neither to the right nor the left, keeping pace with the sound of the shovelled soil.

Eventually, the two men who had waited their turn, like executioners on a scaffold, finished shovelling slagheaps of earth from each side of the grave. They pounded the mound they had created as flat as they could and departed, leaving Meic in the solitariness of his death.

As they wearily reached the boundary of the unfenced graveyard, water was still bubbling beneath the grassy path, slowly forming what, later in the year, might be a tiny stream. In their boots, they made heavy strides whereas the mourners had stepped carefully, trying to avoid breaking the slim covering of grass. Mud seeped from below and filled the careless footprints the men left behind. In late spring, when the water will slip onward a little more boldly, it will attract dogs and the occasional sheep. In time, when the rain becomes heavier and more frequent, it will become discoloured and drain into small pools. Or maybe none of this. It will simply run to nothing.

Then and only then, did Mary Jane come forward. She stepped

slowly, down the shallow hillside, not in a straight line but as if she were following a labyrinth, that only she could see in the swathes of rough grass, to its centre. She carried a few flowers wrapped in an old newspaper. As she reached the grave, the knuckle-white moon arrived ahead of her. Her mother waiting for her. Mary Jane's fingers tightened around the splinter of coal she had taken from the back of Meic's throat.

Standing before him, she tried to recover how, as a couple, each had embellished the other's life. She clasped her belly.

'My love,' she said, 'you are here. Inside me. I will make sure she is looked after.'

As she spoke, in the now rapidly disappearing light, the trees seemed to draw closer. She took the flowers from their paper and placed them over the clods of earth, as she used to lay sprigs of mint over the lamb she cooked for him.

The gravestone, lying at the head of the grave, waiting its erection when the earth had settled, now seemed like a discarded playing card. She walked prayerfully toward it. Each letter of his name cut in the granite seemed like a teardrop.

'How little, my love, have they written about you,' she said, taking the splinter from her pocket.

She wanted to lie with him for all eternity. Then, as if the trees had suddenly pushed themselves forward, she found herself asking whether he would want that. Or if there were someone else, he would want there, too.

Holding the tiny shard of coal as tightly as she could, she knelt again, this time beside his stone.

'Whatever,' she said. 'I pray you find the grace to rest in peace.'

As Mary Jane walked away, the mound and horizontal gravestone quickly dwindled beneath the disconsolate night. She had never felt so alone, so inconsolable.

Ebrill | *April 1881*

February is a detestable month. The sky seems forever grey and low. Whatever snow falls in late January remains, compacted in shiny metallic islands. They are difficult to walk on until they break into sharp shards like fine filleting blades.

In 1881, February extended into March and continued into April. Mary Jane slipped several times on her way through Llanelli, dropping her cases and making a windmill of her arms. A jolt ran through her spine, her calves absorbed most of the pain and, in her thick boots, her feet had no subtlety. If it were not blue cold, she would consider treading barefoot. The booted march of winter always proceeds, slow and heavy, under darkness. Usually it retreats quickly and nervously before the incoming light, but not this year it seemed. Even so, March and April had something going for them which the lingering of February could never take away. Promise of the summer ahead.

Every night for the past few weeks, at what would have been their dinner time, Mary Jane had sat alone at the table. She had not eaten, her appetite had deserted her, but being there, when they would have been together, brought her close to him once more. For the first week after his death, there had been no distinction for her between day and night, simply twenty-four hours to get through. Two or three times an hour she had clasped that small splinter of coal she had taken from his throat. Holding it helped, a little.

That morning, the day on which she had decided to leave, the stove had stopped working as if to agree that everything had ended. Rust had begun to bore a hole in their tin bath. The bucket under the sink stank of damp soap. The scrubbing brush bristles looked sharper than ever. She thought she saw one of the young rats. Fast and agile. Now the rooms were all theirs. They had the rot, the broken panes and the crumbling floorboards to themselves.

But, for all this, Mary Jane was reasonably optimistic on her way to Cardiff. Clouds scudded across the sky. Some looked like streaks of cold, egg plant. The movement gladdened her heart. If anyone could help her, her sister could. She had spent the last couple of months hiding alone in Llanelli. She had little money left. Most of what she had saved had been eaten by the rent, gin and her meagre diet. She hated leaving her rooms because out on the street there wasn't a glance, a gesture or an avoidance she had not experienced. Inside, she felt safe, but she could not stop thinking about Meic and the good times they had had together. In these rooms, she had enjoyed some of the happiest moments of her life. But the 'terribles' returned more often now. They were fiercer, her scalp prickled and her cheeks grew so hot she wanted her whole face to lift off like a mask. They reminded her of all the hideous things she had done, all the secrets she kept. The rats had grown larger, they had bigger families and they were noisier even than those in her own head.

There were days when she lived from nightmare to nightmare. Sometimes they came at night, sometimes in the day itself. In a recurring dream, she lay on the kitchen floor, the smell of her death encouraging the rats to break through the skirting boards and tear holes in her clothes so that they might better reach her flesh. As she raised herself on her elbows, waiting for the nightmare to fall away from her, like the water when she stood upright in her bath, she realised over again that for Mary Jane simply being alive was not enough.

The train struggled out of every station at which it stopped. It never moved as they did in Mary Jane's story books when she was a child. She studied how the villages climbed the hillsides close to the railway line with their straight streets of grey houses, all exactly alike, beneath huge coal-tips. Entering one station, she noticed a tip towering over what looked like a school. Children in similar, dark coats ran about carelessly in and out of different gatherings and through her dirty, carriage window they looked like armies of ants. She wondered what view they had of the world as they copied their letters, recited the Bible, listened to their teacher and played within such an almighty shadow.

Two colliers of middle age hauled themselves up from the platform into her compartment. They might have been men who knew Meic. Each of them was of short stature and shabbily dressed. They greeted her and asked her something but she could not decipher what they said. They threw themselves deep into the bench seats leaving a space between themselves and Mary Jane but leaning toward each other, continuing the argument between them that had started on the platform. They were talking angrily about a pit, Mary Jane thought they said Nelson Colliery, that had been put on stop tap. One of them sat back in his seat, almost as a gesture of despair Mary Jane thought. The other tried to light a discoloured stub of a cigarette, having to purse his lips and bend further forward in order to do so. The match flared angrily and the flame burned his fingers before it lit his fag-end. He spat a morsel of tobacco out of his mouth before trying again. His friend, counting on his fingers for emphasis, numbered three pits which Mary Jane believed must constitute the colliery. She did not want to catch their eyes and kept looking out of the window at the hillsides but all the time she could see their reflection in the glass. The other mentioned somebody called Waldo who was in Number 3. Mention of this name stopped the other man from searching his pockets and he started nodding his head, seemingly anticipating what was coming next. His friend whispered, as if this were a word not to be spoken aloud, 'communist'. Whatever was going on, Mary Jane thought that this one disclosure made sense of everything for them. A magnet bringing all the iron filings together in one swollen heap. The train brakes screamed before a set of signals and when Mary Jane could next hear what they were saying above the train's clanking wheels, they were speaking about someone else and, whoever he was, the stub smoker was listing the properties he owned, from his mansion in Cardiff to his 'ouse in London. A little further down the line, he appeared to be Lord somebody or other and he was taking instruction from whoever to take on the communists in Carmarthenshire.

The train strained noisily over a hill above a long valley into which it descended swiftly, eventually halting, on Mary Jane's side, next to a large farm. From the other side, the view was very different. A dozen or so streets carried their grey stone houses higher and higher toward the pit. Its black, looming, winding-gear dwarfed a small square chapel as if announcing itself as the people's new god. She watched the two men drop onto the platform and as the door slammed, she heard one of them say 'What right as 'e got ...' For the first time since she left Llanelli, she felt the train slip away easily from its station and wondered, as dirty smoke drifted past her, whether 'he' was Waldo or the Lord.

As the train approached Cardiff, there were fewer coal tips. Dismounting from the train and following the other passengers, Mary Jane noticed fewer collarless men than in Llanelli. In her black widow's weeds, she looked a younger version of Queen Victoria. She hated them, she thought they made her stand out like a wrought-iron lamppost. Like the Queen, she was heavy in her bosom and abdomen and slightly chubby in her face. And there were blotches on her cheeks which she tried to hide. She found herself trying to manage a case and a basket on a crowded platform and hoped that it would not be too long before her sister came into view. In fact, Mary Jane's sister was too thoughtful to leave her struggle by herself and met her immediately outside the station. The pavement thronged with families and solitary well-dressed men who had come to Cardiff on business and some of them had to swerve to avoid the two women who warmly hugged themselves, getting lost in the deep emotion of their embrace. Mary Jane seemed shorter and bustier than her sister remembered which she put down to her pregnancy. Her veil fluttered as she spoke until, impatiently, she thrust it up and over her bonnet.

Her sister had been the first to leave the family home in

Carmarthen. She had travelled to Cardiff with the intention of meeting a prosperous man and marry him. That was how many women thought in those days, although there were some who didn't, and she, unlike many others, had succeeded in what she had set out to do. Neither sister had seen each other since shortly after their trip to Paris. Mary Jane's widow's weeds made her look older than she actually was. Her sister felt such deep sorrow for her, unable to think of her as a widow. Widowhood, so permanent in those days, so many lonely years. She passed Mary Jane's luggage to her husband who acknowledged her with an open smile. He was a big, spruce man who swung her case to and fro as if it were an empty box and, despite Mary Jane's own height, made her feel like a pygmy. He was clearly one of the municipality's most formidable gentlemen, she thought. He had a carefully manicured moustache and a beard clearly never allowed to become too bushy or too narrow and wispy. Whenever he said anything, he spoke very quickly as if he had to be somewhere else very soon and he reminded her of her 'father' at the Arms.

Mary Jane's sister and brother-in-law led her through the thinning crowd and made their way into the town. She believed all the women they passed were glancing at her out of the corner of their eyes, and she wondered what this meant. Suddenly, she felt exhausted and unable to say much.

'You will remember the house, we haven't changed it much,' her sister reassured her.

Mary Jane recalled the house easily. It was where she had stayed with her sister for a short while before their sojourn to France. She was endlessly telling Meic about it, almost as often as she recalled Paris, describing it as the kind of house they would have, maybe exaggerating in her own mind its magnificence. In the slow walk there, the town seemed much busier, grimier, than Mary Jane remembered. The people on the streets, especially the ordinary men, began to seem less different from those in Llanelli. The sound of raucous laughter, and occasionally singing, came from the public houses even though it were still early evening. She caught glimpses of women drinking coloured liquids out of long glasses and men of different ages all clustered around oval gaming tables. It did not take her long to realise that she was hearing less Welsh and a strange, strong kind of English with a lilt that constantly rose and fell.

They came to a bridge spanning a broad river. On the far side, where the houses seemed smaller and dirtier than those near her, groups of people from different families were huddled around door steps. Some of the women watched barefoot children groping about in the water. They reminded Mary Jane of the youngsters who would join their parents poaching salmon in Carmarthen, a time when she and her sister and their parents were a family. Others simply stood with their back to the river and watched the passing human traffic. Outside a Christian mission, Tŷ Gobaith (Hope House), men in ragged, ill-fitting suits and flat caps queued for food. Below Mary Jane, the inky-black water slipped by. She began to feel nauseous and a little giddy. She felt her sister's arms around her, steadying her, as they did when she was a child. Her brother-in-law took her basket from her. They decided to enter a café on the street beneath the grey, looming walls of the castle, and to sit awhile.

Mary Jane's sister noticed her swollen ankles and how she was perspiring. She mopped her forehead with a folded handkerchief from her handbag. The café reminded Mary Jane of those near the river in Carmarthen. She may have lost consciousness for a short while because afterward she could not remember her sister and brother-in-law ordering anything, only a waitress in a smart skirt and blouse bringing them a tray with tea cups, a large tea pot, side plates and some cake. Her sister positioned herself easily between her husband and Mary Jane as she poured the tea and divided up what there was for them to eat. Mary Jane felt her edging herself closer to her. They had always got on well together but her mother thought less of the daughter who lived in Cardiff, as if she were no longer a Carmarthen Kelly. Of course, in a way she wasn't. She had married.

She had become a Sullivan.

The quickness with which her sister asked about the baby did not surprise Mary Jane. A pregnant woman had few options. For many unmarried women, the main problem was finding someone to abort the pregnancy. For others, how to dispose of their child. In Ireland, unmarried women, and many married women, too, were forced to drown their child at birth. Mary Jane wanted control of her life, she was driven by ambitions and now she had connections, and for her there was a sister who desperately wanted a child.

Mary Jane's sister lost no time in reassuring her that she could stay with them in Cathedral Road as long as she needed, including after the birth. Her husband listened while avoiding looking at either of them. In the weeks to come, Mary Jane would wonder what he really thought about having another member of the Kelly family and a new-born baby hoisted upon them. They had been married a few years but had not yet had children of their own. There had been an alternative which would have been to despatch widow and child to their mother's in Dublin but each of them knew that their mother was now too unwell to take on such a burden. Mary Jane's sister marvelled how well she appeared to be coping with Meic's death and with her pregnancy without her family to help.

'The truth is,' she later confided in them, 'I find it impossible to live without him.'

She bemoaned the fact that Meic had not lived to see his child and that their child would never see their father.

Her sister and her brother-in-law listened intently to everything Mary Jane said. They had never listened so closely to anyone before, and never would again.

Tachwedd | November 1888

Watch him now. The man who has said more about her than all the others she knew put together. He moves freely on a street where the previous week he had been hardly able to put one foot in front of the other. Two or three of the reporters who crowded around him then, pushing through the constables to get to him, have returned and loiter in different parts of the road. They do not spare him a second glance.

A tall woman whom he has only ever known as Julia, as well-dressed as she always tries to be, is milking all the attention this morning. He notices that the reporter with whom she is talking is jingling shillings in his pocket. He looks away, toward the broken window pane beside the entrance door to her flat. Then he strolls back to it. Very carefully, very mannered, very deliberately so as to attract the reporter's eye. He stares at it, as if he is remembering something. Look at how quickly a reporter approaches him. 'Street scribes' the constables call them.

'I don't suppose you have more you can tell us?'

Yes. They spoke together a few days ago. The reporter's face is studied carefully. Those few minutes of silence are essential. Take your time. Think of something they will pay you for. A few shillings will help the day along. One is thinking how much he needs, the other how much he can afford.

'I might have given you the wrong impression ... you know ... the other evening.'

Is this a retraction or an elaboration? Both are the same to a street man. They are the runners, the knockers and the trotters of journalism who buy and sell to those who have risen to sit at their own desk, who fence what might be printable. They have learned to recognise how people toss information they don't understand the value of onto a tip like household waste. Watch him. He is interested. He has already paid out quite a lot but there are still some shillings left. Listen. He rattles them in his pocket. He'll pay for what he cannot make up, after all he doesn't live around here.

'When I said I used to read her the papers, you might have thought I was saying she couldn't read.'

Listen. Nothing. The sound of coins against each other has stopped. The pocket is silent. Now you have to think quickly or he'll walk away.

'She spoke English but she did not read it as easily as she read Welsh. That was the language she was schooled in.'

'You read her these stories?'

Both of them knew what the other meant.

'Catherine Endowes. She was always asking about her.'

'Why? I mean, any particular reason?'

'The stories were all about how it was she fell on hard times. Just like our Mary Jane.' Listen. He is listening. Intently. He can hear shillings sliding against each other again.

'She came from a family that was quite well-to-do. She was always talking about her links to the Welsh aristocracy.'

'Welsh aristocracy? Who are they?'

''She came from Cardiff,' he said. Then he realised he might have misremembered or suddenly thought this was too precise. 'Or Carmarthen or Card ... something like that. I am not Welsh.'

Welsh aristocracy. The idea was being pondered in time with the coins being turned over.

Look at how he gets the money out of the reporter's pockets.

'You know, the Princess of Wales. That Danish Princess. You know, Alexandra.'

'She knew her?'

'Said she knew her. Had stories about her.'

Shillings, bobs, dripped slowly into an open palm.

Ebril | April 1882

All that is in the future, six years after Megan walked again through the village to their old farm house. She found it hard to believe she was doing this.

She was alone but carried a small child in a bag carrier she had made herself and which now swung gently across her chest. The child slept peacefully, lulled by Megan's rise and fall over the mud tracked road and her sweet singing. But Megan did not feel she and the child were by themselves. Meic was here, too. He was still here. He had returned. She could feel him holding her arm. He was pushing her along. She didn't like that and tried to stride ahead of him but not so far that she could not feel his presence. She had to have him with her and she couldn't cope without him. But this couldn't be about him. It had to be about her.

Despite being much earlier in the year than when she had left three years ago, it was a similar kind of warmish, dry day. But winter was still hanging around like men outside a bar at closing time. Although it was early spring, the late afternoon sky was turning slate grey, the hills squatted like elderly widows and the sheep roamed like the ghosts of long-lost children. There were too many bare branches on the trees and they made her think of the funeral, the grave she had sat by for an entire morning.

She wondered what the house would be like. A wreck with no roof and no shutters or doors, and full of animal poo? The bailiff had said. 'It needs work. But it is habitable.'

As she walked, she remembered, or reimagined, the dresser where their mother arranged their plates and dishes and the drawers underneath, full of needles, cotton and flannel, and, like a treasure, a few pieces of fine silk. She would find a smaller version, a mattress and a cupboard where, like her mother, she could hang her few dresses, stack some shoes and store her shawls. There would be chickens for sale in Llanrwst and sheep in the animal market at

Denbigh. Meic had advised her which were the best days to go. They had bought sheep together when they were younger. Before he went to the mines, long before Mary Jane entered their lives, he worked the sheep with their father. She knew he would follow her around the market. He would find a way of helping her.

As she stepped onto the track that led to the farm, she noticed how high the hedgerows had grown. At one point, she had to lift her skirts, and step over brambles, nettles and thick undergrowth to make her way to the stream. It was hard for her to keep her balance, the baby was waking and stirring and she had two carpetbags to cope with. The bridge across the stream, which now seemed fuller and ran more swiftly than she recalled, no longer looked secure but she risked it.

A few minutes before she reached the house, she saw the white spell that its walls always cast through the trees. Her heart inflated in her chest and the palms of her hands became itchy. Enthusiasm and serious doubt jostled in her head. She didn't want to go any further but she also wanted to run there, as if she were a child again. She wanted their mother and father to be there waiting for her. She wanted her father to be standing beside his first Highland calves. She needed her mother to be proud of the farm they had developed. And her brother had to be proud of her.

As she approached the cottage, she noticed the bushes which crouched between the trees like infantry on manoeuvres. The door needed to be shoulder-pushed very hard. It opened on to a cavernous, white-washed stone room. Although empty, it seemed smaller than she remembered. Megan couldn't think how a family of four had managed to live in such a confined space. The fireplace offered no warmth this time, only a chill that wrapped itself around her bones. It had an old person's grip. There were a few remaining small marbles of coal that might have come from the time they all lived there. The floor was uneven, she didn't recall that, and under the window it yielded to tree roots attacking the foundations just below the surface outside. There were patches of mildew climbing hand-over-fist around the windows and the door frame. Along the foot of the walls, the stone was crumbling into the earth beneath the cottage. A few logs which they had left beside the fireplace when they left were still there but too damp to use.

Her father had said, 'We will leave these for the future.'

She knew that he hoped that Meic would return and work the farm.

She emptied the wooden basket of its logs and lined it with a small, thick blanket, turning it into a crib for her child. She lifted her from the bag around her neck and smelt her. She would have to change her dress. She expected the child to scream but instead she only giggled and used her wide eyes to ask for milk.

Behind her, the evening's darkness was ascending the stairs, a step at a time, and Megan thought she could hear her brother limping around in the rooms above. A web of fine, grey-filled cracks ran to the plughole in the kitchen sink and she noticed that the bucket beneath had not been moved. The house seemed to have measured the time they had been away differently. Three years had not passed at the same rate and in the same way as in their absent lives. The closeness of the ceiling above her head as she climbed the stairs made her realise that she must have been smaller when she lived there.

Megan turned sideward and slipped into the space in which she and her mother slept. Sandwiched between the windowless wall and her mother, Megan was often kept awake by the groan and whistle of her father and brother snoring on the other side of the curtain dividing the room. Suddenly, she heard a noise from downstairs as if bricks were falling into the kitchen. Thinking only of her child, she ran quickly downstairs, two steps at a time and slipped on the final step so as to slide into the soot fall created by the wing-whacking frenzy of a crow that had fallen down the chimney.

Rolling between the fireplace and the sink bucket on which it cracked itself more than once, the bird seemed not quite fully conscious. She ignored the bird and went straight to her baby which had started to cry, eyes tightly closed and her face screwed up like a ball of different coloured wools. There were small specks of soot, like tiny beetles, on her dress.

When her baby had become quiet and calm again, Megan returned her to her new crib and looked around for a towel in which to wrap the semi-comatosed bird, finding instead only a bundle of very old, yellowed newspapers from which she could draw a few double sheets. She managed to lift it, holding its wings tight to its body. When she reached the outside, it began to recover and struggled to hatch itself from her grasp. Its head battered her fingers and its sharp yellow beak bit its way free. As if she held some kind of explosive, she rushed to the long grass at the edge of the yard and dropped it into the deep vegetation. As she returned, she listened to the bird's slow nestling into the long leaves, and noticed the streaks and globules of birdshit on the front of her blouse. Inside the kitchen, she gathered up a few letters, notices and a leaflet. She balanced them across the corner of the sink.

'You must build a fire,' she said to herself 'and brush up this mess.'

She had noticed there was still coal outside, although a lot of it was very damp. But it was not as bad as she feared. About an hour later, the coal which she had laid in the grate was aflame and warmth was rushing out to where she and the baby sat on a small rug on the stone floor. The heat danced around her as it did in the old days. In a rare moment of sheer physical pleasure, she clasped her hands around her knees and watched the flames pushing through the coal like her childhood memories. Before long she had to release her hands and, kneeling at the hearth, push lumps of unburnt coal from the edges of the fire into the flames, slightly stinging her fingers.

'Watch out for those flames,' Megan warned herself, partly out of concern for herself and the baby and partly from fascination with the way the wood and the coal settled into a solid bank of orange-red heat.

Beside the fire's crackling, the house moaned more than she remembered. Outside, the trees swayed steadily and the crow's flapping wings had ceased. Megan rose and went to check. There was a small black body in an envelope of crushed grass. It was very still. A blue bottle had already settled itself beneath one of its wings. Another much smaller fly was slipping speedily through the smaller, softer feathers on its chest. Megan left it and walked back to the house.

Inside, she lit some of the candles she had brought with her in her carpetbag and laid out the travel rug which had kept her warm on the journey. The gathering evening's gloom made her think of the rag rug they had always had in front of the fire which in itself was sufficient to brighten the room. Most, if not all of them, had been made by her mam-gu who created the circular rings of colour by pushing pieces of material from old sheets, shirts and trousers through hessian or sacking with a sharpened, wooden clothes peg. The newest rag rug had always been assigned pride of place at the hearth. Then when it became soiled and scorched from bits of coke, dust and smoke, it would be moved upstairs to the landing and then to the sleeping places. Megan still had pictures in her head of her mam-gu in a high-backed chair near the fire in her house creating mats for her children's homes, her closest neighbours, the chapel and local markets. Gently caressing the child, she promised herself that one day she would make one. She would pass on her mam-gu's skills.

Chapter Fifteen
New Families

Chwefror | February 1881

Mary Jane wished for a different brother-in-law. She knew little about him. If she were honest with herself, although she would never disclose this, she didn't trust him. He had never allowed her sister to return to Carmarthen. And as Mary Jane confided more and more to her sister, he was always there, watching and listening. He was learning about her. All the time, he followed her voice, not the south Wales Welsh which he had grown used to, but the subtler, more melodic lilt of the west that was closer to his Cork way of speaking.

There was something that Mary Jane herself, and certainly his wife, never knew. He had met their father one evening in the Ivy Hotel in Carmarthen. He was a commercial traveller, there on business. Her father was attending a civic function. Throughout the evening, strangers mingled, drank and talked. Among them were these two men, Edward Sullivan and John Kelly. They were father-in-law and son-in-law but strangers to each other all the same. They had not expected to meet at this gathering and were nervous at first, almost anxious. But they were two men from Irish, albeit different, backgrounds who needed to console each other and found they had more in common than they had believed. Two men who might have been friends but one had married into the other's family.

Too much drink had flowed over the table. One man was lonely, the other maudlin.

'You married the better of my girls. You know that don't you? Well, you must do. You had the best of the lot. I knew she would be the first to wed. You had competition, Mr Edward Sullivan. You know that. You do not need me to tell you.'

His son-in-law nodded. He would have liked to have been home with his new wife now. He always wanted to be home with his wife. But he had to travel. He was a man from a good family and there were expectations of him; he must travel and build a business of his own and have a family. But, as yet, he had had no children. He did not want to talk about this. He was drunk, not as drunk as John Kelly, but he could not trust himself. Next year, he told himself, they will have a child. His wife had promised him.

'Yes, you married the better of my daughters,' John Kelly repeated, and would repeat again before the evening was out.

As he said the same line over again, he became even more maudlin. Edward Sullivan was from Cork and Cork people, to his mind, did not trust those from Limerick. He thought John Kelly sounded like a farmer who had lost his livestock. He felt he was being asked to look after the man's prize daughter, that a sale had gone ahead because one man had thought he could trust the other.

'She is lovely,' Edward Sullivan said, almost as a barrier to disclosing any more. His father-in-law sat silently. Nodding. He seemed to be allowing himself some relaxation after the stress of the function. He always found these events difficult. He found the Welsh people difficult. He spent many evenings making friends. No, he was making contacts. He was not a man who valued friends. Like his son-in-law, he was building something. He had clear plans in his head.

It was a while before John Kelly said what he really wanted to say. He didn't want to talk about Mrs Sullivan. He needed to share his thoughts about another of his children.

He took his son-in-law by surprise, 'I do not find, and have never found, Mary Jane convincing, even as a child.'

'Not convincing.' This was something which Mary Jane's brother-in-law did not share with his wife. But he bore it in mind every time his wife talked about her sister and every time he listened to his sister-in-law, when she talked about her Meic, her baby and her aspirations.

'All her airs and graces, and she leaves her home and her family to live with a miner, a former farming boy whose parents could not even hold on to their farm. And she a Kelly. You know what they are now,' he spat, 'shopkeepers in Liverpool.'

For a while, he was silent but then he revealed what he called her secret.

'All those airs and graces. Can you believe it? Going around, making out to all and sundry that she was to be some kind of maid to the royal household. The royal household. Yes. That is what she said. That she had been asked ... and Meic having to live with this kind of nonsense ... with all his mates in the pub mocking her and all her foolishness.'

His son-in-law wanted to ask him more about this secret, but John Kelly was drunk, very drunk. Now wasn't the time.

Settling into the Sullivan house, Mary Jane found that newspapers were scattered here, there and everywhere as if they were ornaments. They were a diversion for her. She would flounce in chairs, on window sills and on the beds, reading them avidly. They were from different months and some from different years. She found herself pondering pictures from places and times she had not ever thought about. She found the Welsh-language papers or the Welsh columns in the English-language papers easier to read. But she had enough English to get the gist of most of them. One morning, she scanned an advertisement for a Ladies Boarding School, where a Mrs Churchill 'respectfully informed her Friends and the Public' that she proposed to undertake 'the education of six young ladies' whom 'she was happy to receive into her family, and who would be treated by her with the same care and tenderness as her own children.' Then from *The Cambrian*, which Meic had read to her regularly, she picked the bones from an article about vice being inherited. A woman who was born in 1740, whose life was spent in thieving, begging and tramping, left behind a progeny which to the present day consisted of 106 born out of wedlock, 142 who were beggars, 64 who were chronic dependents upon alms, and, of the women, 181 who were prostitutes. She closed the paper and folded it through a piece about a royal visit to Wales. It was talking about the furnishing and decoration of the royal reception rooms being nearly complete. She saw herself arranging the Princess's clothes handed to her from her travel chests.

Medi | September 2016

The university buildings line one of the thoroughfares from Cardiff's civic centre. Of course, all of this was only beginning in Mary Jane's day. After the white of the town hall, the law courts and the museum, the more recent redbrick buildings are disappointingly dull. But Mary-Jane likes the avenue of trees alongside the edge of the road and the small green park. Walking alone, standing in groups, even lying on the grass, there are students everywhere. Some of them have what Mary-Jane recognises from her own university days as the air of freshers while others, clearly returners, are much more nonchalant. She is accompanied by the historian with whom she sat in the Carmarthen graveyard and a small camera crew which attracts attention from those they walk among. The historian looks straight ahead, he knows the way to the University's history department and, sure enough, when they come to a flight of steps, with a broken handrail, a tall woman, about Mary-Jane's own age, awaits them. Mary-Jane notices that the camera is beginning to follow her closely again. The director has come to the side and is gesturing to the crew. Mary-Jane is used to camera work but not so the Cardiff historian who makes her way uneasily to greet them. Her Carmarthen colleague seems to have no role other than to accompany her, to provide some kind of continuity between the different venues, and holds himself back. Almost ignoring him, the two women take four or five steps quickly and pass through the front door which is held open for Mary-Jane. Students, a little startled, move aside. Some of them stay and form a small circle. The microphone is held aloft to capture what the two women are saying to each other. A huddle of students coming down the stairs to which Mary-Jane is being directed are noisy and excited. One of the crew tries to shush them with hand signals off camera.

The journey from the foyer to the staircase is taken up with a summary of why Mary-Jane is here and what they have discovered so far. The west Wales historian is having to hurry to keep up with them. Then the filming stops and is not resumed until Mary-Jane and the two historians are sat around a small table in what Mary-Jane thinks must be some kind of departmental library. The surface in front of them is covered with thin folders and newspaper clippings. Mary-Jane knows the drill, they will be passed back and forth in the course of the interview. According to the script, which only the crew and the historians but not Mary-Jane on this occasion have seen, they will be looking to film a specific piece of information. Dr Prescott, seated in a room with which she is clearly familiar, is more relaxed than she was on the steps. She begins with revisiting Mary Jane's early life and one of the questions which the previously filmed scene had left hanging.

Mary-Jane thinks Dr Prescott sounds like a barrister. 'On the evidence of what her friends and associates', this word comes with a slight cough, 'said of her, after her death, to reporters, to the police and at the inquest in Shoreditch, it would seem that not only the status of her father as a foreman ...'

'Or even an accountant,' the visiting historian interrupts.

Dr Prescott hesitates, clearly not happy with the interjection, before adding 'precisely' and then continues.

'Not only her father's employment in the iron foundry but other details suggest that your Mary Jane,' she looks directly at her namesake and the camera reiterates the point, 'had a somewhat privileged upbringing.'

She pauses for effect, the camera relishes her composure, while Mary-Jane imagines how Dr Prescott reacts with her students in their seminars.

As the camera moves from Mary-Jane's face into a longer shot of the two of them, Dr Prescott explains what she means.

'Apparently' (another pause for effect), your Mary Jane (the expression is beginning to rankle with Mary-Jane) was known as something of a linguist, fluent in Welsh, English and French, and a not untalented artist.'

The other historian interjects again, pointing out that training in drawing and education in languages did not feature on the average Victorian school curriculum and would only be available to fashionable young ladies. This interruption is not in the script but the team allow it, for it introduces some energy into the conversation. Dr Prescott's performance on camera is coming over a little stilted which her colleague may have noticed and probably accounts for the fact that Mary-Jane, unusually for her, has not said anything so far.

Perhaps, Dr Prescott realises this herself. Overcoming, what might be nerves, she gets into her stride.

'The man with whom Mary Jane lived in the last few weeks of her life said that she had spent some time in France, with a man, maybe a client, but that this did not work out and they both returned to England. However, it is also likely that she spent some time in

Paris when she was a teenager, along with her older sister, no doubt paid for by her father.'

'On a foreman's wages?' Mary-Jane interrupts this time.

She leans forward at this point. The camera is focused on her. She returns to the questions which she had asked in Carmarthen displaying the persistence for which she is well known as a farming correspondent.

'If her father was well off, an accountant, more than just a gaffer, why did she end up living in rented rooms in a less than salubrious part of Llanelli, eking out her living as a prostitute.'

'A relatively high-class prostitute,' the Carmarthen historian corrects her. But Mary-Jane's familiarity with camera enables her to talk over him and not, like Dr Prescott, lose her thread, even momentarily, 'and married to a collier who might be earning good money compared with the farming life from which he came but was a lot less than she was used to.'

While the one historian looks puzzled, Dr Prescott rises to the challenge. She has the reins again.

'Something must have happened between herself and her parents, probably her father. It is curious that shortly before her death, she told one of her friends that she had seen her father in Whitechapel. Stories about her are not entirely reliable. But it is hard to imagine anyone making this up. What interest would they have in her father?'

'But,' says Mary-Jane interrupting, 'maybe she used the word father for someone else.'

The two historians smiled. 'Precisely,' says Dr Prescott. 'But we need to return to why she came to Cardiff.'

Mai | May 1881

Only a few weeks after Mary Jane's arrival in Cardiff, and while she slept in one of the upstairs bedrooms, her sister had a hushed conversation with her husband. It reminded her of being at home with her family, there were so many secretive, whispered conversations behind closed doors. If truth were told, she believed she had failed him as a wife. She had known before they married that he wanted not so much a family, as she did, but a dynasty who would take over the business empire he was building. As she spoke with him, he was seated behind a table on which samples of the latest imports were spread, together with notes as to which were proving the more popular and which were in demand in the western seaport towns, Cardiff, Bristol and Plymouth, and in the capital city, London.

Mary Jane's brother-in-law knew every thread of the cloth industry, which made him suspicious of Mary Jane's boasts about the future she intended for herself. He tried to cherish his wife's affection for her sister, as he might with any one of what he saw as her idiosyncrasies, but Mary Jane was not the kind of sister-in-law he wanted. Nothing could have prepared him for his wife's revelation that afternoon.

'Mary Jane has asked me, asked us, if we will adopt her child once it is born,' she whispered to him over the dyes and patterns that, until then, were consuming his attention.

Unable to respond and shocked as any man faced with this proposal might be, he removed his spectacles and sat back in his chair.

'Mary Jane feels that we are the kind of parents that she would like her child to have. She doesn't feel that she will be able to care for it in the way she thinks it should be.'

'Take Mary Jane's child into our lives!' He was exasperated. 'I have always wanted a child, but our child and we will have a child of our own, I am sure of that.'

'No, we will not,' his wife interrupted him. They had both thought this but neither had admitted it to the other. 'I will never have a child,' she said. 'I will never be able to give you a child.'

'I will never be able to give you a child.' Her words poisoned him, as deadly as arsenic. All he could think to ask was how could she be so sure. By the end of the sentence he was speaking softly, trying to comfort her, to reassure himself, to bring his life back on course. That is it, he is thinking, this is an aberration. She is depressed. She did not mean this. 'How can you be so sure?' he asked her again, and for a third time, becoming angrier. Angry at the prospect of bringing up Mary Jane's child and at the prospect of his dynasty ending before it had begun.

'A woman knows. Trust me,' she said. 'This is our chance to help my sister and for us to have at least one child, a child to whom you can leave the ... business that you are working day and night to create. The Sullivan dynasty of which you dream.'

But all he could think about was how the Sullivan dynasty, as he saw it, would be founded upon a secret, a lie. He wanted to implore her to think about the kind of person Mary Jane was and what, through her body, she might pass down to her child. But he knew that was a discussion he could never have with his wife. Instead, he asked her how they could seriously be the child's parents with Mary Jane in their lives, in its life. He implored her to think about her brothers and sisters. They were a large family. Everyone would know. Had she considered what they would make of this?

Of course, she had considered all of this, with Mary Jane and in her own mind. There was so much that she and her sister had worked through.

'Believe me,' she said, 'when I say that that will not be an issue. She intends for us to have the child, as our child, if we wish. As for the rest of the family, they will be led to believe that eventually I had the child for which we have been trying.' Her hands were clasped tightly and her screwed up eyes held back tears. 'They will know it only as our child. Besides, Becky is with my mother, Shawn is in the Scots guards, John is in Carmarthen with his father. When do we ever see them or hear from them these days? We are all in different parts of the country, leading our own lives and bringing up our own children which is what God intended for us.'

'But it will not be our child,' he insisted, thumping the table. His wife waved her hands in front of his face to quieten him, not wanting Mary Jane who was upstairs to hear anything. 'Mary Jane's child will have her features', he continued, 'her personality. Every time we look at her, we will see your sister. I will see her child. Hers not ours. Not mine.'

His wife was shaking her head vigorously in what to him looked like despair.

'Do you think,' she asked him, 'I would not want to see my sister in our child, the sister whom I loved as if she were my own child as we grew up? And it is not just Mary Jane we will see in her, and learn to know, but my whole family together with Meic and his family.'

She saw him crumple in his chair. Placing his hands over his eyes, he complained, that that was all very well for her, but he would never see himself in her or any of his family. She and her family, Mary Jane herself, will turn up features like heirlooms, talk excitedly about how their family lives on in their son or daughter. But it will mean nothing to him.

Mary Jane's sister became gentle and sympathetic. She loved him, cared for him, and she wanted him to know that would not change. She spoke as a woman who had discovered the powerful bond of love between a parent and child and wanted to live it.

'Do you really think you will not see yourself in our child?' she asked. 'A child is formed not just from their mother's body and the blood that runs from its mother, but the love it receives, the home in which it is able to feel it belongs, what it absorbs from those around it. It will begin as Mary Jane but it will become you and I.'

He had never heard his wife talk so passionately and with such conviction. She made him feel suddenly very shallow.

'I am anxious,' she continued, 'when I think what the child will draw down in its mother's blood and her body. I know my Mary Jane and her sufferings. I know that when it is born, and I look into its tiny face, I will see the emptiness that we have both observed in my sister's face. But as her child grows up in our home, with you and I, that emptiness, I am sure, will disappear. It will become us. It will look, feel and know that it has come from us.'

His anger had subsided. He had leant forward and, holding his head in his hands, was reflecting, deeply.

'What about Mary Jane?' he sighed.

'You have to trust me,' said his wife. 'I will be the child's mother. You will be its father. Father. That is all we must think about. Our child will grow up with us and have their own family. We will have grandchildren and great-grandchildren. Imagine that. You will have the dynasty of which your family has always dreamed.'

'Founded,' he said sadly, 'on a secret.'

'But not a terrible secret,' she suggested soothingly.

He nodded. But in his mind was a wish. A terrible wish. He did not want Mary Jane alive. She, her child, was a threat to everything.

Medi | September 2016

Is it really MJ's great-great-great-granddaughter who sits in a small office in Cardiff University? Mary-Jane is not sure. But she feels she is getting closer to Mary Jane. Her life was the life of many women at that time; leaving home, a short-lived marriage, having, for want of any alternative, to turn to prostitution. Mary-Jane knows of some friends in university, not many admittedly, who faced with a seven-year degree, cumulative bills and fees, worked as prostitutes. There were things that still worried her, issues that were not settled. Could this MJ really be Mary Jane Kelly? Amelia had shaken her up. Suppose, she thought to herself, MJ was a deliberate ambiguity. Did that point toward Megan Jane or to someone else entirely? And if it were Mary Jane Kelly, how could she be her great-great-great-grandmother when no one has spoken of her having a child. If she did have a child, what was the likelihood, given her work as a prostitute, albeit a higher class of prostitute, that its father was Meic Davis and that he was her great-great-great-grandfather.

As she recalls the details of Mary Jane's life, her eyes begin to well up with tears. The camera is there to catch them.

The next papers are passed across the table, statistics of the number of women involved in prostitution in Carmarthen and Llanelli, the location of the most popular brothels based on recorded court cases and the mention of certain hotels and inns.

It is time for Dr Prescott's colleague to interrupt again. 'Of course, while the conditions of the poor caused the ranks of prostitutes in industrial south Wales to swell, some of these women came from middle-class families.'

'There is no specific evidence of Mary Jane working as a prostitute in Llanelli or Carmarthen. But look at these figures. Notice the hotels and inns that are mentioned. We know that she worked in one of them and we know that maids in them offered men services. Think about Mary Jane's story, a woman forced to leave home for whatever reason who became a maid in a hotel where we know what was made available to men with money and time on their hands, hungry for sex, and then living in rooms with a miner. Consider the lives of women like Mary Jane, how they struggled, how they were treated by men, and other women.'

'So, why did Mary Jane come to Cardiff?' Dr Sullivan asks.

At this point a dialogue opens up between the two historians which the camera conscientiously captures and will be slyly edited for the final programme.

'We know nothing for certain but, again, a very likely picture begins to emerge when small pieces are placed together,' says the Carmarthen historian.

He begins to itemise the evidence on his fingers.

'When she lived in London, she spoke of having 'family' in Cardiff. Who were they? Not her parents, that is for sure.'

This time Dr Prescott interrupts. 'She told her landlord that she received regular letters from her mother in Ireland.'

'It is likely,' her colleague continues marking a second point on his fingers, 'that this 'family' was a brother or sister, most likely a sister.'

Mary-Jane had been doing some homework. 'Some historians have said that it was a relative in the sex industry in Cardiff that introduced her to prostitution. She said as much herself.'

'But she frequently distorted details to draw attention from the real truth. It is likely that she entered prostitution in Carmarthen or Llanelli,' he replies.

Mary-Jane smiles. She accepts this as being the case. Besides, she does not want her great-great-great-grandmother moving to Cardiff to work as a prostitute. Everybody says she was ambitious. Mary-Jane is wondering what has happened to this.

Dr Prescott picks up the gauntlet. 'She spoke about a sister, of whom she was very fond, who led a respectable life and travelled from market to market. This sister was probably married to a businessman, someone who had started out as a commercial traveller, and was more likely settled in Cardiff when Mary Jane was widowed.'

Her colleague marks this on his fingers as the third point of fact, or near to fact as anyone was likely to get.

'So, as a widow, she came to live for a time with her sister in Cardiff,' Mary-Jane says, drawing some of the threads together. Then she nods to camera, adding 'that makes sense.'

'Except,' responds Dr Prescott, who is being studied closely at this point by her colleague who is clearly forcing himself not to leap in, 'there are several intriguing, additional pieces of information.'

'She said she spent about six months, may be longer, in an infirmary.'

Her colleague, unable to control himself any longer, interjects, making the appropriate scare marks to camera with his fingers, as he repeats the word 'infirmary'.

Dr Prescott remains calm and authoritative, laying out the facts as she might if she were indeed a lawyer.

'There is no record of her staying in an infirmary or even an infirmary as such,' she says. 'But this is not to say that this story is a fabrication.'

'What do you mean?' asks Mary-Jane.

The Carmarthen guest is very quiet. Surprisingly. Mary-Jane expected him to leap in. It is as if he is waiting to see what Dr Prescott has to unveil.

'Well, not long after she arrived in Whitechapel, she apparently talked of having a child, two or three years old.'

The camera moves to a longer shot which takes in the other two faces together. Mary-Jane is stunned.

'That would correspond with her trip to Cardiff. In searching for a record of Mary Jane having been in an infirmary in Cardiff, historians have unearthed several places, such as the Protestant House of Mercy and, more likely, the Catholic Convent of the Good Shepherd, to which unmarried women, often from the middle class, were sent to have illegitimate babies.'

Mary-Jane is now very interested. This is the piece of news for which she has been waiting ever since her meeting with the historian in the Llanrwst graveyard. Where, she has been asking herself, was the child which enabled Mary Jane to be her great-great-great-grandmother.

'So,' the other local scholar summarises, 'Mary Jane was not only a widow but pregnant following Meic Davis's death in the mines and had a relative to whom she was able to go in Cardiff.'

'May I be sure about this,' Mary-Jane interrupts, 'you said Mary Jane told people she had a child who was three years old. Are you suggesting, the child was still alive when Mary Jane was in Whitechapel? But maybe back in Cardiff.'

'Your great-great-grandmother, Mary Jane Kelly's daughter.'

Mary-Jane's face remains a little stiff. There is something else on her mind which she does not reveal. She is thinking of her mother. And she is wondering if when she was christened as Mary-Jane, her mother knew where the name came from. Her name joined her with her ancestor. The hyphen separated them.

Gorfennaf | July 1881

Mary Jane's sister made her way through the hospital. The nuns looked so pristine in their white, immaculate caps and aprons. Everywhere there were flights of stairs, cheaply furnished rooms, uncomfortable benches and high-backed chairs. Woodwork was painted chocolate and the walls a dull cream. Everyone sat in the rooms seemed stiff, cold and silent as if they had been waiting a long time. They seemed like the forgotten.

A nun showed her to a bed with understanding, if not kindness, expressed in careful, silent gestures. But she did not speak. She knew why the woman had come. Distressed as she was, Mary Jane's sister noticed how all the nun's seemed to have the knack of averting their eyes without being nasty, as when a young woman passed them in her bed gown with a terrible rash over her arms and hands and her face hidden beneath livid, purple blotches.

Mary Jane was asleep. Her baby lay in a tiny basket on a table beside her head. After a few minutes, during which her sister gathered her thoughts, she stretched out her arm toward her visitor. She was pleased to have had her sister back in her life again these past few months. The birth had left her exhausted and she could hardly lift her head from her pillows. The damp air made the sheets cling to her body. Her sister touched her hand resting on the mattress and then bent forward and kissed it.

'Do you know what this reminds me of?'

'No, continue please,' her sister laughed.

'When I was a child and you cared for me that evening when father broke my hands with the piano lid.'

Her sister's face darkened. There was a period of silence between them as if Mary Jane's sister did not want to be reminded of this. She turned away from Mary Jane to her baby beside the bed. Then she looked back to her sister's face.

'Are you sure?' she asked.

'I love her, but I cannot look after her. I never wanted a child. I am not ready to have a child. What kind of life will she have with me? No father and her mother with no money.'

'You will have all those things in the future once you have settled in London.'

Sinking her head deeper into the pillow, Mary Jane sighed and muttered something, possibly about all the talk being over.

'I thought we had agreed,' she said, putting as much energy as she could muster into her voice. 'You both want a child,' she continued. 'You can't have a child. That is what you told me.'

At this point Mary Jane's sister let her hand fall and clasped her own hands tightly together.

Mary Jane continued. 'I don't want, have never wanted, a child. Yet I have a daughter. I would like her to be your child. Please do this for me. Please take my child for both our sakes. For her sake. She needs a home.'

'I can't be her mother.'

'Yes. You can. You were mother to all of us. She must know you as her mother. She must not know about me.'

Tears started to swell in both their eyes.

'Remember what we agreed. You must tell the others that you have a daughter. A most beautiful daughter. You must tell them that I died here, in an infirmary in Cardiff. Of the fever.'

'Cannot we tell them the truth? I mean ...'

'No,' said Mary Jane, 'I left them years ago. They have been dead to me and I to them. Apart from you, I have had no sister. They blamed me for what happened to our mother and the way father turned.'

'That is nonsense,' said her sister.

'It is not nonsense. You are far too kind. I was difficult. I am difficult. I do not trust myself. I have never trusted myself. I am scared as to what I will do to this baby. This innocent child.'

Mary Jane felt her sister searching every inch of her face, retrieving memories and trying to understand them, wanting to think differently about Mary Jane from the way her sister thought about herself.

'We will love her, Mary Jane. I promise you that. She will have a happy childhood and when she grows up, she will marry someone who will love her and she will have children of her own. And grandchildren.'

'I know she will. With you. But not with me.'

The baby stirred, her eyes still closed but not as bud tight as before. She waved a hand above her small covers tucked into the sides of the crib. It was as if she wanted to feel the touch of her mother. Mary Jane reached out and clasped her hand and gently joined it with the baby's hand. The baby moaned ever so quietly, ever so contentedly. Mary Jane's sister found herself smiling and crying at the same time.

'Take her. Take her home,' said Mary Jane. 'I have nothing left. The nuns are expecting you to leave with her. I am not sure I will leave this place.'

'Don't say that,' her sister interrupted.

'Well, if I do,' Mary Jane conceded, 'take me to the house we agreed. I don't want to come to your house.' Then she laughed, as faintly as her sister had ever heard anyone laugh. 'Your house in Cathedral Road is a family home now.'

She raised herself up on her elbows with such difficulty that her arms actually shook. From the table beside the baby, she lifted a neck chain hung with images of the saints that she believed protected her.

'When she is older, please give her this. From you, not from me. I hope they do a better job of protecting her than they have me.'

Her sister reached over and eased them from Mary Jane's hand.

'Mother gave you this,' she said, surprised Mary Jane would part with it.

'She was drunk,' Mary Jane remembered. 'It was my birthday

and neither of them had bought anything for me.' She paused, and then repeated, 'She was drunk,' before lapsing once again into silence. Seconds passed, then she spoke again. 'But I have loved the saints. I wrapped them and asked Meic to give them to me as if they were from him. I held them close to me all the time I waited for news from below. When they brought him up, I wept into them? I cried with them. It was the only time I have ever felt heaven crying with me.'

'Your ... my ... daughter will love these saints too. I will see to that.'

'Make sure she goes to mass,' sighed Mary Jane. 'I stopped going to mass. I am a terrible sinner.'

Her sister did not know whether she laughed or coughed when she said this. But at that moment, she was filled with love for Mary Jane and for every woman who had given birth in that place.

As her sister left with the necklace curled up in one hand and the baby's crib in the other, Mary Jane's eyes became smaller and her gaze seemed to fall back into the contentment in her face. Then she closed her eyes. Her sister would have gone on expressing her gratitude but she realised there was no more to be said and it was like thanking the steel bed frame or one of the chairs.

A nurse, opened the door but she neither acknowledged Mary Jane's sister nor her child. How many times had the nuns seen an unwanted baby carried away like this? When the door closed, and Mary Jane's sister's footfall could be heard on the bare floor boards outside, the nurse moved to the bed and straightened the sheets without ever looking directly at the young woman beneath them. As she made her way around the bed, she stopped at the small table on which the baby had been placed but then hurried away as if there were something there that would contaminate her, as if an unforgivable sin had been committed, a crime against the Virgin Mother herself.

Hydref | *October 2016*

Mary-Jane has in mind a different approach. She will walk through changing rooms, as if she were joining her mother in the local swimming pool. She will leave off the generational clothes that distinguish her from Gwen. She will join her mother in her reality. That is what an article on the internet has told her. Do not contradict patients with dementia. Go along with them.

She sits as usual at her mother's bedside. Gwen is looking so much older. Her hair, no longer bushy, is thin and straggly, as if she has just taken off a hat that she has been wearing all day.

'I have fed the cat,' she says.

Gwen's eyes flicker.

'Oh, thank you,' she replies.

'I have opened one of the tins you bought.'

'Yes.' Gwen appears to be uncertain.

She raises her head for Mary-Jane to place a pillow behind her back so that she might sit up a little. That appears to be a good sign. Recently, she has just lay flat.

'She will like that,' Gwen adds enthusiastically.

'She enjoyed it. I have never seen her clear the plate so fast.'

'She is such an old cat. My daughter bought it for me. Did I tell you that?'

'That was very kind of her,' Mary-Jane observes, wondering who she was now and in which of her mother's realities she now found herself. 'Does she still live at home?'

Gwen seems surprised as if there is something nonsensical about the question.

'She is a nurse like you. You both wear the same blue …'

She cannot recall the phrase 'T-shirt'.

'What's her name? Is it Gwen, too?'

Her mother tushes her. She is smiling. But she cannot seem to remember her daughter's name.

The nurse rises from her chair and walks over to the family cards. She takes down her own and reads the name inside, aloud. This has to be handled very carefully she tells herself.

'Mary-Jane. That is a lovely name.'

Gwen smiles once more. She seems to be enjoying this conversation. She seems more present to Mary-Jane than she has been for a while.

'You would say that wouldn't you,' she prods her. 'It is your name, too. You are both Mary-Jane and you are both nurses.'

'Why did you choose that name? My mother named me after a great-great-grandmother, maybe, a great-great-great-grandmother, too.'

Gwen lapsed into silence at that.

'Yes,' she said. 'So did we.'

She is quiet again.

'Did you close the curtains,' she asks.

Mary-Jane was her daughter again.

'Burglars will be watching. Waiting to see if the lights are on.'

'Yes,' Mary-Jane assures her.

'Don't put the cat out. Not tonight. Youths will take her.'

Mary-Jane feels she may be back among the rabbits. She is expecting to be asked if she has chased them off. But her mother talks to the nurse again.

'How did she die? Your great-great-grandmother?' she asks. But she is quick to correct herself. 'I mean, did she die young?'

Mary-Jane wonders. Then tries a direct approach, from the nurse, not herself.

'Why do you ask?' she attempts.

'My daughter. We named her after a great-great-grandmother. I told you, didn't I, that she wasn't even thirty before she died. She had children. But, even in those days, that isn't any age.'

'Several of my grandparents died young,' nurse Mary-Jane volunteered.

'Yes,' said Gwen. 'In your family.' Her voice had grown very faint.

'I'm not young, am I? Not like you. I wish you could meet my daughter. You'd like her. And you both have the same name. And the same grandmother. That is unusual, isn't it.'

'Will you tell her about that? When she comes in. About why you christened her Mary-Jane.'

Gwen summoned up enough energy to lean forward so that the nurse could take away the extra pillow and she could lie flat.

'No,' she says. 'She doesn't come. She's a nurse you see. She has no time.'

Mary-Jane is fairly sure now that this dementia has been in the family for genrations. That a great-great-grandmother had died at an early age may be a sign. Her doctor had said that this form of degeneration was rare but there have been cases. But people died young in those days from a variety of cause. It might not have been because of this. She would have to discover more about MJ's mental state, her great-great-great-grandmother. Maybe the historians would unearth further clues.

'Nurse,' Gwen called. 'Nurse,' she repeated, as if not believing she was there, 'please put out the light. I will sleep now.'

Chapter Sixteen
Fences

Gorfennaf | July 2016

Mary-Jane's range rover is parked in a farm yard with which she is familiar but where she is not always welcome. Opposite her, is the barn conversion in which her uncle lives in exchange, he says, for his meat-processing services, but Mary-Jane believes for the money he has put into the place, a kind of sleeping partner. The farm is run by a farmer who is well known in the area for his contempt of vets. There is a joke in the surgery that Prothero is a Welsh version of the stereotypes in Yorkshire's *All Creatures Great and Small*. As she sits, folding the legs of her jeans tightly into her socks, she cannot help think that this was how the Yorkshire vet who wrote the books might have felt. Her boots make her feel like her feet are being clasped by a cold hand.

Prothero has a deadpan expression on his face which confirms what Mary-Jane already knows, that he has been expecting the senior partner in the practice who is a man. She stands up and pushes her feet as far as she can into the shoe of the boot. She and the farmer maintain a stare that neither want to drop.

A voice comes from the side. She sees a child dressed in clothes that look as if they are from a previous century. Blood is rushing to Mary-Jane's head and she feels momentarily dizzy. She thinks she is hallucinating.

'Are you coming over?' Prothero calls to her.

'You do not know me,' she says. 'And you do not know yourself.'

Then she vanishes.

Mary-Jane puts her hand to her forehead. She is feeling confused but alert enough to hear Prothero asking whether they are waiting on her partner Dr Cuthbertson, adding that in his opinion that would make her delaying worthwhile.

Prothero has forgotten that Cuthbertson doesn't make visits anymore. He has appointed vets like Mary-Jane to do that kind of thing. He has long tired of farmers, like Prothero, who would rather shoot their sick stock than pay vets to treat them.

Mary-Jane is no longer looking at Prothero. She is gratified that farmers like him are a dying breed. On her way to the field, she can hear him thinking that she should stick with looking after those small critters that city kids keep in cages, and they should send us a real vet. She wants to say something to him but the poise and beauty of a velvet black highland cow stuns her. Prothero's daughter steers her to the gate while her father looks on sternly. She waits for Mary-Jane who slips the gate's bolt and steps up to the animal, her boots squelching loudly.

'Isn't she a beauty,' the young woman says.

'Yes, she certainly is …' she agrees, pausing to try and remember the girl's name.

'Megyn,' she says, stretching gingerly from the hips and forcing an awkward smile.

Mary-Jane nods in acknowledgement.

Then she asks her what the problem is as she parts the curtain of hair to study the cow's eyes.

'No use to us, that's what the problem is,' Prothero shouts from behind. 'She says,' Mary-Jane realises that he is referring to Megyn, 'call the vet. I say we need old Ned and 'is slaughter truck.'

Mary-Jane looks him squarely in the face. She says nothing.

'She's lethargic. Not often like this. And there hasn't been any milk for a few days,' Megyn offers.

'But she's on her mobile before I can ring your uncle,' her father continues.

The silence between them grows more awkward. The cow's lips are easily lifted and the animal hardly seems to notice someone messing about with her mouth and tongue.

'A job for Cuthbertson. He might save this cow from your uncle.'

Megyn and Mary-Jane look at each other. What passes between them only women might recognise. They sigh in unison, Mary-Jane much more loudly.

'I am going to take some blood. Get it sent off to the lab.'

'You know what it is, don't you?'

'Not uncommon.'

'Will she be alright?'

'Yes, if I am correct.' They both look at her father who is finally making his way over.

'She's magnificent, isn't she?' he says. 'She comes from a herd in Monmouthshire which was started on a farm 'ere in Llanrwst. Long, long ago. Even before my father's time.'

'Come over to the car and I will explain everything.'

His daughter turns to take the cow to the sheds and her father slaps her on her buttocks as if he had missed the hind of the animal.

The vet and farmer walk over the yard. For a millisecond, Mary-

Jane thinks she sees that child again. But this time it is the sun in her eyes. Prothero seems to want to get closer to her, as if all that before was a charade.

'I think, Megyn worked it out. What was wrong, I mean. That is why she phoned you. She is bright you know. Really interested in science and all that stuff.' Then he hesitates. 'But do not misunderstand me. She's no softie. She's my daughter. A farmer at heart. She will send them to the knacker's yard if she must.'

Hydref | October 2016

It is a bridge to which they come often and do not usually cross without stopping half way to contemplate the river. Mary-Jane is concerned about Amelia and Amelia knows she does not want Mary-Jane to interfere in what she is doing. One of them might have seized the moment and confided in the other. But neither does so. Amelia senses that Mary-Jane is thinking about her and Mary-Jane believes that this is irritating her.

Amelia is preoccupied with what she and her friends have agreed. They must take action. They have swapped suggestions and have selected one, one that frightens them. But they all want to go ahead. Her smart watch tells her that someone has been approached and she has been told what she must do. Amelia does not want Mary-Jane beside her.

Amelia knows that Mary-Jane does not like her uncle and she hates him for the business in which he is involved even though she accepts that this is what farming is all about. But she recognises that Ned is her mother's brother and that he and Mary-Jane will be the last surviving Sullivan's after her mother's death which they both know is not far away. What a mess, she says to herself. She curses herself and curses Ned Sullivan's niece for being involved with her. She curses how she feels and what she believes. She wants to undo what she and her friends have done, and what is going to happen.

But she can't. Deep down, she doesn't want to.

Chwefror | February 1881

One afternoon, Mary Jane's sister returned to the infirmary. She had steadied herself for dreadful news but Mary Jane's face positively shone from inside a nest of pillows. Her eyes were wide open, as if there were a vision of heaven behind them. Her lips were no longer blistered and the blotches had all but cleared from her cheeks and forehead. She had never seen her sister look so young since she came to Cardiff. She tried to tell her about her child whom she had left sleeping happily at home with their maid. Mary Jane placed two fingers over her lips, closed her eyes and asked her sister to sing to her.

She chose a pastoral they had learned years ago in Paris with words so sweet they seemed fringed with flowers. Mary Jane's mouth stretched in a tight line of perfect contentment. It was as if she were listening to something for the first time which came not from the past but somewhere in the distant future. There is no point trying to reconstruct the words that passed between them for it was really a matter of the mood they shared and would each carry forward into their separate lives. They were like separate branches forking from a tree and one of them would soon break off.

Mary Jane knew that the only thing that she could give her baby was life. It was no coincidence that she gave back to her sister the kindness that she had shown her. It seemed so unfair that someone with such love to give could not have a child of her own. They both knew how hard life was for women. But there was a spirit in them that through this child would be passed on. Life had given Mary Jane some happiness with Meic. But then it was cruelly snatched from her, as it was for so many colliery wives. She believed that, in handing her child to her sister, she was placing it beyond hurt. Not wanting to be a mother, she wanted a different kind of happiness. A happiness even greater than that which she found with Meic. The Princess was in her mind. But she knew that the happiness she wanted had a large fence around it. She had fallen in love with someone who was out of reach, who had a wall around them, too. She had found something with Meic, in his ability to connect with animals, which occasionally gave her relief from her troubles. When she thought of the Princess, she knew that they could be banished. Banished for ever. She did not know who she was. She had never known who she really was.

That evening, Mary Jane did what she had been planning for some time. As quietly as she could, she rose from her bed, took advantage of an open window and slipped into the night. One of the nuns tried to find her and her sister and brother-in-law joined in the search, losing themselves in parts of the town unknown to them. But Mary Jane had vanished.

Awst | August 2016

The street in which the veterinary surgery is situated has little to commend it, a few cafes, charity shops and a closed-down bank with a boarded cash machine. She remembers something she read recently: 'Mae stryd fawr yn newid ond nid yn marw.' (The High Street is changing but it is not dead). She scoffs.

The café which Mary-Jane has selected is opposite her surgery and does not take cards or fifty-pound notes. Chance would be a fine thing Mary-Jane thinks. As she takes a seat near the door, the lighting above her head is blinking and the irregular fluctuations are magnified in thin metallic strips on walls around the room. Through the windows, she watches a homeless man with a Dickensian overcoat and an emaciated whippet settle on a blanket near the surgery. She has seen him before. He scrabbles around inside his rolled up sleeping bag and finds a paperback book with a creased front cover and a back cover folded in two. He is always reading. He holds up a piece of cardboard with something written on it which she cannot quite read. She notices that he has placed an empty, rusty baked-beans can near one of his feet. The sole is coming away from the bottom of his boot.

A stout Labrador is being taken into the surgery with an asymmetrical gait suggesting that it is in considerable pain. It makes her think about the way people develop relationships with domesticated animals, organising their lives around them, and intensifying the cycle of health, fun, dependency, loss and bereavement in which everyone lives. Y gylchred bywyd. (The life cycle) She tries to identify the client but she cannot recognise her. This worries her slightly but she tells herself that with so many colleagues she may never have treated this dog and if she can't remember her, it is nothing of significance.

She normally brought a novel with her to read while she sat alone in cafes but because she is meeting Amelia she chose not to do so. Everyone else, even those in couples, are staring at their mobile phones. She thinks about retrieving hers and checking to see if Amelia has sent an update. The flickering light above mirrors her state of mind. There are two people in her life now. One is a ghost who follows her like a live human. The other is a human who haunts her like a ghost. Remembering MJ again makes her think about the shortness of human life. People on the whole live longer than non-human animals but she has heard of a cat or two that had lived to twenty-six years which was about as long as MJ in human years. Two thoughts cross her mind. How life can be shortened by disease and how human life is inextricably connected to memory and cognition. Thinking of her mother, and herself, she ponders how life can fail long before it ends. But Mary-Jane pushes this thought to one side as if she were pushing a used teaspoon to the edge of her saucer. She tries to think about things differently. As a vet, she works with different life forms in mutual reliance on each other. There is beauty in that.

Mary-Jane sees herself at times as she now believes Amelia sees her. She does not want Amelia to think ill of her. Amelia has emotional needs. She tries to remind herself of that. She has desires, too, but she is less demonstrative. Every time they meet or Amelia stays over, she updates her on what she has done and what she needs to do. She is conscious that it all sounds as if she is reading from her schedule but she cannot help herself. On more than one occasion, she has seen Amelia's eyes blank over.

But there is another side to Amelia from which Mary-Jane always feels excluded. In bed, they sweat and exhaust each other and then lie limp inside each other's skins as if they are one being, not two, but as soon as Amelia is dressed, she pulls down the shutters with her T-shirt and sweaters. As she disentangles her clothes, it always seems as if she is freeing herself, ready to leave their shared world and enter a space to which Mary-Jane has never been invited.

Mary-Jane has made three calls and sends three texts and still there is no answer from Amelia. She begins to worry whether she is avoiding her. Having arranged their meeting, Mary-Jane was late, having been delayed by an emergency, but Amelia now is no-show kind of late. She wonders whether Amelia is coming on her motor bike and starts to listen for its ropey, grumbling exhaust. She signals the waitress and is soon served a soup and a black coffee. Amelia eventually messages her that she is on her way.

The waitress notices that there is nothing casual or relaxed about Mary-Jane. Her personal space seems to irritate her. She sweeps small crumbs from her bread roll into the palm of her hand, then brushes them onto her plate and arranges and rearranges the condiments. The waitress casts her quizzical looks as she moves between the tables. She notices that Mary-Jane is staring at a notice on the table about eggs. It says: 'We only use cage free eggs in our ingredients.' This irritates her. For a while she thinks of complaining how misleading this is. Customers might think that cage free meant free range which it doesn't. The eggs might come from hens crammed in overcrowded barns. She has seen such places on farms she has had to visit.

Mary-Jane remembers how only last week Amelia had stayed all night. It had been lovely to wake with someone beside her. Amelia's legs were curled around her own.

'You feel it is important to make a difference, too,' she had said.

It seemed such an off-centre and corny thing to say that it made them both giggle. But now, as she is waiting for Amelia to arrive, it does not seem so groan-worthy. Mary-Jane reflects on how they each see the world differently from the other and how Amelia had accused her of having much more of her future mapped out than she had.

'You are all sorted out, ta very much,' she had joked, unclasping herself in order to rise from the bed and start dressing for work.

The truth is Mary-Jane says to herself, you have it all wrong. I want everything to have a clear prognosis. I am a vet for heaven's sake.

But Mary-Jane's head is full of uncertainties, about her uncle, who grows darker and darker; her mother who is leaving her; MJ the new phantom that has come into her past and tears at her present; and the enigmatic Amelia. She doesn't feel she knows the people in her life anymore. And she doesn't know whether this is because of them or something hatching within herself, inherited from her mother and from those before her. She slips off her shoes and presses her feet onto the cool, slate floor beneath her table. It doesn't give her the connectedness she feels walking outside in the fields, in the woods or beside a stream. Why should it? She wants to take a few hours away from the surgery and let her toes ripple the long grass or soak in free-flowing water.

Out of the corner of her eye, she glimpses Amelia breaking away from someone with whom she has been walking. She does not have enough time to see this person fully, but she looks to be an elderly woman who limps into the small vegetable and fruit shop into which she has gone herself many times. She is familiar, but

Mary-Jane cannot place her. She thinks she is not one of her clients. But, yes, she has seen her before. She asks herself why Amelia was strolling with her. Maybe she belongs to one of the groups to which Amelia belongs. Amelia has some papers in her hand which, although Mary-Jane did not see them change hands, she feels certain had come from her.

But, then, as she watches Amelia hurrying, before stopping to cross over toward the café, she realises how obsessively suspicious she is becoming. She tells herself that when Amelia arrives, she will have to be careful. This might be a difficult conversation as it is. Perhaps her delay in answering her phone is a sign. She starts to worry whether their relationship will end. Amelia has always had the air about her of someone who has already secretly packed and is ready to leave. But she must know why Amelia has cooled toward her, whether she has said something, behaved in a particular way, or whether she has discovered something about her which she doesn't like. Or maybe it is just that there are too many years between them. Amelia is a young activist, student politics cling to her, somewhat desperately in Mary-Jane's opinion, as if they are afraid she will grow out of them. Mary-Jane thinks of herself as a successful professional who has learned so much in having to bend a whole community toward her ideas.

When she arrives, Amelia is flustered and does not seem enthusiastic about their meeting. Mary-Jane has the sense that she would rather be somewhere else. But she hands Mary-Jane a book in a paper bag.

'I thought you would like this,' she says.

The bag is sealed with a small square of Sellotape. She holds her breath as she peels it off, uncertain as to what might be inside. She is reminded of lifting the lid of a box which has been brought into her surgery, nervous of what she is going to find.

She slides out an antique book with a green cover and no title, only an embossed picture of a horse. She opens it gingerly, delicately turning to the title page. *Y Meddyg Anifeiliaid.* (The Animal Doctor) It is written by John Edwards who is a member of the Royal Veterinary College in London and John Edwards who is a member of the Veterinary College, Edinburgh. She wonders if they are father and son as she searches for the date of publication. There isn't one as such. It was published in Wrexham. There are two prefaces, one written by one of the Johns in 1816 and the other by the other John in 1837. Father and son, she is sure.

'I saw it and thought of you, Animal Doctor,' Amelia kindly mocks. 'And who knows your MJ might have read this.'

This last remark is delivered in an offhand kind of way as if it were something she had not thought of until now. Still, it makes Mary-Jane feel slightly uncomfortable. Not quite a threat but a playful thrust between the ribs.

'I doubt it.' Mary-Jane replies, perhaps too hurriedly. After a pause, she changes her mind, 'But, yes, it is possible, I suppose.'

Every moment with Amelia now seems too direct, too raw. She seems impatient with Mary-Jane's nuances of mood and feeling. Mary-Jane is wondering if Amelia is finding her too concealing, as if she were an elder sister who keeps hiding her make-up.

Amelia sits for a while in her anorak with the hood pulled up over her head. She is clearly still worried about something and for a while Mary-Jane fears she is not going to stay. She looks at the menu, mutters under her breath about the number of meat dishes and then pushes back her hood and begins to slip out of the anorak.

'Are you thinking of breaking up with me?' Mary-Jane asks dryly.

Amelia is wriggling her arms free of the anorak's sleeves and ignores her. She allows Mary-Jane to reach out to take the coffee she has ordered on the way in. Before the waitress leaves the table, she rushes in an order of vegetarian spaghetti bolognaise.

'Why do you say that?' she asks but not with the strength of surprise and protest that Mary-Jane had been expecting.

Mary-Jane does not answer immediately, but studies her as if she were an x-ray she was sharing with a colleague.

'I do not feel we have been comfortable with each other lately,' she says.

Again, Amelia does not seem that surprised and does not disagree, making Mary-Jane continue, 'You seem to be very moody around me. Have I done something?'

Amelia is flipping through pictures stored on her mobile phone. Just as Mary-Jane is becoming impatient with what she sees as indifference, Amelia hands it to her as if she were in the witness box and the phone were an exhibit for the prosecution.

'What is it?' she asks, nonplussed like one of her own juniors. She cannot decipher the photograph.

'It is a horsebox,' Amelia blurts out leaving Mary-Jane none the wiser for the moment.

Amelia's plate of food arrives and the spaghetti reminds Mary-Jane of the three-course meal that was delivered to her mother in the care home earlier that month.

'Don't you see,' Amelia says, frustratedly, this is a picture of a horsebox and a horse being led from it.'

'So?' retorts Mary-Jane.

'Look at where it is,' Amelia instructs her. 'It is outside your uncle's slaughterhouse.'

'How do you know that? I mean why did you take this picture,' she blusters.

She studies the screen while trying to enlarge the picture's background. The horsebox shrinks diagonally to the left and what was background comes to the fore, but Mary-Jane is no more convinced that it is the slaughterhouse. Eventually, she returns the phone and rearranges the salt and pepper once again. Amelia is still not used to Mary-Jane's obsession with ordering and reordering things around her. She twists a string of spaghetti around her fork.

'I would like you to visit the slaughterhouse,' she says coldly and deliberately, sounding more like Mary-Jane than Mary-Jane herself.

'Why?' Mary-Jane asks, snatching the phone from her and studying the photograph once more.

However many times she looks at it, she cannot be as certain as her friend that this has been taken outside her uncle's business. Turn the picture whichever way, the horsebox obscures most of what is behind it.

Amelia moves uncomfortably in her chair and reaches clumsily for the salt. There is silence between them. When Amelia has something on her mind she cannot be stopped. Mary-Jane knows this even from the relatively short time they have been together.

Amelia tears a corner off her olive roll and begins to butter it. Mary-Jane notes to herself that an Italian would eat it unbuttered. Buttering bread is very British, she thinks. Amelia lets her fork slam down harder on her plate than she had intended. Mary-Jane can see that her mind is elsewhere. It is a condition that she is suffering from at present, but she is also very nervous. All the time they have sat together she has been looking over Mary-Jane's shoulder, watching people in the street, as if she were a fugitive fearful of being spotted.

'What are you up to, Amelia?' Mary-Jane asks accusingly.

'Nothing,' she blurts as Mary-Jane notices she is beginning to perspire.

'Well, I am still looking into this,' she continues, sounding like one of Mary-Jane's historians. 'There are bits and pieces, you know, from everywhere which need to be brought together.'

Mary-Jane feels she is being fobbed off. 'I do not know, Amelia. I do not understand what you mean by looking into something. What are you looking into?'

'Don't you think this means something? Why would there be a horse being taken from a horse box outside a slaughter house?'

Mary-Jane senses that Amelia is ready to leave the rest of her meal and rush off rather than talk with her.

'You must tell me why you were there to take this photograph?' she asks again.

Amelia stirs the spaghetti, watching the sauce become darker as she mixes it. She is weighing how much she should reveal. 'I didn't,' she snaps.

Perhaps Amelia had forgotten that, as a vet, Mary-Jane is used to gentle, and sometimes not so gentle, interrogation. 'Who took it?' she said.

Amelia squints and looks at her as if she is focusing the tip of an arrow.

'Someone I know.'

'Evidently,' Mary-Jane lisps as she tries to sip her coffee. She decides to wait and allow it to cool, while Amelia slides chopped up vegetables and tomato sauce into her mouth.

Mary-Jane has the voice of a peeved parent. 'Then who did and why do you have it on your phone.'

Amelia's arrow is in flight.

'Look,' she says, 'I want you to visit your uncle's business. Please do that. Then talk with me.'

Amelia's life is rigidly compartmentalised, she does not feel the need to share everything, but there is nothing sly or slippery about her, Mary-Jane reminds herself. She wonders if anyone in any of the boxes that make up Amelia's life ever sees the whole woman. What Mary-Jane decides she can say about her is that she is defiant, tough and obstinate. Thinking about Amelia this way, Mary-Jane suddenly realises, from this perspective, that MJ starts to make sense.

For a few moments, Amelia considers telling Mary-Jane everything, everything about the photograph and everything about the slaughterhouse and the horses. Everything. But she decides only to repeat, 'Please go there and look for yourself.'

Diwrnodau blinderus, nosau aflonydd. Troubled days, disturbed nights. Mary-Jane's mother's words come back to her, revised. Little black specks begin to gather in the corners of her eyes.

Medi | September 1933

I wish we had not been standing infront of this bush. The berries are half-eaten by the birds. Mam-gu is sitting on a kitchen chair. Her ankles are swollen and they make her feet look very small. We are standing on each side of her. She is holding Rhianwen in her lap, a small bundle of wool with a hat mam-gu has knitted to keep off the early autumn chill. Branwen Siân is the same age as I was when I gave birth to her. I have not seen a photograph like this before. Four generations of women. I cannot believe I am a grandmother. I want to see a young woman ready to eat the world raw. But I look like my mother. My face is unbearably dull against the light. The interplay of shade enables me to see Branwen Siân's chestnut legs. She is barefoot, as usual, and around her feet the grass surrenders to flesh. She is the handsomest of all of us, like a goddess standing at the dawning of a new world.

Chapter Seventeen
Another Line

Ebrill | April 1944

I have most difficulty seeing in the slanting afternoon light. I can make out Rhianwen shouldering her bag but although I know her mother is at the gate, I cannot really see her. Rhianwen is impatient to be home. I can understand that but each time I find her leaving more difficult. I do not know if it is my fading sight or that with every visit, she seems taller and fuller than before. She takes after her mother but I think she has her great-grandmother's kindness. She has the imagination that her mother had at that age. She loves storytelling. I do not believe even half of what she tells me.

In my mind's eye, I see her walking down the hill clasping her mother's hand. Branwen Siân has taken off her shoes and stuffed them in her leather bag which makes Rhianwen seem even taller. She has married a farmer and already my granddaughter is talking with her mother about how they will develop the farm when the war is over. Nobody now thinks we will lose the war. Her father is in a reserved occupation, so throughout the last five years she has not been without a father. That was the worst moment of my life. I knew what the telegram said before I opened it.

One of the harder things about getting old and losing my sight is that I rely too much on my memories. It is like having a library of books all of which you have read, some of which you love rereading and others you simply can't bear to open. Then there are the books from which some of the pages have been torn. I sit rubbing my fingers up and down the inner binding where there used to be leaves. Nothing can bring back what used to be there.

    Rhianwen has broken free of her mother's hand and, running ahead of her, she demonstrates how she has learned to cartwheel. I wish I could have shared my daughter's joy in her at that moment. In the photograph, Rhianwen's legs are candles arising from the skirt which has fallen down over her chest and most of her face.

Medi | September 2016

It all comes back, as we all knew it would, to those letters, initials which might be Mary Jane's. She cannot delete the possibility that they are not Mary Jane's initials. Suppose they are Megan's initials. Everything changes but then nothing necessarily changes. All you have is a sister who loved her brother and a brother who is fond of his sister. There's nothing new in that.

    But suppose the letters are saying something else. Mary-Jane looks to the camera. Imagine Mary Jane taking her child to her father, making him a promise, all the time knowing that he might have wanted a child with someone else. Or she might have considered giving the child up to his sister. She might have come here, debating.

    Whichever way you think about these initials, Mary-Jane says to the camera, behind them she feels is the greatest of all sacrifices, an act of unselfish love. Or is it unselfish, she asks rhetorically. She is making him a promise that his daughter would have a future.

    Mary-Jane stares at the gravestone. Then she admits that she now feels that she is a part of that promise, afraid also that it is with her that it all comes to an end. Past, present and future converge in her, a country vet. She can see that she has the kind of future, maybe, that Mary Jane had wished for herself and had promised Meic his child would have .... The camera is absorbing all of this. It is excellent television. This is someone really speaking with the dead, to lives that couldn't be lived being lived through others. It is about promises and dreams. Mary-Jane now feels closer than ever to Mary Jane and to her mother and all her grandmothers.

After the filming, on her way into the surgery, Mary-Jane sees the homeless man near the doorway again. He is reading a book, propped up on his sleeping bag as if he were in a comfortable, warm bed. He smiles and wishes her a good day. For the first time, she steps out of her way and stands over him.

'What are you reading?' she asks, before explaining that she has noticed he always has a novel in his hands. The one he is reading is not in good condition. She is not sure but some pages might be missing from the end.

He explains that it is a book about animal terrorists and those who seek to catch them. The cover is turned round and lifted so that she can read it. She thinks she has seen it in the town's bookshop window. The photograph behind the title is dirty like the hand that holds the book.

'Why do you read so much?' she inquires. She expects him to say that it passes the time; a life on the pavement, she imagines, can be very boring. But his face suddenly comes alive. He tells her that he enjoys reading and that it keeps his brain alert.

His broken boots are on their sides next to his legs. He has thick socks and there are no holes in them. She thinks about the condition of the feet inside them.

'How did you become ...' she searches for another word as if the one she has in mind is politically incorrect or offensive in some way but nothing comes to mind, 'homeless?' She wants to see him as more than just a homeless man. He must have had a life before this. Maybe he has a story to tell her which makes sense of why he is here. Maybe it doesn't.

He answers much quicker than she thought he would, as she also feared he would not answer at all. Why would he share himself with a stranger in the first few minutes of meeting her? He had had a motorbike accident, he told her, and eventually lost his job. A motorbike? She had not thought of him having a bike. A picture came to her, like a photograph, of him straddling a shiny bright Norton, which he rides to work every morning, his smart clothes in a rucksack on his back. His partner and he had quarrelled more and more and they separated. He moved in with his mother. Imagining returning to live with her mother, she could understand how dreadful this may have been. But someone, he says, half muttering, burned down her house.

She opens her purse and takes out a five-pound note. She hesitates for a moment, wondering if she should give him a ten or a twenty. Afterall, he is no longer a homeless spectre. He has a story in which he saved to buy a bike of which she is sure he was very proud, fell in love but became part of a couple who came to feel trapped and, after they separated, suffered terrible violence. What, she asks herself, had happened to his mother. But there are too many questions. She does not feel ready to enter his story. Who knows if he is telling her the truth anyway? Like her research into MJ, she feels there is a truth here somewhere. She is sure of him. Not everything about him, but he has a story. That must mean something.

He follows her movements but then waves the closed book in front of her. 'No, no, no. You do not have to do this?'

'Please. Buy yourself something to eat … or another book.'

She watches the note disappear into the fist he has made with his other hand, like a small pet mouse into its paper nest.

She has never seen someone's face brighten so quickly. He repeats his gratitude over and over and does not take his eyes off her until she has slipped into the surgery. She feels content with herself, what she sees as her act of kindness warms her inside. She makes a plan to find him a new pair of boots and a few paperbacks.

Awst | *August 2016*

This is only Mary-Jane's second visit to the Prothero farm. When Megyn Prothero invited her, spelling out the day and time so precisely, she suspected that Megyn's father would not be there. She waits in the small sitting room in the farm cottage as Megyn makes them tea. It is as if every object in the room – the candlesticks, jugs, plates, even the Bible – belongs to her father. She cannot see anything that she thinks would belong to Megyn, or her mother for that matter. Megyn is wearing a long dress with sophisticated stitching, the kind only a successful professional woman or a professional man's wife could afford. She knows that Megyn is neither.

There are pictures of Highland cattle on the top of a chest of drawers. When she enters with the tea tray, Megyn notices that Mary-Jane is studying them.

'How long have you bred Highland blacks?' Mary-Jane inquires. 'I forgot to ask you the other day.'

Megyn is pouring tea through a strainer and does not answer immediately. She reaches out to Mary-Jane with a cup and saucer in one hand and a plate of biscuits in the other. Mary-Jane takes the tea gratefully but refuses a biscuit. Megyn looks down at the plate she has returned to the table as if she is reckoning inside her head.

'They have been in the Prothero family for generations,' she says, as if she has given up on accuracy, and invites the veterinary surgeon to sit. 'The herd can be traced back to before the First World War.'

'All that time!' Mary-Jane finds it hard to believe. 'This must be one of the oldest herds of Highland cattle in Wales,' she gasps.

'Wonderful, aren't they?' says Megyn, looking for Mary-Jane's agreement.

'Then, your great-great-great-grandfather' (she pauses

meditatively) 'must have started the herd. I wonder why he chose them.'

'Why?' asks Megyn.

'Well, as opposed to Welsh Blacks.'

As Mary-Jane raises the cup to her lips, she ponders that MJ would have been alive at that time, although living in a different part of Wales. She does not waste time thinking they may have met. But immediately it occurs to her that Meic Davis's family would have been farming in north Wales around then, too. It is a train of thought that is interrupted. Megyn is thanking her for coming and is beginning to explain why she has invited her.

'I wanted to talk with you, about something personal.'

Mary-Jane places her cup into the centre of her saucer and turns the handle so that it is at an exact 90-degree angle. She adjusts the spoon so that it precisely parallels the handle of the cup, as Megyn watches her curiously.

'I would like to follow you,' she continues, making Mary-Jane smile.

'That wouldn't be wise,' she says. 'I couldn't advise anyone to follow me.'

For a few seconds, Megyn joins with Mary-Jane's merriment. Then, she places her own cup on the table near the plate of biscuits, making Mary-Jane wanting to align the two and bring them closer to each other.

'I mean that I am thinking of becoming a vet like yourself, and in a farming community like this one.'

Mary-Jane is interested. She leans forward and listens carefully as if she is hearing a client describe their pet.

'I know it is difficult for women to work as vets in a farming community. I am aware how you have found it. Well, I know what my father thinks of female vets.'

Mary-Jane is thoughtful, carefully positioning her cup alongside Megyn's, almost as a symbol of solidarity between the two women. As she does so, she wonders how much to say.

'It has been difficult for me,' she confesses, 'but, as you say, you know that. However, I enjoy being a vet. I have a scientific, clinical mind. I love operating. The other stuff, the sexism and everything, that is changing. We can undertake close combat in the armed services now,' she laughs. 'And there are many women vets, admittedly more in the towns.'

'I would like to work with large animals. Cattle. Horses.'

Mary-Jane raises her eyebrows.

'That is unusual,' she says. 'Most vets, men and women, seem to prefer to specialise in small pets. That is where the money is, I suppose. I am fortunate in that I have something of both. But the small pets, that is where most of my work is.'

'Is it difficult for a woman in vet school?' Megyn asks. 'There are only four of us in our science class.'

'I didn't find it so. I went to Liverpool and in my year, we outnumbered the men. But it's a long course and expensive. I was fortunate, my parents supported me. Is your father behind you?'

Mary-Jane read the answer in Megyn's face before she answered.

'He doesn't know,' she says. 'He wants me to take over the farm.'

'Follow your great-great-great-grandfather. Continue to build the herd.'

'Great-great-great-grandmother actually.'

Mary-Jane avoids a conscious reaction. But maybe there is

surprise in her eyes. She wants to ask Megyn more but she does not have to. Megyn is forthcoming.

'I am named after her. Megan Prothero. Different spelling.'

Mary-Jane translated her name into initials. 'MP'.

'She had the farm and then married into the Prothero family. It has been a Prothero farm ever since.'

'Why do you want to give up the farm?'

'It is too hard. There aren't the markets there were. And when we leave the EU, who knows? More and more people are turning vegan or simply reducing the amount of meat in their diet.'

She stares out of the window, maybe reflecting as to what to say next. Possibly listening for her father's truck.

'People are suspicious of meat.'

'What do you mean, suspicious?' Mary-Jane asks, feeling she has slipped into an argument with Amelia.

'Well, people today want to be certain as to what they are eating. Even around here, folks are worrying about the meat in their food. You must know that.'

'I know about the slaughterhouses,' says Mary-Jane. 'At least some of them.'

This wasn't true, she had not entered a slaughterhouse for some time. That was her uncle's province.

'Look, I like what you said about the way you work with large and small animals,' she says and then laughs, 'a balanced portfolio. You should be in business but not with Roger Ailes.'

Again they laugh together. Mary-Jane thinks to add, 'Vets need good relationships with their bankers, I promise you that.'

'So, you would not entirely discourage me,' Megyn suggests,

flashing her a grateful smile.

'I would not discourage you at all. I would not advise any woman against doing what she wants.' Again, there is a pause and she adds, 'Being a vet demands so many different skills, personal qualities. You have to be a good doctor, relate to people as much as animals, work with a diverse range of colleagues in diverse communities ... and you have to be a good scientist and technician. I would not do anything else.' Another pause. 'Although,' she continues thoughtfully, 'I need a change ... but,' she inserts quickly, so as not to give Megyn the wrong idea, 'within veterinary medicine itself. I want to do more veterinary science.'

Megyn continues to give the impression she is staring at Mary-Jane. But she isn't, she is mulling over what Mary-Jane is saying. But then she jumps, as if she has suddenly re-entered the present.

'I had better change into my yard rags. Mr Prothero will be home soon.'

Mary-Jane is amazed that she refers to her father as 'Mr Prothero'.

'I'd like to drop by the surgery and talk with you some more. Maybe you could advise me on courses. And show me around. I'd love that.'

Mary-Jane agrees willingly. She decides that she likes Megyn.

When she drives away from the yard, she sees Megyn in jeans and sweater heading to the sheds. Something about Megyn worries her. There is something not quite right. She sees what she thinks is Mr Prothero's truck on the top road and puts her foot down.

Half an hour between the Prothero farm and the surgery, other thoughts are crossing her mind. But she dismisses them.

'Megan is a common name in Wales,' she tells herself.

She thinks of mentioning it to Amelia.

'Don't be ridiculous,' she hears her say.

That night, Amelia is not staying with her. She dreams about Megyn and, like all her dreams, it is very troubled.

Prothero is emptying a small chest that he has found among Megyn's belongings into the centre of her bed.

'Have you any idea about how much is here?' he asks her.

She has, but she is afraid to say.

'Who else knows about this?' he persists.

Again, she is afraid to reply.

'What do you think your mother would say? You have kept all this from me. She must be turning in her grave.'

'What are you going to do?' she asks.

'You are what I always thought you were. All your high and mighty talk of going to uni, becoming a vet. As if we can afford that.'

The dream does not end there. But Mary-Jane cannot remember anymore.

Mehefin | June 2016

Ned Sullivan. He's been hibernating all his life behind a library of western books. We've coaxed him out now. Here he is in the real wild west. Look at him, in his baggy suit and cheap, tan brogues. He might be in a Manhattan speakeasy. It might be the 1920s.

He walks through the bar like someone in a dream. He passes women and men whom he has never seen before. One or two of the women wear body-hugging cocktail dresses and more than one man has a sharp-cut suit. A couple dance together in the middle of the floor with their eyes closed. They are both women. Most people do not want to dance. The couple lift their eyelids to watch him for a few seconds.

In a corner of the room, one woman sits waiting him, stylishly, within a space which defines her. He has never met her; he has no idea what she is supposed to look like but he knows she is waiting for him. He sucks on an ice cube from his drink, sensing hungry-smelling men and women prowling behind him. He is out of his depth. This is not a place to make a mistake.

She gestures him closer. It is then that he notices a silver cigarette lighter with a swastika which she turns over and over again in her fingers as if counting time. Two drunks crash into each other as they clear out of everyone's way. He feels as if he has been called to the centre of a circus ring. The star turn. Everyone is waiting to see what she will do with him. Tic toc toc tic. He reaches her table and is about to sit down when a hand stops him.

Imagine her. She smells of sweet and sour bitters. She has cheeks the colour of brandy which disguises her age and her forehead is lined like limestone in the effort to remember his name, perhaps. She motions him to sit as if words are at a premium. Her hair is glossy and expensive and her fingernails are painted black, matching the swastika. She straightens herself as one of her men come from behind him and places a sheet of paper before him as if it were a plate of food.

Dates run into each other as he scans the schedule. All the time he is reading, men stand at his shoulder. From the dates, he can see that he is committed for the next twelve months. This is not something that he had expected but he is afraid to argue. He folds the schedule to put it in his pocket. That in itself is enough, as if confirming that the contract is agreed. She rises without meeting his eyes and makes as if to walk away from him. She is much taller than he is. But then she turns and says the only words he will ever hear her say.

'I do nothing but mischief.'

It is the closest he has ever come and will ever come to virtual fucking. He puts out his hand but hers simply closes over her lighter. Sometimes in life there are irreversible decisions. Ned knows that he has made one. The room parts for her and the dancing couple release each other and fall in behind. The ring of people becomes tighter the nearer she steps to the door. The schedule is like something hot in his palm. After she has left, he decides this is not a place to stay longer. He slopes to the door himself and as he does so, he notices the beat of the music picks up which is strange because ever since he entered, he has not been aware of music.

Outside, he experiences a freaky hallucination. Cowpats are spread through the street like landmines. He would have laughed but all the time he can hear the lighter with the swastika hitting the unprotected table. He refolds the paper, this time into four quarters and fingers it deep into his inner breast pocket. It will be found like that when his rooms are searched. A trickle of rain begins as the headlights of a taxi select him. He pats his pockets for his change purse and steps into the road raising his hand. The car stops beside him. For a moment, he considers sitting up front with the driver but decides to take a back seat. As he falls into position and locks the seat belt, he begins to breathe again at a proper pace. He listens to Jeremy Paxman ripping someone apart on the cab radio. He wants to speak with the driver but he is unable to think of anything to say. In the silence, Paxman's sarcasm gathers momentum. OK, he thinks to himself, what do I do now?

Tachwedd | *November 2016*

Ned searches among the assortment of jackets on the coat rack near the door for a free peg for his hat. Eventually, he gives in and places it on a table. Like his western heroes, he always wears hats but he knows that these days very few people do. When he re-enters the lounge, he notices Mary-Jane is in the kitchen. There is a mug of coffee waiting for him. It has no milk in it, as he likes it, and is slightly grainy like the light outside. Mary-Jane suggests that they sit near the window and she follows him with a plate of scones, jam and cream. Squeezing himself into a chair, he notices guttered candle stubs on the window sill. She pulls her chair closer to the table and settles herself opposite him. Since Amelia entered her life, she has been very moody, depressed at times.

They have spent a few hours walking together but the opportunity had not arisen when he felt comfortable asking Mary-Jane about her friend. The last time he saw her, she was standing in the small gravel path along the side of the surgery and he was bidding her good luck with the next part of her programme. He does not say anything immediately and concentrates on spreading his cream and jam. He realises that he doesn't know which to spread first, the jam or the cream. That could make a conversation breaker in the silence between them. As it is, they both sit watching the gathering storm outside. She says that it is a northeaster. There are specks of snow in the air already. He remembers the blue-black clouds over the hills when he left home that morning. After a while, she begins to confide in him which is unusual.

Cars outside run through the fusing snowflakes. Neither of them can remember snow this early in November. He tucks a napkin she has handed him into his shirt to protect himself from the strawberry jam. As he spreads the cream with his knife, she sees her father at supper taking up his knife and cutting his steak into irregular bite-sized pieces. Her mother was never much of a cook in her opinion. Her memories, she tells him, are of meat juices carrying blood to diced carrots and chopped greens, all with the taste of the earth boiled out of them. Ned wipes his thumb and forefinger in the edge of the napkin. He reminds her too much of her father, not physically but in his awkwardness and his uncomfortableness. She remembers the family table. How her father would purse his lips, push back his plate and drum his fingers waiting for her to start eating her meat. Her description of the meat juices makes her uncle think about his business and he tries to push it from his mind.

'How are things with Amelia?' Ned asks remembering how full the coat stand was.

She shakes her head.

'Sometimes I feel she is so young,' she complains.

'You are young yourself,' he laughs incredulously.

She only partly smiles. 'She can be like a child. I respect her vegetarianism but she is so,' Mary-Jane thinks for a while, 'so militantly anti-meat. Sometimes I think, despite what we say about loving each other, that she resents me. No, hates me, for working with sheep farmers and having an uncle who runs a slaughterhouse.'

This sounds pointed, probably more so than she intended. Ned screws up his eyes. He wishes he knew how to pursue this conversation. He looks around her flat as if there is a solution to be found in one of its corners, waiting for him. Yes, he thinks, he would be depressed here. It is so small compared with her mother's house.

Eventually, he returns to the conversation. 'Amelia is not a country person, from the city isn't she?'

'Isn't she just,' she says aloud but sounds as if she is speaking to herself.

He hates cities. The hills have a hold on him. He loves being able to ride out among them of an evening, when the shadows are long, or at weekends, especially on fine days with the sun coppering his face. Like the men in his westerns, he feels he can ride where he chooses. This isn't true of course. He shares these thoughts with her and then stops short; stops short of telling her how there are always places where ancient hills become a prairie, and the tracks he follows become the old Concho River, flowing down from Cheyenne country. That is where he lives, not in the converted barn on a farm he part owns or in the slaughterhouse, but in the west.

'Amelia was born in Dublin but brought up all over the place. She finished her schooling in Cardiff.'

'Born in Dublin,' Ned picks up. But Mary-Jane doesn't know what to say. She would have been more interested if she were raised in Limerick.

A horse outside his slaughterhouse. That only makes sense if someone were letting Ned see their horse. Selling it. Amelia didn't know what nonsense she was talking.

Mary-Jane shares her uncle's love of horses. When she was a child, she and her uncle went riding together, something she never did with her father. On one of their rides, they came across a sheep's skull, not quite complete but bleached Windsor-swan white by the sun. He told her it was a horse's skull, maybe to see what impact that would have on her. On that ride also, he reminisced how, when he was very young, her grandfather placed him bareback on a Welsh cob. It was, he said to her, the most precious moment of his childhood.

All this was before Mary-Jane and her uncle grew more distant. It coincided with his increasing obsession with westerns. Sometimes, she felt that when he remembered his childhood, he was not riding among the Welsh hills but out on a prairie somewhere, his horse shod in rawhide, dragging travois poles, following an old war trail.

'Is Amelia a fresh air kind of girl?'

'Yes and no,' she says. It seems to sum her up, she thinks. Then she continues, 'she likes a walk and she works on a farm in all weathers planting and pulling veg.'

'Not a real farm,' he wants to interrupt, but asks instead about her archery.

'That is largely indoors,' Mary-Jane points out. It is one of her pursuits that most interests her.

Ned is still worried about his niece's concern with their ancestry and this woman she calls MJ rather than Mary Jane. She knows her name is Mary Jane so why does she insist on calling her MJ he keeps asking himself. Her mother was always like that. Keeping everything locked up in her head. Perhaps, he thinks, they should talk about this now. But he decides to wait and see what it is that is revealed to her through the television company. Instead, he returns to the conversation between them about her mother when they were out walking.

'It must be hard for you as well as me,' she says, listening to him. 'I am sorry, I forget that. It is kind of selfish of me.'

He turns up his collar, beginning to feel the cold near the window. She knows that her uncle and her mother rarely spoke. They grew apart from each other. A characteristic of the Sullivan family she tells herself.

'I enjoyed speaking with you, about your mother. You made me realise that I should have stayed by her, especially after your father died,' he tells her.

'I wish there was a record of how the Kellys became Sullivans,' she responds, turning and looking at him intently as if he knows something that he has not disclosed.

'There are so many Kellys in Ireland. It is like looking for Davises in Wales.'

She tells him a little more about her visit to their house. How it was really strange that there were drawers where everything was jammed inside and, now, she is unable to sort out anything in her head. He looks puzzled.

'Sometimes, I feel our deaths, the way we die, build up slowly through our lives. That our deaths do not arrive from nowhere, we invite them in. There are small things, if we spotted them, telling us that this is how it will all end. I thought that when my father died, too.'

Outside, the snowflakes are painting war streaks down the evening's dark face. He finds Mary-Jane difficult, he cannot relax with her. She makes him feel awkward and, in their conversations, they seem to dance around each other. So much is always left unsaid. He doesn't realise how difficult he is.

'It is like aliens,' she says, suddenly confusing him and letting him remain so for a short while before clarifying, 'I mean, here's me and you searching for them, for a particular one, and you would expect at least one of the Kellys to be researching their family tree and coming after us.'

Ned frowns his way into his own silence again. She has touched a chord. She sees that. Words are floating around him like the snowflakes on the other side of the glass. 'Researching us. Coming after us.' She is beginning to think that she has discovered his secret. She is trying to imagine what kind of nerve she has touched.

However, this is not going anywhere. It is late and time he made his way back to the ranch, as he calls it.

As she watches him negotiate the slippery pavement, she observes a frailty in his step which had not been there earlier. The pull of the hills. She thinks of him at home again, changing his clothes and reading one of his westerns.

Ned drives back slowly, desperately trying to see through the snow, now blizzarding like arrows, anxiously trying to keep track of the road and identify the buildings that erupt in his windscreen and fall away behind him. As he nears the village, telegraph poles appear like crosses. He wonders in a moment of foolishness whether he should pull over and wait for the snow to ease but he fears he could be stuck for ever and a day if he did that. He shakes his head violently every time he senses himself falling asleep. He remembers reading somewhere that the whiteness of snow can comatose you. Maybe, he thinks, it is becoming too warm inside the car. He turns off the heating, allows the cold air to enter from outside and takes off his hat.

A half-hour later, the car suddenly skids and nearly slides into the side of an old house. It reminds him of the home in which he lived as a child. There are lights on in all of the rooms except for one, and he imagines that he is a child again and that this is his room. As he slowly manoeuvres the car back to the road, he remembers his father sending he and Gwen into the front room on Christmas eve. They each had a long narrow package beneath the tree. They competed to see who would get the paper off first. Inside each, there was an air rifle. Gwen was as excited as he was. She turned the gun over and over in her hands. Then she and Ned rushed into the kitchen and both gave their father an enthusiastic joint hug. He gently eased them away.

'Nawr, dwi eisiau dy weld di'n dysgu saethu fel fy nhad a fy nhaid. Marcwyr yr oeddent'.

(Now, I want to see you learn to shoot like my father and my grandfather. Marksmen they were).

Ionawr | January 2017

There is a myth, she reads in a book about the Whitechapel murders, that a neighbour who refused Mary Jane money for food that last evening is cursed to walk the earth in search of what is most distressing and wicked. It is a book written by a local historian. There are no excerpts from reviews in it. She searches for the publisher's name but there are only the details of the printer. There is no source cited for this myth. It could simply be someone's imaginings. She thinks how this could slip onto the internet and be trafficked around the world until it became gospel truth. Or be a truth that no one else would dare publish because it was too bold to be told. She continued reading. Every year, on the date of Mary Jane's death, she must return to keep vigil in Whitechapel but only those who have evil deeds to their name can see her. 'Who knows?'

the author ruminates. It is alleged that she seeks someone to pass on her curse to. Amelia closes the book, and thinks about some of the things that Mary-Jane has mentioned to her. How she is beginning to feel someone is following her, that she is being stalked, that someone is coming after her.

PART FIVE

LONDON

*Everything possible to be believ'd
is an image of truth.*

William Blake

Chapter Eighteen
The Boutique

Mai | May 1883

It was difficult to see clearly into the shop from outside even on the brightest of days. What you saw was mainly light striking polished wood. Inside, there were made-up dresses and once you moved beyond them, rolls and rolls of fabric, of every material, colour and thickness, stored as if they were all military maps printed on canvas. They caused Mary Jane to think about her brother-in-law and ponder her sister surrounded by clothes and materials from all around the world from which she could take her pick; how her child was swaddled luxuriously in cloths from India of which even Alix would be envious.

The counter, which ran throughout the shop, was made of rosewood, highly polished and smelling of beeswax. Each assistant had her own place behind it to which she would return and stand after having served a client. When Mary Jane first entered the shop, it made her feel drab and dreadfully depressed. She immediately changed her name to Marie Jeanette. She spent part of her first wage on powdered paints and fox-hair brushes together with a few sheets of paper which she could barely afford.

The shop was surprisingly busy. Every hour men and women came and went. Some of the customers were confident and determined, they went straight to the material they wanted. Others seemed much more tentative, as if they did not really have the money to spend there. But it was the men who really surprised Mary Jane. They seemed to be familiar with specific women who worked there and when they entered, the assistants appeared to know whom they were and came forward to welcome them, while the others knew to hang back, even keep out of the way. These men were guided out of the dim light inside the doorway to a quiet spot at the rear of the shop where assistant and client whispered together, smiled a lot and touched the fabrics, and, eventually, each other's hands and shoulders. Mary Jane wondered if the Dr Hamilton whose 'medicines' her mother bought was among them. She had always imagined him with a top hat and well-dressed.

One morning, Mary Jane found herself in the window at the far end of the upstairs stock room, able to survey the grey, awakening city below. She had come to work early and none of her colleagues had arrived. She had washed, dressed and left her room as soon as it began turning light outside. The silvery clouds gilded by the rising sun made the buildings temporarily shine. It was the kind of light she remembered from early-autumn mornings in Llanelli. Being in the shop at this hour gave her an opportunity to reflect on things, on what had brought her here. But she did not want to waste this opportunity. She told herself that change was important, and she craved changes to suppress all the dreadful events in her short life, to dispel her anxieties, and the darknesses which she never wanted to return and possess her again.

She liked being in this room, looking out at the capital, her body filling with a gentle rush of discomforting pleasure. She was not used to being in the shop at this time and certainly not by herself. Most of the nearby shops were, like hers, still closed although a handful had already opened. A few hansoms passed noisily in the direction of the Embankment. No one turned as they did in Carmarthen to notice the smarter carriages rolling by.

Her memories were still coming, like the hansoms, but not so aggressively. Yet all the events that had brought her there, all the people, some of whom she dared not mention to a living soul, stood around her still, she felt, like patients in an infirmary waiting their turn. She wanted to complete her inventories of the cloths which she had started the previous afternoon. That was why she had been left with a latch key, but some of the thoughts that crowded her would not leave her and would not let her get on with her work.

The contrast between the different parts of the street which she never found in the towns of west Wales was compelling. She could have stood in the window for hours just watching, as she did in her aunt's house in Paris. The variety in the street and the richness in the buildings gave her a different sense of time. On her way to the shop, a bright, cold joy seemed to float above the puddles left by the overnight rain. It made even the dirtiest parts of the street pleasant to the eye and the brisk morning almost spring-like.

The elegant manners of Oxford Street, the flashing finery of city ladies and the passing smells of expensive perfumes had begun to intoxicate her. They made her feel young again. She saw herself in the stockroom mirror with painted lips, black peeping eyes and high-laced boots. She had started to pluck her eyebrows and they rested above her eyes like small strips of cotton thread. She had to dress this way every day for work. At last, she felt that she was herself. Marie Jeanette. There was no one here to accuse her of putting on airs and graces.

For Mary Jane, this was one of the oddest sensations that she had experienced, finding herself alone in rooms normally full of people and noise. How good it felt to be all alone, to be able to talk to herself in this way, to walk about with nobody's eyes on her. Here, in the early morning, she could daydream without interruption. As she stood in front of a full-length mirror, she seemed so much taller than she thought. She remembered the Princess of Wales making her way along her line of dresses and how she was dressed by her ladies-in-waiting for every occasion. This was a lovely, pleasant memory which she did not mind. She wanted it to squeeze out all the others. She, Marie Jeanette, able to think about the Princess. Every occasion changed who she was, the way she was seen and how she behaved.

Mary Jane never found anyone in the Arms, or in the whole of Llanelli, who recognised this and thought like she and the Princess did about clothes. For her, clothes were like names, they reflected the time and place in which they were worn just as names became imprints of everyone who used them, sometimes contaminated by them. Mary Jane herself no more liked wearing the same dress over and over again as she did using the same name endlessly. She changed her name to stop others, through over familiarity, defining her in ways in which she no longer wished to be defined. A different name gave her the opportunity to be new. Changing names, she now realised, was like moving to a new town or city, travelling to a new country, acquiring more than one language, entering a place where others did not know you and you did not know yourself.

As the hour progressed, more shops opened. She watched people arriving in the street, followed them with her eyes, observed how nobody seemed to notice anybody else. So, they come, ladies clutching their bags to their chests as if they were lapdogs and lapdogs as if they were bags. She studied the stooping ostrich feathers, printed parasols and stiffened crinoline and wondered about making a list of all the things she would sell in her own boutique one day. Marie Jeanette of London and Paris. In the forthcoming hours, the street would be all commotion, voices, movement, pushing and pressing, fumbling and frustration. It would have energy and urgency, distance and engagement, even vilification and violence. She could see pedestrians passing each other quickly like empty passing words. London was an exciting but deadly city. A place where there were more deaths than births. Yet it kept growing and growing like a giant octopus. Each street a new tentacle.

She felt that coming here was like an act of gravity. Since she had arrived, she believed that things had improved for her. She no longer hankered after the child she had left with her sister. In fact, she thought that helping her beloved sister in this way was one of the best things she had ever done. The stretch marks had almost disappeared and she no longer experienced abdominal pains. Even her fingers seemed more flexible. But the gin-soaked debauchery, the other side of the West End, beckoned her, as she feared it would. The taverns and the gambling houses in Llanelli had become so much a part of her as would Oxford Street, with its cacophony of round-the-clock activity, noise and smells. All so different but also the same. With all of that, the gambling and whoring dens, the public houses and the boarding establishments, the old melancholy returned. A sense of futility began to creep up on her once again.

She still had lots of stories. Others, especially men, told her how much fun she was. But there were times when, once again, she no longer felt in control. Then it was that the nightmares stayed their longest. She didn't have to be asleep. In them, she watched herself, a frightened, damaged young woman who had no idea where she was or why she was there. With Meic, she was able to invest her life with meaning, similar to the way in which she drew different vocabularies together to make herself sound sophisticated and worldly-wise. But once again, there were times when no anecdotes would come to lift her in the way they used to. In such moments, one memory anchored. It was a recollection of her standing beside Alix. They whispered conspiratorially about clothes, men and themselves. She told Meic about her association with Princess Alexandra and others, too, when the opportunity arose. These stories made her feel proud and important. A girl with fingers that never grew straight had achieved what others envied, confirmed how different she was and would be in the future. She became excited every time she saw Alix in the papers and she believed that one day she would be beside her in the Illustrated News. When she had had too much gin and her life was becoming overcomplicated, and the 'terribles' had their tightest grip on her, she would try to simplify everything by recalling herself as the Princess's maid. Everyone laughed because they were impressed, she told Meic in her dreams, not seeing how many laughed in disbelief. And on one occasion when she talked about the Princess, elaborating on their brief encounter, she did not see the couple who listened and watched her, who listened to her more intently than anyone else but, like them, were trying to get the measure of her.

One morning, while she was again alone in the shop, she took a pencil and drafted a short note. Then she inked over all the letters, taking special care with the loops, until they all seemed consistent. If you looked closely, the pencil was still there, behind every upward and downward stroke as if it were some kind of ghostly presence, something that had entered, or was about to intrude, into the moment. But to Mary Jane who was not used to writing and was immediately impressed by the formalisation of her letters, and the manifestation of her thoughts on a clean sheet of expensive paper from the boutique owner's desk drawer, it was good enough. But she would never know how later, much later, her note would pass among, and be read by, others. How one person in particular would study every word, every spelling error, every juxtaposition, in coming to their own conclusion about Mary Jane.

Hydref | October 2016

Mary-Jane passes the brooding Catholic church. It is where she and her mother used to celebrate mass. When she was a child, she remembers, she always enjoyed the ritual, everything was always so ordered, so neatly sown together, and she relished dressing for it in her heels, her best blouse and her skirt. In the church's musty gloom, she participated in a solemn, impenetrable mystery she was too young to understand and leaving the old building was like stepping out into a bright, new hay field in the sun. That was the part she loved most of all.

She has always liked to stand by herself in the open air in the evenings and let the night darken around her. Life would be unbearable if it were not for moments such as these, when she felt most herself. But it isn't often that she comes to this part of town. It is late evening and night is not far off. She can hear the shadows rustling. Over in the distance, room lights are coming on in rapid succession like playing cards being turned over. A heavy truck gasps up the road and growls like an aroused guard dog when it reaches the entrance to the yard before coming to a halt. Startled, Mary-Jane slips down behind a low wall. She cannot see much but she can hear the slaughterhouse gates being dragged apart, horses neighing and panting heavily as if they know where they are. When she does pluck up the courage to look, she sees them being dragged, breath smoking around their nostrils, into the building. So Amelia was right. She drops back on her haunches wishing she wasn't there. The truck's headlights pick out a slug trail like a quartz streak glistening on a piece of rock. Dozens of ity bity mosquitoes orbit a smelly drain.

On the roof of the slaughterhouse, bats line themselves like pirates waiting their signal to move. There is a big aerial booster. It protrudes out of the grey slate like an elongated telescope. She starts to believe that someone is watching her, their eye pressed tight against the lens. Eventually, two men climb into the cab and steer the lorry in a tight circle as quietly as they can. Stones crackle beneath the thick tyres and she can hear horse coughs gargling in the last minutes of life. She wants to get nearer to peer inside the slaughterhouse almost as much as she wants to disappear. After the truck has left the yard, she notices that the slaughterhouse doors have been shut fast. She waits, her head in her hands, listening to the last death throes. Twenty minutes, or maybe thirty, pass before she has sufficient courage to creep as close as she dares to one of the windows. The panes of glass are grimy and protected by wire mesh, but she can make out three or four figures carrying and hacking boulders of meat in various cross sections, heaving carcasses on and off heavy hooks and chains. Even from outside, she can taste the blood, flesh and muscle. It reaches into her nose and slides down the back of her throat. It strikes her how quickly and conscientiously everyone seems to be working and she wonders how many deliveries there have been this week. She can hear them shouting at each other, one voice at least sounds like a woman's she thinks. The relentless thud of cleaver against bone frightens her. As she turns to go, a skull larger than a manhole cover swings close to her face, so near that its eyes stare at her. She hides behind her hands. The head hovers for a minute or so, as if in a nightmare and then passes out of sight. A loud horse's neigh seems to come from behind her. But there is nothing, only another wing of the lit-up building and the remorseless thudding, punctuated by the jangle of chains.

That night she cannot sleep. She thinks only of the slaughterhouse, her uncle and what he is doing. She has the sensation of a mare pushing her long bony nose into her hands, she can smell the sweetness of her breath and feel the dark wells of her nostrils.

Mawrth | March 1883

He stepped out of a hansom at the place and at the exact time they had agreed to meet. He looked the same as he did when he first entered the shop only this time, he carried, rather than walked with, his cane.

The boutique owner had pulled her away from the counter to whisper in her ear that this was a man, a very special gentleman, she was to look after. As she did so, she kept looking from one side to the other, as if the shop had invisible eyes and ears.

Like most of the men who milled on the pavement around the door of the club, he was sharp suited and wore a top hat, a lapel overcoat and a luxurious silk scarf. He had removed his gloves and even in the gas lamplight, she could see how arthritis had gnarled the knuckles and the lower joints on some of his fingers. Mary Jane had wandered a little from the door, having felt conspicuous standing in the same place as she waited the agreed hour. She was dressed more expensively from when she worked in the shop. She had chosen her clothes carefully, based on her experience of this type of elderly man, and hidden beneath a cape, was a copy-cat image of what she had seen Princess Alexandra wear. He greeted her with a long, well-rehearsed smile, for this was a man used to buying the attentions of women much younger than himself. He touched the brim of his hat and took her arm. Then he guided her up a few steps into a hallway and, eventually, into the main room. It was magnificent and expansive. There were two large chandeliers, standing lamps, thick-veined pot palms, leather sofas and mahogany chairs. In the different shades of light, Henry, as he asked her to call him, became slightly younger than he looked in the dappled daylight of the shop. She was a little scared but also thrilled at being in the club. Wealthy men of all ages, some looking no more than boys, slouched on sofas with women who listened and laughed as they were meant to. When prompted, Mary Jane asked for whisky which made his eyes sparkle and inspired him, for whatever reason, to grasp her waist tightly.

'Ah, I am so much older than you,' he said, somewhat wistfully. 'When I was a young man, ladies did not drink whisky but today ...' He did not finish the sentence, but simply raised his eyes to the ornate ceiling and gestured playfully with upturned palms.

A barman brought a decanter and two glasses to the corner into which Henry had manipulated her. He undid her cloak and placed it across a deep plush seat next to them with such care that she believed he was imagining it were her. Before inviting her to take a seat, he stood back from her, as if she were a painting, and admired her. He told her how much he liked her eyes. How magnificent they were. How they shone like the inside of oyster shells. His pleasure in her claret-red dress, low-neck and embroidered décolletage was reflected in his face. As they sat and drank together, he laughed and told amusing stories, pausing it seemed only to blow a steady stream of cigar smoke into the standing lamp.

While pretending to listen to him and making the appropriate and expected responses, she observed women, like small costumed mice, slowly coming in on their own or in twos or threes. They stood near the bar and waited to be approached by a lone wolf or be invited to join a pack. Before long, the room swelled with them. They wore the kind of dresses that Mary Jane sold in the boutique and looked as if they had been bought for them. They looked glamorous and expensive but they did not move or hold themselves as if they really were. They all entered with the same deadpan expressions. From different parts of the room, men, who clearly did not see them as expensive at all, studied them. Some rose and invited them to join their group, others snapped a waiter to do it for them. As soon as a man spoke with them, they flashed a smile and mounted a different kind of face. In their gatherings, the men were raucous and loud. Some of the women joined in with this straight away, as Mary Jane remembered she used to do in Llanelli, others were quieter and more demure at first. But it didn't take long before they too became noisy and entertaining. The louder the women became the more the men enjoyed their company and the more they were passed around the group and from one group to another. Mary Jane knew exactly what it was like to be on the roundabout. More and more women were whirled upstairs.

Mary Jane wondered how she compared to them in these men's eyes. She felt diminished by the bulky furniture. How did her companion really see her? Sometimes, he looked at her as if she was the kind of woman he would walk out with only at night. At one point, he asked her how, coming from Wales, she had joined the boutique. She confided that she had received a royal invitation, forgetting that in the Arms she had been told explicitly that the Princess knew nothing of the contents of the letter she was handed. Forgetting that she had been told not to recall the Princess's visit and her work for her. She expected Henry to take her to a room. But she knew he would be polite and dignified when he did, unlike the travellers at the Stepney Arms. Their room will already have been reserved and she could see herself approaching it in her mind's eye. He would touch her buttocks over her skirt, gently tighten his grip on her waist, and steer her to the end of a long corridor. She knew from experience that the room would be small and a little unkempt, different from the opulence and the magnificence of the foyer and the bar in which they now sat.

As she looked around, she remembered that the only people who really cared for her were a long way away or dead. In the course of the evening, a tall, bearded man, with narrow eyes, emerged from the shadows and placed a bottle of whisky beside the decanter. It seemed strange but her companion appeared not to notice. She did not think about it until, in a pause in their conversation, she read the label, Old Irish Malt Whisky. For a split second, she saw it as a cryptic message to herself. Henry eventually noticed the bottle but not, it seemed, the niceties of the label. Turning his whisky tumbler round and round in his hand, he told her how much he loved cognac and how it always reminded him of Paris. Despite the whirligig, the extravagance and the fact that he would soon have his way with the young woman he thought he had chosen, he seemed someone, a little like herself, always wishing for something else. Paris was the one thing they had in common or Mary Jane led him to believe they had in common. He talked excitedly about the city, as did she, and how the French capital was changing which made her think of her aunt and the time she spent with her. She knew a little at least of the Impressionists and Paris theatre and how they pointed toward a new future. As he took up each of these subjects with an eloquence with which she could not compete, she made a note to herself that, come the turn of the century, she would be in Paris again. She found herself calculating that if her gentleman friend was as old as he appeared, he probably had little more than a decade of life left, and that in the new millennium which stretched in front of her, his passion for cigars and young women would be long gone.

Age and his own mortality entered the conversation as many times as the waiter came and topped up their glasses but never for very long. Whatever personal fears he had for his future, or the lack of it, he hid beneath his evident affection for the sensual things in life.

'If tonight is good …' he said, letting his words deliberately hang, to instil in her fear of what would happen in the shop, with his custom and her position, if it were not. *If tonight is good* meant only one thing and it was all about him. It all rested like her hand in his lap. He lifted his voice and continued, 'If tonight is good, you and I shall meet again … maybe in Paris. You know Paris, but not the Paris I can show you.'

As she conjured up the Paris he had in mind, she surveyed the evening unfolding all around them. Under the great chandeliers, the whole world seemed suddenly modern but so uncivilised. Noise, frivolity, promise and threat rushed from sofa to sofa, corner to corner, and music of different kinds flooded under the doors from private parties beyond the walls.

There was nothing small and delicate anywhere. Everything, like the decade itself, was brash but alive. So much thundered around her. So much yearning and grasping. This was it she thought. This was what London, at least, thought the 1880s should be. It was as if the capital were casting off Queen Victoria's weeds for ever. Everyone was saying they had had enough of her mourning and melancholy. They wanted the age of Edward and Alexandra. Suddenly, Mary Jane felt so alive. In London in the 1880s, no one stopped, no one paused, everything was there, ready to be pulled out of the air. All the smiles in the room seemed large, everyone knew what was coming, everyone was ready to embrace it when it arrived.

But everywhere men were buying, women selling. Everyone

appeared expectant but no one seemed satisfied. Everyone seemed to watch or participate. Henry hovered on the edge of his chair, getting closer and closer, like a hawk about to pounce. The man who brought them the whisky hid in the throng. At one point, as the room whirled around and around, she thought he was kneeling beside her chair and asking her questions. But she was dizzy and confused.

In the early hours, she was where she had known all the way along she was going to be. She liked his smile which relaxed her when they entered the room which was exactly as she had expected. She was used to men of his age and class and all too familiar with their sense of superiority. He watched her strip and directed her as to how she was to behave and move. She felt that she was on stage in a rehearsal. Clearly, he liked being in control. There was nothing unusual in that. With a wide, open palm, he gestured her to stand behind a chair and pressed her back firmly until he saw the curve in her spine. She whispered to him, as she used to do with Meic, that she liked assertive men. It was a dangerous thing to say, risking seeing a smile where there was no smile, overlooking how the pleasantest face can hide the terror beneath it.

He was behind her as so many men who paid for her had taken her. In the Stepney Arms, she had been advised, gentlemen always liked to enter through the back gate. But it meant she would not become pregnant. He commented on her beautiful rump, admiring her heart-shaped buttocks. Like so many who had had sex with her, he repeated her name over and over again. As his rhythm became faster, her name was whispered more curtly and by the time he climaxed, if indeed he did, it was nothing more than a confusion of sounds. Looking over her shoulder, she saw him red-faced and panting, no more able to regain his steady breathing as he could pronounce the syllables in her name. The explosion of letters from his mouth had more force than his ejaculation. But he seemed satisfied and grateful. She had given him a good time. When he was dressed, she noticed that he was able to say her name again but, as he talked to her, he held his cane tightly as a walking stick again, as he had when he first approached her in the shop. She was experienced in the postcoital kindness such men need and she found that he was easy to flatter. He talked again about taking her to Paris. She kissed his cheek, offered a genial smile and assured him how lovely that would be. From his reaction, the pleasure in his eyes, she knew they would be going.

Gorfennaf | July 1890

Megan loved walking in the countryside above her home, it made her feel part of something larger than herself, which included her brother and Mary Jane. Hill House hold. She belonged nowhere else.

She remembered the first few occasions, after her return, when she strolled through the town. She felt awkward and attracted curious stares as if in coming back she were behaving in some unfathomable way. People who knew her from the past cast what she thought were disapproving looks at her child, snuggled in her arms. They made her feel that she had done something very wrong and had been sent to walk the streets in some kind of disgrace. Occasionally, she might see children barefoot, playing between carts, and she saw the occasional carriage. Through the comments she experienced, she became only too aware of the terrible power of the community look. They were thinking, well, that is Megan Jane, what should you expect. How hard it was, being conspicuous.

In the hills it was very different. She often walked there with her daughter. She was small for eight years and Megan had to stoop slightly to take her hand. It was tiny but she believed that it was her Meic's hand in hers. On this afternoon, she was not alone. She was leading someone who had a blindfold over his eyes. This was a game Megan and Meic played in school and every Christmas Day. But Edward Prothero had never done so. He was not walking easily.

One hand was extended and held by Megan. The other he kept waving around in front and beside him, imagining hedges and ditches. Unlike Megan's sure tread, he was hardly able to move one foot in front of the other. She was taking him to the rim of the quarry, but he did not know that. All the time Megan was watching, caringly and carefully, but he did not know that either. She was thinking about her brother and about her father. And she thought of Mary Jane.

The thick grass came to an end and there was a dirt track which they had to cross. They did so slowly because he was terrified of walking forward into what he could not see while her feet had to avoid bits of stone and clotted dirt. Eventually, they came within a few yards of the quarry. Megan felt him resisting her now as if he sensed that she had brought him somewhere dangerous and he did not entirely trust her. One step became heavier than the one before and he felt the ground falling away. He did not know this part of the landscape and, after a few more steps, she told him to stand still. He could feel that the air was colder and there was a breeze from which the hedges had protected him. She let go of his hand and he could sense a new urgency in her voice.

'Cadwch yn llonydd,' (Keep still) she said again, using the person which she would use with a stranger which added significantly to his unease. He was in seconds of tearing off the blindfold when he felt Megan standing very close to him. As she lifted her hands to the blindfold, he welcomed her breath on his face.

'Peidia â symud,' (Do not move) she whispered, this change of person and her proximity, so close to him now that he could hear her heart beating, reassured and excited him. 'Cariad,' she added and kissed his cheek before the blindfold and the darkness fell away. The light came like a hot poker and it took a second or two for him to take in the vastness and the beauty of the landscape in front of him, the way the quarry stood before them like a vast healing wound, everywhere the grass returning.

It all made him unsteady and she slipped her arm around him. Just beyond their feet the earth dropped away and this made his chest heave.

'Thank God you are holding me,' he whispered, his voice trembling a little which brought him a reassuring squeeze from Megan.

'Daeth fy mrawd a minnau yma yn aml iawn,' (My brother and I came here very often) she sighed.

In being brought to a place that was so personal to her, and to her brother, he felt that he was being admitted to something that for her was spiritual, a sanctuary, where the present dropped away into the past but only fell so far.

She asked him, nervously, if he felt Meic's presence there. He didn't but he said what he thought she wanted to hear. He didn't answer immediately but waited in the silence between them, watching the sky stretching toward a far-off horizon. They made him believe for a moment that yes, he could feel Meic alongside them, so that is what he said. She nodded. Clearly it brought her relief even if deep down she did not think he could.

She pulled gently on his hand and steered him away from the rim of the quarry. The view was magnificent but a part of him was content to move further back. At first, he seemed heavy when she pulled him alongside her but, after a few steps, she found him much lighter. She was reminded of helping her father move Velvet through their yard. As they walked, she pondered how her life, and Meic's when they all lived together as a family, was one of action as much as contemplation. She looked up into Edward's face and pressed her head against his shoulder.

'Well, Mr Prothero, credaf y bydda ti a minnau'n cydweithwyr,' (I believe that you and I are fellow travellers) she confided.

This was certainly what he wanted to hear but he wondered if she would have felt the same if he had not told her that he could sense her brother beside them. That thought did not linger and, in response, he kissed her forehead just below her hairline.

'Cenhedlaeth Newydd am Hill House. Byddaf yn dysgu popeth yr oedd fy mrawd yn i wybod.' (A new generation for Hill House. I will learn everything that my brother knew) She squeezed his hand tightly and, remembering her daughter at home with a friend waiting for her, she started to move forward sprightlier.

Then she stopped and turned so that she was directly in front of him and again looked up at his face. He noticed that a film had crossed her eyes and that she cast them downward. Without raising them again, even when she had finished, she asked him, 'A fy merch, Mari Siân? A fydda ti'n ei charu hi fel dy blentyn di hun?' (And my daughter? Will you love her as your own?)

As he answered, he placed his fingers under her chin and gently persuaded her eyes upward. 'Dw i eisoes yn meddwl amdani hi fel fy mhlentyn.' (I will always think about her as my child)

He had never seen someone's face light up so quickly and so deeply. She placed her arms around him in a loose hug. 'Mae hi mor bwysig i mi. Dwi'n gweld ...' (She is so important to me. I see ...) she stopped as if she had no more vocabulary to bring into her throat. All she did was tighten her arms, and squeeze him, really hard.

Mai | May 1884

As soon as Mary Jane crossed the threshold, she sensed the atmosphere. Madame Lanette Chasseur was beside the counter and two of her assistants slouched in the shadows at the back of the shop whereas normally they would have been stood to attention.

'What are you doing here?'

She smelt the lingering, stagnant perfume of the gentleman with whom she had travelled to Paris, a venture that didn't work and lasted only two weeks. Clearly, he had only just left and Mary Jane sighed, realising that she could not have chosen a more inopportune moment. Chasseur would have been told everything that happened and did not happen between them, all no doubt elaborated from his point of view.

'It didn't work out,' she replied, well aware of the limpness of her words, but she was testing the water.

It was cold. Icy.

'But what are you doing here?' the elderly woman asked, making a point rather than posing a question.

Mary Jane cast a glance at the two women with whom she had worked ever since she had arrived on the doorstep with what she embellished, in her own mind, as a royal note of introduction. Slowly, they straightened themselves.

A small girl, ferret-thin with a sickly pale face, slipped through the gap created by the unclosed door as if she were a cat home from her nocturnal prowling.

'I do not need any more girls,' the proprietor said with an accent on her last word which underscored its ambiguity. The sarcasm surfaced like thickening spit. 'I thought you would be staying in France. You are French after all Marie … Marie Jeanette.'

She stepped closer than she had ever done, even when she introduced her to her special gentlemen. Mary Jane could hear her arthritic joints clicking as she did so. She smelt of her mother's medicine bottles that she and her sisters had discovered, the crushed pills that she never licked entirely from around her mouth, and the syrups she drank from glasses meant for port. Madame's lips were pursed as if she were about to gob in Mary Jane's face. Slowly, while keeping Mary Jane in her sight, like her father used to do when he punished her, she searched for a waist bag beneath the folds of her skirt. Eventually, she brought out a handful of coins which she pressed deep into the pocket in Mary Jane's jacket. Mary Jane had no opportunity to count what was there. She saw that it might be sufficient for a week's food but not enough to buy rent anywhere. Then she found herself being shoved toward the door.

'You do not work here anymore.'

Mary Jane was sick with shock. She had not expected this and now realised how stupid it had been for her not to do so. Madame Chasseur's face was impacted hard with her hatred. Whatever she had been told about Paris, it was enough to trounce her in the madame's eyes.

The door smashed shut behind her like a huge breaker crashing on rocks. As she watched the women inside gather in the centre of the shop, her ears filled with the sound of the street.

Pounding one hand into another like a pestle and mortar, she had no idea what to do. Collect what belongings she could carry from the rooms she shared and could no longer pay for and run? But where?

There was nothing colder, lonelier and more discombobulating than a London street when you have no one and nowhere to live. She listened for voices between the trample of horses, people recognising her, not believing it was possible to be so outcast. A young woman passed her in paper-thin clothes and rags bundled around her feet. What was she doing in this part of town? Roedd hi'n hanner llyfr. She looked like some of the women who worked the kitchens in the Stepney Arms. But who was Mary Jane to dismiss her so unkindly as 'hanner llyfr', as simple, as her father called her once?

There was a hotel opposite, much higher than she seemed to have noticed in the past. It was hard for her to focus on anything. She could hear the different voices in her head quarrelling as they often did.

She is telling Meic how she will convert the building opposite them in Llanelli's main street into the grandest hotel in west Wales. He is laughing, clipping her wings, reminding her where and who she is.

She knew they were all watching her from inside the boutique, waiting for her to move on, seeing her as no more than horse shit that someone needed to shovel and clear. She wondered whether the hotel opposite needed a maid. She had good references. No. She had no references at all. Slowly, she moved away, pressing her hands inside her coat even tighter than the frowns into which she squeezed her face.

A few hours later, clutching a bag with all the possessions she had, Mary Jane, no longer Marie Jeanette, continued, randomly, purposelessly. Here and there, a few lamps still burned but at the guttering end of their life. Momentarily, a thick smell of pork fat trumped every other. She found herself wading from one colonising smell to another. They led her to a passageway where there was nothing for her but to collapse on a bail of straw. Her life came to her in pieces.

She is swinging her legs, watching her father dressing in his civic best, wishing he would pick her up and hold her, shaving-brush close, to his face, pressing her so tightly they could hear each other's blood circulating.

But when this cleared, as if smoke has been washed from her eyes, she realised she was trapped, homeless and afraid, on a London thoroughfare, like an untethered horse. She breathed in warm memories but they were soon choked by the smog and dirt in the air. She dropped into seconds of sleep, like someone falling off a cliff. But whatever she recalled behind her closed eyes did not linger, one reminiscence chased out another, and she woke again to the present. She returned to the rumble of horse-drawn traffic, handcarts and barrows, the shouts of street vendors, shoving crowds and dogs snarling at each other. Rising and stumbling down a quieter, straw-strewn, redbrick passage, she passed door after door, desperately wanting one of them to open and to be invited inside. Occasionally, she stopped to catch her breath and removed her bonnet to cool herself from the head down. Her chest rose and fell with each gasp like a pair of bellows. She knew how threadbare she must have looked.

Like a Greek warrior in the stem of his ship, he watches his daughter's progress. Is he not her father? Her true father. He knows before she does where she is heading. In his head there is relief. Whatever were they thinking to bring her here, he says to himself.

There were not many people in this passageway and those she passed had drooping shoulders and a shambling walk. Everywhere, there was the vinegary smell of defeat. She continued and continued, impelled forward, as was always the case, by a deep inconsolable longing to be more than she was, to be what she felt she could be. There were still so many unturned cards stacked against her but she refused to believe that.

When she reached the next thoroughfare, she was not far from Hackney. Cart after cart from its factories and warehouses, over laden with cheap oak cabinets, black lacquered drawers, bureaus and dressers, began to pass her, the rumps of their horses whipped almost raw. But she headed to the East End, dodging street hawkers, stumbling over beggars and elbowing gangs of thieving children. Eventually, everything changed again. A violin told her she was not far from the markets and the rundown, ramshackle shops and soon they appeared: bric-a-bac stores, butchers with cheap cuts and offal-filled pies, bakeries with brick-like loaves, even heavier than they looked, bakeries with scones and griddle cakes shedding currants like mouse droppings, cabinet makers, and flower stalls with irises and roses in the first colours of summer. The violin bow had little sophistry, dragging one chord into another, but there were coins in the boy's upturned cap.

A song from a public house lassoed her towards its doors. She was familiar with this kind of place. She had money, which she had still not counted, to buy a hot brandy and a boiled egg served in pig ears' broth. After she had rested, she pressed forward, through even more chaotic crowds, until there were more songs. They sounded different. She was back in Llanelli. But this was Whitechapel.

By this time, she looked so different to when she arrived for work that morning. Roedd wedi ei thrynnu drwy'r drain. (She had been pulled through a drain) So, she thought catching sight of herself in a glass panel.

By late afternoon, she was drunk with no capacity for thought. She roared with the others. They had found her and she had discovered them. In this kind of place, she knew how to dance the tables and twirl herself, like a corkscrew, deep into the eyes of the men who watched. They lifted their heads from their conversations and watched her like dogs with pricked ears, amidst the slapping of bare and sandaled feet on table tops. She was among them, inviting them to pluck her out of the dance as they might a pheasant at market, and they did. That is exactly what they did, guiding her, as she laughed into their faces and itemised outloud the handsome features they never had, into alleys and passageways no wider than a whore's bed. There they fumbled, some succeeded while others failed entirely but never realised. But nearly all of them paid. Sometimes, a trickle of bobs. Nearing midnight, one exhausted woman collapsed on another and they took her home, criss-crossing from one house to another, hesitating on thresholds, stepping in and out of streetlights and sending shadows leaping up the walls. Now, she was one of them. She would pass months, years, with them, lose her mind with them as they did with each other, love, fuck and quarrel with them. All the time, she was waiting, watching for an opportunity, for her chance, she said to herself.

Medi | September 1885

I used to see her sometimes in the palace grounds, her younger children charging behind her. Then, she seemed at her most joyous.

You would not want to interrupt, she was with her family, but occasionally we exchanged spirited words. She had the most loving smile and enjoyed banter. But when her mouth closed and her lips slipped from even the merest trace of a smile, I knew I had to leave. I shrank back, behind the men in uniform attending to the shit her dogs left behind. As I passed through the palace, no one noticed me, well not like she did. The rooms were decorated with tapestries and pictures. There were battle scenes with bodies decapitated, gutted and disembowelled. Men in hats with high plumes rode on horseback above and seemed pleased with the carnage. In summer, the cry of the children chasing each other drifted through open windows. Once or twice the Princess came upstairs to her inner rooms before I left. I listened outside the door to the rustle of dresses, the impatient clink of hangers as clothes were swished together than just as swiftly pulled apart. I could see her looking at each of her dresses in turn, studying them, selecting them, discarding them. When she was half-way around her wardrobes, there were murmurings. I would have loved to have helped her dress. For nights after seeing her, I lay awake wishing for what never could be but felt so near. I worried for her. She was so lonely, isolated and unfulfilled.

Mehefin | June 1885

It was a fine day in early summer. Mary Jane was feeling positive about her life for the first time in years. She had even sent her sister her Whitechapel address and received a response, telling her that the Severn Tunnel had opened and the train journey to Cardiff, if she wanted to visit, would be only four hours. She wondered if her husband knew about this. Clearly, her sister was encouraging her to return to Wales. She said that Princess Alexandra had been doing much, like the Queen, to encourage nurses to train in Wales. That was the only blot in the letter. She had been thinking of training as a nurse or with St John's ambulance as Meic's sister had done but she wished that her sister had not mentioned Alexandra.

Mary Jane turned down a narrow street beside furniture factories keeping an eye on the clouds drifting like weeds into a river of blue-grey sky. This was not the street that she had intended to take but she knew that she would end up near the market. Baby's clothes in a basket outside a draper's shop made her think about her child. Not her child but her niece. That is what Jane will be being told. She would be four years old, getting on five.

The street turned into a darker lane than she had expected. She closed her fingers on the bag that she was carrying. She was not dressed as well as she used to be and she knew what kind of woman she would be taken for. She was conscious also of the coins that she had in her pocket.

The warehouses were so dark they made her think that they were built of liquorice. She laughed at herself for this silly thought. After a while, the buildings became so close that two people could hardly pass each other. She lost sight of the precious sky which had made her think she was back in Carmarthenshire. Eventually, the passage became a lane again, opening on to the market. Insolent, young swells took off their hats and bowed mockingly before costermongers who threatened to box their ears. A man swinging a dead, feathered goose from the neck zigzagged then skipped past her. A vendor whose head barely touched Mary Jane's waist almost tripped her. She struggled not to spill her basket of mackerel, two of them that landed at her feet glinted like silver hat pins. A boy rushed around them both with three dead rabbits tied together by their hind legs. Women appeared carrying packages of offal which leaked into the road. The smell of butchered meat from the densely packed stalls began to turn her stomach.

She paused to look at the sky again and cast her eyes around the market. She had not seen a market as thickly populated as this even in Carmarthen. Everywhere was busy. Opposite her, butchers outside their shops stood resentful of all this weekend competition.

Everywhere joints, legs, necks and heads were framed by hanging carcases and ringlets of sausage. Rounds of black pudding arranged like medals decorated the marble slabs and, deeper inside the butchers' premises, pigeons, chickens, geese and rabbits hung from ceiling beams like trophies. She began to think of herself stripped and slaughtered. The butcher opposite stood in his whites with his hands on his hips beside his two sons, one of whom had his arms folded defiantly across his chest. Behind them, hand-drawn signs advertised pickled tongues and potted meat. All three of them looked as if they knew one day that the sign above their shop would read not 'James Morgan' but 'Morgan and Sons', displaying the family testosterone like the organs laid out on the ceramic counter. It was the kind of business on which the empire had been built. The type which provided the stamina, force, vitality and, in their whiteness besmirched by blood, the racial strength on which the long-serving Queen had always depended.

Mary Jane noticed a different kind of boy, resting on his bicycle not far from the others. He was much thinner and had a pristine apron. There was a basket full of bread over his arm. The loaves smelt wonderful and reminded her when she used to visit Meic in the bakery at Llanelli before they lived together. All four of them turned to look at her as if they were staring from inside a painting.

As Mary Jane walked on, the Welsh newspaper which she used to read regularly in Llanelli was reporting a terrible accident. The husband of the owner of the Stepney Arms Hotel, where she had worked, had been shot. While out pheasant shooting, in a party that had included associates of the royal family, he had been struck in the face. The bullet had pierced his left eye and at the moment he was critically ill. But, of course, she did not know this.

Mary Jane was fascinated by the market, it reminded her of the one in Cardiff. Cardiff market was originally the site of the goal, the gallows had once stood at what was now one of its entrances. But Cardiff must be forgotten now. The market here stunned her in the variety of food it served: hot-eels, pickled whelks, oysters, pea-soup, boiled meat puddings, kidney puddings, and eel pies. Some of these had been available to her in Llanelli but never in such variety and number. She searched among stalls selling oranges, roast chestnuts and ginger beer for her favourite, hokey-pokey, which she remembered on days out with her sister. There was even a stall selling exotic animals and birds. She studied a parakeet with rheumy eyes, a misshapen lower beak and only one tail feather and thought of how Meic would have made contact with the deep sadness behind its eyes. At the back of the stall, there was a nearly-dead snake curled like a deflated cycle wheel. She stopped at the oyster sellers, she had fallen in love with oysters when she and her sister were in Paris. But, these days, at a penny each she could not afford them. A trader in a small coat, handed-down topper and corduroy trousers, who reminded her of a man from whom they had bought them regularly in the French capital, was opening some for a young couple. She prided herself on having learned how to open them correctly from a Frenchman. The woman was holding a child in her arms who pointed to the ones she wanted. Her father held a shell to his lips like a miniature soup bowl. She was better dressed than him, in a large crinoline skirt, cotton jacket with large sleeves and narrow wrists, and a felt bonnet. They reminded her of herself and Meic.

Groups of young men in sloppy trousers and jackets, waistcoats and woollen scarves were gathered around the ginger beer seller. He was pouring it out of barrels on which he had written 'The Best Drink Out'. Few of those standing around him were buying and most seemed to be hiding in the small crowd with eyes on different parts of the market. As she looked around, she had the sensation that this was not a good place for her to be.

As she made her way from the throng, she noticed gentlemen in tall hats and women in silk dresses making their way from eateries and hotels and horses drawing cabs then … Nothing.

An arm around her neck forced her head down. Momentarily,

she blacked out. On regaining a half consciousness, she was still being held but standing upright. Sweat, perfume and beer. Then a voice which she thought she recognised. Someone from Whitechapel. A small crowd began to gather. Someone spluttered her name. Above the clip-slip of horse shoes striking the polished cobbles, she caught some of the shouts sparking around her. The hustling and jostling became more intense. Opinions were batted and returned from different directions. She felt like she was in the middle of an auction and she was for sale. The girth of the gathering expanded. And all the time, Mary-Jane had no idea as to what was happening.

Held by the collar and dragged as if she were a doll, her blouse rose up her chest, making her increasingly naked above the waist. Her ashen face was pushed toward the crowd to feed its appetite for scandal. Her bonnet had fallen and disappeared under a horde of stamping boots. Someone will snatch it and slip away. The crowd's chants of disapproval became louder as they were told she was a sneak thief, working away from her home turf, part of a gang. The outrage becomes even louder as she is publicly searched and everything emptied. The evidence was pocketed but no one noticed.

Fearful that the crowd would attract the constables, they hauled her to a passageway and there she was discarded. All she could do was draw up her legs, bury her head in her knees, sobbing and weeping. The crowd had dispersed. They all had a story to embellish. Now, again, Mary Jane had nothing.

Gorfennaf | July 1958

A murmur among the crowd runs like fire spiralling through kindling, at first a faint glow than suddenly a leaping flame. The marathon runners are not far from Westgate Street now. I can see myself rubbing Gwen's shoulders excitedly, as her father, I remember, encourages her to press her knees tighter around his neck. Her small teddy bear, without which she will not go anywhere, is hoisted above her head. Behind her is a large sign that dwarfs everyone, announcing Greyhound Racing, Saturday and Monday.

    The toy's face has only one eye and the other is a loose thread awaiting me to attach another button as soon as I can find a good match. I remember, I had it in mind to try the drapery counter in Howells if we had enough time. I never found a perfect match, not even a good one, and she went through childhood with a bear with a misplaced eye. But she loved her just the same.

    Within minutes, three runners thumped into view, almost on top of each other like the three greyhounds in the poster above them. Behind them are eight or nine more who cannot seem to break from each other and run as a pack. Gwen and her teddy are attracted by them, maybe expecting them all to collapse on top of each other in the road, while my eyes are on the leader who has passed us but is slowing down. His legs appear to be getting heavy, as if he is running with coal buckets on his feet. The two behind are catching him, they have legs like racing dogs, striding into the shadow behind him. They will catch him I was thinking. I was sure of that. I do not have another photograph. This was the only one my brother, who was in the crowd opposite us, managed to take.

Chapter Nineteen
Nearer?

Ebrill | April 1986

She is beautiful. I expected her to be standing but she is lying ever so comfortably in the straw. Her brown legs end in white socks that look cream in the photograph. Her nose is resting in my father's hand. I remember how she kept closing her eyes and my father kept tickling her under the chin to wake her. My father is in his corduroy trousers which he cherished since the 1970s. This means he had dressed up for us to go and see our foal. Yes, this was as good as sartorial elegance got for him. He has taken off his farm boots and is in thick woollen socks, so that he could pad close to her without startling her. This photograph must be before he beckoned me forward. I still remember the softness and the exaggerated length of her ears. There is a blaze, like a haphazard streak of white paint, which divides her face into two unequal parts and in the next photograph, where she looks to camera, one eye is perfect and tranquil, while the other is less oval, sharper and somehow more daring. I hate myself for seeing this in such a gentle creature. My father said that I could name her. I chose, Heddwen. I think it was on that day, at that moment, I chose to be a vet when I was older.

Medi | September 2016

Mary-Jane is heading into the East End to find the district in which her great-great-great-grandmother was living before she was murdered. In a street in Whitechapel, she meets historian Joanne

Flaxton-Brown. She is an independent, local historian and scholar who has written a book on the victims of one of England's first and most infamous serial killers and teaches in the adult education programme of a local university. They sit in a café opposite where one of the streets on which Mary Jane lived had been. To add a note of realism to the scene, the introductions between them are interrupted by the arrival of tea and coffee in plain white mugs as is the custom.

Joanne is what some historians label, a little unkindly, a Ripperologist. She has studied not only the lives of the Ripper's victims but the murderer's modus operandi. She dislikes the way in which some recent histories try to disentangle the murder of the victims from the remainder of their lives. This is particularly true in Mary Jane's case where she has attempted to reconstruct her life, weaving between what facts there are, what Mary Jane said to others and what, given the social context of the age, is more than likely the truth of her life. Joanne likes to describe herself as a historian who is sensitive to the vibrations in the scholarship.

She begins their interview proper by asking how Mary-Jane feels about what she has discovered.

'I am still in a state of shock,' she says, half-laughing, as if to disguise her embarrassment about how she feels and what she thinks she may have already revealed to camera. There is a pause between them. The camera comes closer and the microphone hovers overhead like a huge bird. Mary-Jane is encouraged to add, 'I feel so much for Mary Jane and I cannot get over how she died. What a horrible death.'

Mary-Jane looks to camera as she does in her own programmes when they cut to the chase. 'I had a faint awareness of the Ripper, but I know much more about the East London killings now.'

She pauses and Joanne nods sympathetically. Mary-Jane feels much closer to her than to the other historians with whom she has met. But this makes her cautious. She has enough experience of camera work to know she must be true to how she wants to be seen. She can read Joanne well enough to know that this is not what she wants. Joanne has a clear idea as to where this part of the programme is to head. Her stay-stuck-in-there-and-just-wait attitude is similar to Mary-Jane's own.

'I never thought I would be connected to the last victim of England's most notorious serial killer.'

'Maybe she wasn't,' says Joanne. All interviewers are card players. Wait long enough and they will deal from the bottom of the deck.

Mary-Jane tries to match the card Joanne has dealt.

'Yes, I know,' she says. 'I have read some works that suggest that Mary-Jane was not the last victim.'

'I am not convinced that your great-great-great-grandmother was one of the Five even.'

Hearing another person refer to Mary Jane Kelly as her great-great-great-grandmother reassures Mary-Jane. There is a pause, which the camera does not ignore, before she pounces on the gist of what Joanne says, aasking her why she is not convinced.

'Some historians have suggested that your great-great-great-grandmother's murder was not the work of a serial killer but that the first four women were intended to make people think that there was a serial killer at large, while your great-great-great-grandmother was the targeted victim all along.'

'Is that what you believe?' exclaims Mary-Jane astonished.

'No, but there are incongruities in the whole Ripper serial killer narrative that perturbs me as an investigative historian,' she continues with her soothing, reassuring approach.

She has Mary-Jane's attention once again. They are talking to each other as fellow professionals.

'There were similar crimes reported throughout the 1880s, such was the nature of the streets at that time, which makes me wonder about the way an individual killer was singled out. But be that as it may, the murder of your great-great-great-grandmother was similar to the others in some respects but significantly different from them in many others. Her murder was so much more brutal.'

Joanne pauses, leaving the programme to dwell, in the silence, on the word 'more', before continuing.

'Of course, it also took place in Mary Jane's own room. There is no evidence from the other killings that given the chance to be indoors, the Ripper would necessarily have extended the butchery in this way. Intriguingly, the subsequent killings which some historians have attributed to the Ripper were back on the street and more in line with the first four murders. If the conventional Ripper narrative is correct, that the Ripper had been heading toward the really brutal murder he wanted to enact all along and found that he could do this in his victims' rooms, he would not have returned to the street and less brutal killings.'

It is Mary-Jane's opportunity to be calm and thoughtful. Her logical, veterinary science brain is turning over and weighing the possibilities.

'You are suggesting, then,' she offers, 'that my great-great-great-grandmother was killed by somebody who wanted to copy the Ripper murders that were being reported at the time as the work of a serial killer. This is different from suggesting that the whole Ripper thing was a conspiracy from the start. I must say that I find this more believable.'

Joanne nods. The camera continues to study Mary-Jane before turning back to the historian.

'There is something else,' Joanne says. 'Those who knew your great-great-great-grandmother observed that she had an unusual knowledge of languages compared with the others who lived in Whitechapel, although it may have taken only a few words in French, German or Welsh to make them think that, and that she seemed to be of a higher class.'

'That would be in line with everything I have been told all through this programme,' says Mary-Jane.

'She had many names, Marie Jeanette, Fair Emma, Ginger.' She pauses again. 'I wonder where that came from? Maybe from *Black Beauty*. She called herself Black Mary, too. And, so many stories.'

Joanne hands her a sketch of Mary Jane. She is very well-dressed, leaning against a wall which may be near to where she lived, and challenges the viewer from beneath a fine bonnet which has what looks like buttons above its rim and a feather protruding from one side, enhancing her height.

She is beautiful and elegant, different from the somewhat bloated but not unattractive woman whom Mary-Jane has seen in books about the Whitechapel murders. Her left-hand rests on her hip and Mary-Jane notices her knuckles seem pressed hard into her waist while a few of her fingers extend backward and her hand is not tightly closed as one might expect.

Mary-Jane comments that she looks younger than in other illustrations of her which she has seen.

'Whom does she remind you of?' Joanne asks.

Mary-Jane is unsure and the historian slides in front of her a picture of Princess Alexandra, the Princess of Wales, who was to become Queen Alexandra at the beginning of the twentieth century, which, to judge from the way in which she is dressed, was drawn around the same time as the picture of Mary Jane.

Mary-Jane is not sure of the point being made. She notices how similar their faces are.

'Like many middle and upper-class women, Mary Jane mirrors

what the Princess is wearing. But perhaps too closely.'

'Do you think she met the Princess?' Mary-Jane asks.

Joanne shrugs. 'The fact that she copies the Princess so much must raise questions of that kind. But, it also suggests her aspirations and her confidence in herself as a woman whatever time in her life this was drawn.'

Mary-Jane picks up the two illustrations and studies them closely. She and Joanne are walking the same tightrope. Joanne is excited. 'And,' she says, almost triumphantly, 'when she turns to prostitution in London, it is not in Whitechapel, not at first, but in central London.'

Mary-Jane notices that Joanne uses the phrase 'turns to prostitution'. She asks her to explain that.

'Some historians have suggested that when your great-great-great-grandmother first came to London, she worked in clothes shops. What she may not have known is that many of these were fronts for high-class prostitutes and were run by Madams. The young women who worked there met, or indeed were paired with, wealthy men whom they accompanied to private parties and bars.'

'Once again,' Mary-Jane suggests, 'my great-great-great-grandmother may have found an opportunity to eke out the income she earned more legitimately, not as a hotel maid this time but as a shop girl.'

'Hotel workers and shop girls were perceived by men, wealthy men, in the same way. They were tarnished with availability, seen as willing. They were sought out by soldiers from the nearby barracks and by careless, upper-class men who had no scruples about using women, abusing them, and then dropping them as soon as they felt like it. And yes, many ended up in the streets and brothels of places like this.'

Joanne stares out on the streets as two centuries before Mary-

Jane's great-great-great-grandmother may have done.

Mary-Jane watches an overweight man in a knee-length coat making his way down the street opposite, studying the numbers on the doors, and wonders about him.

'But there still remains the unanswered question,' Mary-Jane observes while the camera is following their eyes onto the world outside. 'How did my great-great-great-grandmother join this elite sex trade?' she asks.

'Somewhere in her life,' Joanne surmises, 'she must have met somebody who provided her with an introduction. Somebody who thought she was sufficiently trustworthy and classy to work here. They must have been convinced by her, by the way she spoke and carried herself. Someone may have recognised that she was sufficiently familiar with, and knowledgeable about, clothes and fashion to work in the boutiques around Kempton Barracks and Brompton Road. This was an area frequented by the army, particularly officers who could afford to shop here for their mistresses and wives, by actresses and the artistic set.'

'Maybe she met somebody when she worked as a maid in Llanelli,' suggests Mary-Jane closely following the line of Joanne's argument.

Joanne ventures a further thought, one that she knows will come as a surprise.

'Your great-great-great-grandmother may have accepted the invitation with a considerable degree of innocence. Reading between the lines, she comes over as a naïve but ambitious young woman, somebody who wanted to make something of themselves in a world controlled by men and where women were kept in their place rather than encouraged to better themselves.'

Joanne suggests that this would resonate with professional women like herself and Mary-Jane even today, 'When young, ambitious women, like your great-great-great-grandmother did manage to move forward, they were often ridiculed and despised for it. We might think things have not changed for many of us.'

She pauses. The camera moves around them.

Joanne continues: 'It is my suspicion that your great-great-great-grandmother was deliberately murdered, maybe by a man who was deranged and violent, who had done this before, but possibly acting on the instructions of someone from a fashionable set among whom your great-great-great-grandmother moved for a time. Someone intelligent enough to plan a murder that would be attributed to the Ripper and have sufficient influence to carry it out, or rather have it carried out.'

'But why?' asks Mary-Jane.

'That is difficult to answer. Maybe she saw something that she should not have seen. Maybe she became garrulous — your great-great-great-grandmother did have a reputation in that regard. She was prone to behave outrageously when she was drunk and even when sober she could be more than one person at the same time, if you understand what I mean. Maybe she became careless, untrustworthy, revengeful, too maverick. Perhaps she turned out to be different from how she was originally perceived and was begun to be seen as dangerous. She mixed with people with reputations and reputations have to be protected.'

'You are suggesting there was a large secret in her life.'

'Or in someone else's life of which she learned and which, through unexpected twists and turns, led to her murder.'

'To her being silenced,' Mary-Jane affirms.

The camera ceases. The microphone is withdrawn. The crew stand around the table contemplating what they have. The director comes forward to talk with Mary-Jane. They will need to record her thoughts outside in the park.

Hydref | October 1888

Mary Jane had not left Whitechapel for over two years, certainly she had not returned to the West End since the attack upon her. The more she thought about it, the less random it felt even though all the others told her that East Enders were not welcome there. She had a companion, Joseph Barnett, a brooding man with sly watchful eyes but she was relaxed and safe with him. He felt the same, but what he didn't know was that this would be their last evening together.

He had brought them home a meal, a platter of roast meat. When she began her life with Meic, Mary Jane turned herself into a connoisseur of the kitchen, a cook extraordinaire, the like of which he had never seen before. That evening, she didn't care about what or how she ate. Perhaps she had come to the end of exhaustion where all one craves is food and sleep. Juice and blood ran down her arms, congealed around her fingers, as she cut and tore the small joints of meat apart. Joseph had never seen her eat this way and realised that he had not even seen her lips glistening with grease before. Meic had enjoyed gnawing legs of chicken with his fellow miners, worrying all the time about Mary Jane's reaction if she had ventured on them and found him eating like this, especially chicken. It was his secret which she never discovered. Mary Jane set out the bones beside her plate in order of size as she moved from one piece of meat to another. Joseph noted that this seemed to satisfy her at some deep level.

She and Joseph spoke very little. She was struggling to keep awake and they were content to stare at each other. They had never had sex and this scrutiny of each other might have been a substitute for that. But, usually, it wasn't like this. Normally, they talked extensively, or at least Mary Jane did. There was a difference between the stories she shared with Joseph when they were at home of an evening and those which she embellished in The Bells, laughing, screeching and gasping for breath, one syllable slicing the next, as she unfurled them. With Joseph, she unwound them much more gradually, like a ball of wool. She had a knack whereby her words filled the entire room like lengthening shadows. She always talked about the past and hardly ever about the future as she did when she first arrived in Whitechapel. It was as if she wanted to confide in him as much as she could and was in a hurry to do so, as if it were her way of hanging on to herself, the history which had made her and which was disappearing like daylight slowly slipping behind the horizon. Strange, then, that when he came to talk to the press about her, he only pulled out the bare bones like the blade from the shoulder of lamb they were now devouring between them.

Neither he nor Mary Jane had enough money to keep the fire banked up and the room quickly became cold. Mary Jane pulled her shawl high around her shoulders and found a blanket to cover her legs. She was tired but she dared not sleep because to sleep was to dream and then the noises would start. She had memories which she wished she didn't have, which she could wipe away like chalk on a blackboard.

Joseph started noticing things like the bowl into which she periodically dropped coins for the rent as if they were random thoughts. It was empty except for a few peanuts. The room had two beds, each wide enough for one person, and on one of them, she had spread a yellow-stained coverlet of purple and gold, as if she were imagining she were in a royal bedroom. There was a distinct smell, too, of wet wool from a bucket where she had placed her clothes to soak overnight.

The door opened suddenly behind Joseph, whose hands and mouth were filled with a pork chop. A mushroom-shaped pool of light fell across his face and into the space in front of Mary Jane making her look up and he to twist awkwardly in his chair. The door closed, the pool of light disappeared and the latch fell noisily. A young woman, part silhouette, stepped through the half-lit room toward the grate. Joseph had never seen her before and Mary Jane barely recognised her in a fur hat with a matching wrap around her shoulders. She introduced herself to Joseph as Julia but all the time kept looking at Mary Jane whose eyes, he quickly saw, flamed with the suddenness of a struck match. Whether this interest was in Julia herself or in her furs he wasn't sure. He immediately thought the latter because Mary Jane asked where they had come from. But there was a deep bond between these women, they lived by false flattery and devious wheedling.

As Joseph returned a half-gorged chunk of meat to his plate and spat bits of bone onto the table, Julia laughed and explained how she and her friend had skinned a miserly drunk dressed as a woman, who wanted to paint them together in his lodgings, leaving him naked in an alley behind Cleveland Street. She tossed the hat to Mary Jane, who grabbed it excitedly in both hands, and twirled the wrap like a bunting around Joseph's neck. She loomed over hm. Her teeth were creamy white and slightly misshapen like tiny pieces of chipped cuttlefish.

'Emma's taken the rest of his clothes home with her to keep in her wardrobe.'

Her voice had a disarmingly sharp pitch, her vowels an icy edge.

'What about his purse?' Joseph asked.

Something flashed in her eyes. His words seemed to carry a suggestion of something, but not anything that Julia could immediately decipher. She unsettled him. He found her intimidating with the inquisitive nose and distrustful marble eyes of a fox. Her whole body was drawn in attractive lines, and she knew it. She positioned herself so that the light from the small lamp near her showed her to her best advantage. Her sprawling limbs fascinated him, maybe she knew that. Desire and jealousy stirred in him but he stifled both. With her eyes firmly fixed on him, she stretched down through the front of her blouse and pulled out a bundle of notes followed by a handful of coins, like a magician drawing rabbits from a hat, and let out a huge whoop as she let the coins shower the middle of the room and the notes float down like snowflakes. Then she and Mary Jane clutched each other and danced, Mary Jane clogging on part-chewed meat she was forced to swallow. Taller and younger than Mary Jane, she showed herself to the room, lifted her skirt for Joseph and circled her female friend. Her black hair hung loose down her back over impossibly pale shoulder blades. Mary Jane was uncontrollable, tears of joy rolled down her face. Joseph closed his eyes, part in disappointment and part in exasperation. Mary Jane had never seen him behave so coldly to her female friends. The two women concentrated on each other and ignored him. Clearly, Julia expected to be spending the night with them. After a while, she cast a sly, sidewise glance at him which he did not notice but Mary Jane did because it was to her she was sending a message. She no more expected Joseph to be there than he her.

'Am I alright to stay the night,' she asked Mary Jane. 'If he sees me on the street tonight, he will take a knife to my guts.'

There was much that Joseph could have said. But he chose only to caution her that the hour was long past midnight and the streets were especially unsafe at present. Lifting a final mug of heavily diluted wine, all he had managed to bring, and offering none to Julia, he went to the other bed, leaving the fur trailing behind him. He lay on his shoulder, his back to the wall and drank while staring at the two women. Mary Jane poured some of her drink down Julia's throat. She spat it out, and wiping the moisture from her lips, declared it cat's piss.

'What's become of you, girl?' she giggled. 'Your Julia's been gone less than a week and this is what you have done to yourself.'

She picked up a piece of meat which Mary Jane and Joseph had left untouched and, hoisting it high into the air between her finger and thumb, slowly lowered it, exaggeratedly, between her thick, red lips. When the meat was far enough into her mouth for her to suck and chew, making a juicy sonata with the movement of her jaws, she turned to have a sidelong stare at Joseph. He ducked her eyes.

It was probably in that moment that Joseph decided to leave, even though he knew how much Mary Jane depended on him and how far the two had allowed themselves into each other's consciousnesses. Thanks to the drink, he slept the rest of the night and did not hear the way the two women's bodies slipped and slithered together, not in love perhaps, but gratitude for a space where they might be together, however confined and restricted it might be. Mary Jane pulled a blanket over them, the air beneath was clammy with the smell of their own sweat. She pulled her legs up under her as if she were a foetus. In the dreams that came, she made elaborate patterns from what she had been spinning that evening.

The dawn came on the back of a strengthening storm, unnoticed by Mary Jane and Julia. But the new influx of cold air suddenly woke Joseph. A moth made a stain of light and a shadow on the ceiling. He rose and in dazed, stupefied steps made his way to the door, casting disgusted looks at the intertwined limbs and hands in the other bed. Either because they were entangled or because his sight was too fogged with sleep and wine, he found it difficult to determine which head fitted which body. In the midst of its frantic circles, the pale wings of the moth became a woman's face. As he left, Mary Jane's hand slid softly over Julia's chest. She found herself embraced by her limbs, each leg almost the length of her entire body. Mary Jane herself had filled out in recent years and, in certain lights, she looked like a man, broad and stocky as her father had been.

She shivered beneath my hand. I felt for her, she for me. I desired her. I slid our sheets to one side so I could see the whole of her. I tried to press closer to her without fully waking her.

The opening of the door was a shock, cold and rain hit Joseph in the face, like the smack of leather on a horse's back. It closed slowly behind him, stopping sharply at its latch, but he did not turn to pull it tighter. Nor did he think of the women he was leaving inside with their door resting so vulnerably on only a thin strip of morning light. The wind whistled through the fine gap with the pitch of a bakery boy but it did not wake them. Joseph lowered his head and pushed himself forward into the street. He felt the icy rain lurch toward him, jolting over wooden boxes, a stranded cart and the body of a dead cat. He had another room he knew of, he was angry, and he kept walking into the sharp pain.

Hydref | October 2016

Mary-Jane has gathered a staff around her who are in awe of her. She has charisma, her confidence beguiles everyone she meets. Like a new brand of caffeinated drink, she has an energy the town has not seen for a while. But few people think the same about Amelia. With her zip fastened under her chin and most of her face hidden by her hood, Amelia seems intent to avoid eye contact with people she passes in the street. She is so different from Mary-Jane and that is what worries her colleagues. When they talk about them as a couple, if indeed they are, they realise that they have no idea where Amelia has come from. She has appeared suddenly out of nowhere.

Amelia and Mary-Jane can be jealous of each other. Mary-Jane willingly admits to that. Each scares the other at times. Three things are often said about Amelia. She is a vegetarian, she speaks Welsh when she chooses and she has cold hands.

Mary-Jane is thinking about Amelia and how others see her one early autumn afternoon. The sun lingers on the communal lawn beneath Mary-Jane's apartment, arm in arm with Amelia's circle of winter pansies. The end of the Indian summer. The afternoon seems reluctant to leave like drinkers who cannot quite believe it is closing time. Mary-Jane is inside the kitchen putting new teabags in the caddy and lining up clean cups near the kettle. She sighs deeply and lowers her head as if she and the kettle are whispering conspiratorially. When she stands upright, she catches sight of herself in the chrome tray beneath the kitchen cabinet. She also sees Amelia in the doorway. For a few seconds she panics, momentarily fearing that she might have been speaking her thoughts outloud. When she realises how silly she is being, she laughs to herself.

'What's up?' Amelia asks, unusually cheery.

'Nothing,' Mary-Jane replies. 'Just a careless thought.'

Amelia's mobile phone sings on the hall table which makes her suddenly and inexplicably angry. She strides back down the stairs into Mary-Jane's small, private hall, muttering.

There is a mood between them which they both sense but neither of them can mention to the other. The other day Mary-Jane arrived home and found Amelia playing on a computer game. She had never seen her take an interest in them. She seemed mesmerised by an alien exploding on the screen. As she talks on the phone, Amelia watches the carpet change colour in the fading daylight through the front door. Mary-Jane listens to her, talking increasingly faster in a conversation that is clearly becoming more intense. Eventually, she steps outside through the foyer onto the drive. Mary-Jane has an idea whom she is talking with. Her voice is careless and loud. She switches on the kettle again so she does not have to listen to her. She feels Amelia has a life which they do not share and belongs to a circle which is vague to her. It worries her.

Mai | May 1886

She wrote him letters. I wanted to hide them. I knew he loved her but I don't believe he wanted to love her. We loved each other. We were dependent on each other. But there is a love that is different from the love that we allow ourselves. You know that. I sought that love with her. I knew that she was looking for it, too. I stopped being critical of him, of the way he spoke about her, of his lapses into something he was aware of but didn't understand. I do not know what to say about this love. Do not laugh at me. I am not that drunk. I have only had ... Shit, I can't count. It is risky, you told me that, even dangerous, like standing on the edge of a cliff. I am not at all sure it is love. We are all hemmed in. That is what I think. Yes, I do believe that. But some of us open the door, that door that few of us have ever thought of opening or even seen. A self which is our forbidden self steps through. Forbidden because family, society, culture, everything you really want to fuck up, depends on it being so, and remaining that way. Yes, I did believe they loved each other but I think she loved him more than he loved her. What I discovered ... what did I discover ... ah ... the thread between them ... an invisible stinking thread made of fish gut ... stop, stop laughing ... I'm serious ... either of them could have reeled it in. For that reason, he came to want her to stay away ... far ... away. I know I cannot have my love and she knows that she cannot have hers. He knows she cannot have him. We returned to our beds and lay beside each other. That at least was real. Everything is where it should be. Christ, I am drunk. I'm Catholic. We have our secrets. Every woman in this room has her secrets. We love each other for them. Everyone has secrets, the whole world trundles along on secrets, occasionally slipping on them, being thrown by them. I grant you that. We have to be grown up about this. We all lie, everyone hides something. But lies do not a person make. None of us is ever wholly visible, even to ourselves. You have all gone quiet. I can hear that carriage horse outside the window farting. O God, did you hear that. They must feed the old thing on cabbage leaves. Know the true centre, that is what I used to tell him. We are all trying to get by. Even my Princess. My Princess. Stories. We all have our stories and stories have many threads, many twists and turns. They are all lies but none of them are untrue. My stories are about me. Marie Jeanette. Me, the person.

Julia could not sleep. She slumped against a bundle of unwashed clothes, an ostrich feather still plaited in her hair, listening to the different voices from the night before, obsessing how similar they all sounded. Looking around the room, her eyes took in the other women, all in various stages of undress. One of them lifted up her skirt to dry her eyes and another blew her nose in the hem of her dress but no one cared. Slowly they came again into focus. Maria was lolling against Theresa; her eyes were as dead as two pennies. She always slept with her eyes open which Julia found disturbingly eerie. Theresa, one side of whose face was tattooed with smallpox scars, had cast off her shawl and shoes even though a steely chill edged its way through a broken pane. Her spine was hunched into a slight, half-moon stoop, a birth defect, and she had lived with a haberdashery of assorted insults, razor-keen jibes and bruising barbs. Mary Jane, too, was asleep. There was sufficient snoring, mutterings and heavy breathing to persuade the still drunk Julia, or Catherine as she was sometimes called, that she was not in the middle of a battlefield. The dawn was loitering outside, she could smell it, as if it were uncertain as to whether to peep inside. They had all drunk from bottles and cracked glasses which lay discarded between and underneath lifeless limbs. She recalled their stories in the same memory as the leftover scraps from The Bells, how they had swapped intimate details of each other's bodies, laughed off bouts of the pox, guffawed at what men took home to their posh wives and choked while telling of a man dressed as a woman who had had more than one of them. Here they felt safe, entering each other's lives, weaving their different stories, exchanging kindnesses of all kinds. There was no one to block them or bloke them, as Mary Jane once said. But they remembered their pasts, even yesterday, not as something that had been lived, certainly not enjoyed, but had had to be reckoned with.

Julia wondered whether she loved them, whether they loved each other. Or was it that they were all trapped together in a never-ending cycle of drink, prostitution and despair.

As the dawn inflated its brightness outside, Julia closed her eyes while some of the other women began to stir. Theresa's head felt as if it had been sliced into two imperfect orbs and Maria pulled a blood-stained cloth from between her legs. Here the real battlefield was coming to light. Mary Jane lay on her back remembering little of what she had said in the early hours. Heavy rain scraped the windows like finger nails but no one else heard it. No one stood. No one gathered their clothes together. In truth, none of them had anywhere to go. It was Mary Jane's room and they often came there. The dawn pawed the dirty curtains, no more than thick canvas, to get into the room, where the walls changed to different shades of dark. Yellow shadows fell about on the floor like drunks struggling to keep on their feet. Noise from outside tried to fumble its way into closed ears. Men with loud voices clapped the shit of another morning to come to heel, lifted shutters, unloaded carts, turned over barrels and banged open doors. A hobnailed boot crushed the head of a young rat while others rolled away chaotically like dropped coins. Repeated stamps reduced the rodent to red pulp and broken bones.

Eventually, Maria took the pennies out of her eyes and blinked.

Chapter Twenty
Cut to the Chase

Tachwedd | November 2016

A decision is being taken. They all sit around a circular table watching her. None of them dare look away. Her face is partially hidden by the smoke circling her shiny, black cigarette holder. Her legendary silver lighter with the swastika on one side is turned over and over beside an onyx ashtray. When those outside the 'family' are forced to watch this somersaulting, they have reason to worry. Like the dream of a black cat, it is a symbol that treachery is at hand. The ashtray is beginning to fill. There is so much tension in the room that some of those at the table find a strange solace in noticing such things. Dark grey, pinpoint size bits of tobacco fall, and are buried, in miniscule flakes of white paper.

Then, one hand allows the cigarette holder to rest on the edge of the ashtray while the other continues to play with the lighter. It twists and turns faster and more violently. The strike of metal on wood is exacerbated by the scary silence. The swastika looks as if it will jump free of the lighter and rush from one to another marking them all for having failed her.

The name of Mary-Jane's uncle is spoken aloud and repeated for no one's benefit other than her own. It turns head over heels like the lighter. Eventually, she stops manipulating both his name and the swastika.

'This cannot happen,' she says. 'We have an agreement.'

She starts to twist the lighter again, this time very slowly as if she is counting.

'How many horses do we need to send him?' she asks.

No one need answer because she has that detail on the sheet of paper in front of her. She is thinking outloud. Her mind is turning slowly. No one with any sense would speak now. The lighter says as much. She is calculating euros, euros that like the horses need to be disposed of. But now, there is this other problem. One person cannot be allowed to break his contract with her. She cannot be seen to be weak.

She unfurls what she expects from them. They listen carefully and watch the lighter beginning to turn faster again. She wants to grab the attention of the media. It will start with the Welsh news, then it will spread like a virus through the channels and across the internet. No one will switch on their smart phones without seeing it. Those employed by the family will know that this is a warning from the family. The family is making its voice heard. The lighter is brought down hard on the table.

Medi | September 1888

In the East End, Mary Jane was seen as Irish even though she had always thought of herself as much Welsh. She told everyone how she had been born into a reasonably sized Catholic family. Nothing unusual there, but she tended to exaggerate the number of brothers and sisters she had. Or because she was Irish, others placed her in the kind of family they thought of as Irish Catholic.

She changed by the day in Whitechapel. She became shorter and fatter. Red and grey-white blotches discoloured her face and there were small boils at the end of her nose and on the point of her chin. She didn't seem to care. Days no longer had any value for her and she no longer had the energy to reinvent herself.

Home, a shared room with a broken pane of glass, is only ten minutes distant but she is hurrying. Watch her carefully. What is she afraid of? Who or what has she seen? Is she rushing from someone? The lanes and thoroughfares are hectic and noisy. Walk down them. Can you hear the sound of your own footsteps? She can. There is an echo to each step she takes and it comes from behind. In her hurrying, she is trying to outpace it. People block her path, frustrate her, create a space in which eventually she sees a face she thinks she knows. Mary Jane does not know what she is witnessing. She does not realise what is happening around her. There is a hand extended to her elbow. It guides her as it did once before.

Hydref | October 2016

Mary-Jane's uncle is outside with his dog. She takes the opportunity to look at his desk. She wants to take a closer look at what he has collated about MJ. The folder is there but as she flips through it, disappointingly, there is nothing she has not seen before. His diary is very near it. Through the window, she can see him running over the lawn with his pet. Furtively, she lifts the book, carefully noting its exact position. That is easy for her. It was out of alignment with the folder. The diary smells of his sweat and aftershave. She opens it slowly, reluctantly, as if it were a virus, before having the courage to turn to the current date. Cursorily, her eyes scan the pages as she moves backward through the last few weeks, then the last few months. As she expected of him, most of the notes inside are messy and difficult to read There are appointments marked 'Dubliners', they seem frequent and regular but he has only entered them in the diary fairly recently. A number of evenings and nights have roughly-drawn circles around them and the word 'horse' usually followed by a number written in a slanting line. She does not have to ask herself what is being recorded.

'Bastard!' she says.

She wants to read more but she is too fearful. She can hear that the dog is on the rear porch. She returns the diary to its resting place. On the desk there is a framed photograph of herself, as a child, and her mother with him. She wants to pick it up and hurl it on the floor.

Tachwedd | November 1888

Mary Jane was the first to see the stranger. He strode quickly even though in his face he looked tired and exhausted. His neck scarf was very creased but was made of the finest cloth. She knew it had come from the Far East and believed that she had handled it somewhere, maybe in Madame Chasseur's shop or at her sister's house in Cardiff. She wasn't sure. Every now and then, he stopped and spoke to a girl beneath a gaslight before moving quickly on, hardly stopping. Clearly, he was searching for someone. After a while, he hastened to the corner of one of the alleys, choosing a spot from which he could see both sides of the street without being noticed. His head moved from side to side, he seemed nervous, anxious. Mary Jane did not like the look of him. She had met his kind often. Like the Princess's man she met in the Arms, he was someone in a place where normally he would not be. A constable became visible in the gaslight, then disappeared before appearing again beneath the next lamp opposite to where the stranger stood. Neither acknowledged the other. Mary Jane noticed that while the stranger relaxed against the wall, he did not put down his bag but kept it firmly clasped to his chest. She wanted to eat, she needed enough money to re-enter the pub. She would have gone over to him except that he seemed to be looking for someone specific.

A hansom stopped beside and then behind another, blocking her view. A man, exceptionally tall, stepped out onto the road and then reached inside the cab's gloomy interior to help a lady down. They gave instructions to the driver who looked from left to right and back again, and then turned to focus on the street through which he had just driven. The couple moved away. Their eyes met with the stranger but only briefly. There was a sense that something was happening. Women crossed the street to speak with acquaintances. Those who remained alone stepped further back into the shadows. Mary Jane thought she saw the stranger shake his head as the couple passed him. A slim woman now stood beside Mary Jane.

'I have the chills, tonight,' she said. 'I need a warming tonic.'

Hydref | October 2016

Evening is coming and the end of daylight is beginning to swirl around her. She feels someone following and at one point turns, expecting to see Mary Jane. There are people walking swiftly, alone and in groups, crossing the road, dodging traffic, running futilely after a bus that is already pulling away from the kerb, trying to raise an umbrella against the first heavy drops of rain. But there is no one she recognises, no one watching her as she expected. Soon, the cold, sharp air cuts into her. Her confidence, the courage that has made her what she is, drains from her as if a vein in her wrist has been gently opened.

A metallic rattling hits her under her face. She twists sharply and an elderly woman in a chaotic assortment of clothes and smells demands small change from her. Mary-Jane thinks she is a woman she has seen in another life. But that doesn't make any sense. She pushes her away. This is something that she would never normally do. She is screamed at. She moves on quickly. In a doorway, another beggar, who has seen what she has done, this time a man, curses her. And beside him, for a split second there she is, the woman she has known all along has been following her. She knows it is her. The tin can is pushed like a dagger into her throat. She hurries onward. She sees the evil curses falling around her feet like coins which have no currency. The beggar man stands screaming in his own space. Mary Jane, for she is sure that this is Mary Jane, has vanished.

Where does this leave her? The recording for this week is over. What should she do now? She imagines another street one hundred years before. Or she thinks she does. Lamp-lit beer houses slowly filling, horse-drawn carriages smartly turning, the same beggars imploring passers-by, shop lights going down, gentlemen striking stones with their walking canes and ladies adjusting their umbrellas.

Mary Jane is in a maid's uniform, partly hidden by the cloak she wears, which exactly matches her bonnet. She has no time to stand and watch. She hurries home. She is expected. Someone has asked her to dress as a maid. Nothing unusual about that. It brings her, and the other 'girls', a little extra.

But look again. Is this Whitechapel? Or a street in Llanelli? There is the passageway that took her to the side door of the Arms. Is it the same thoroughfare? It is more built up and chaotic than the one in which she walked home to Meic. But it is the same street. There are more warehouses, barrows, even pack donkeys, boys no more than ten years of age shouting their wares and more women imploring men who do not stop. That woman who sat begging every night is still there, continuing to look up into people's faces as she did Mary Jane's as if she has something to tell them. Imploring them, for their sakes to stop and speak with her. So few do. But then, look, this is not Llanelli.

And there is someone here, whom we missed at first, someone very attentive. Mary Jane passes very close to him, but she doesn't notice him either. She has seen him before but this time nothing registers. Feel how very cold the street has become. Watch men turning up the collars of their coats. Notice the swirling skirts rising far above the ankles of the women who look about, knowing at last they are being watched, that they are of interest. See the men whispering to one or two of them behind their hands. One of them has a name. He is looking for someone very particular, who has just bought a new bonnet. She is on the street. Somewhere. That much is known. Better for her if she had stayed on the street in Llanelli and had not come here.

But Mary-Jane had to follow her. We know that. She had no choice but to come here. It is too late for her, for any of us, to turn back. There is someone here who is determined, fixed in their purpose. Any time now, they will come forward. Mary Jane doesn't know it or perhaps she does. Is this what Dr Sullivan is waiting for? To see who steps out and confronts Mary Jane.

Rhagfyr | December 2016

A torch light creates a small pool of light, now and then casting eerie shadows as it creeps near the wall. Every twenty seconds or so, it is extinguished as if someone is allowing their eyes to get used to the dark or waiting for someone else to move. The ground beneath their feet is uneven and the beam oscillates between finding firmer footing and showing the way ahead. Eventually, it lights a gap between one of the barns and the outhouses, revealing a gate to a paddock. A large black mass is just distinguishable in the far corner.

The torch beam proceeds slowly, hardly moving when it concentrates on ruts of caked mud. The bolt in the gate screeches when it starts to turn. Two living creatures listen to each other, trying to detect signs of movement. Slowly, breathtakingly slow, the bolt is released, turning to left and right to ease the noise, quiet enough not to disturb whoever else is there. But the black mass of muscle moves again, releasing shadows that worries the bars around him. Heavy boots occasionally miss a rut and slip on shreds of slimy straw. The two living creatures are suddenly within metres of each other

But others have been listening, ears carefully attuned to the new sounds, to new motions in the ground, to dawn flickering on and off. The moans start, chase each other high into the hills then fall back around the yard.

The windows in the farmhouse light up, two or three at a time. Megyn is pulling the waist band of her jeans together and reaching around her thighs for the belt buckle. She has dragged socks from different pairs onto her feet. She doesn't use her wall and ceiling lights but relies instead on her mobile phone's torch. It is very bright and the darkness is dispelled up to six feet in front of her.

She takes the stairs two or three steps at a time, slipping on two of them in her socks. Outside the house, she lets the torch loose in every corner of the yard. The low grumbles continue and the raised horns try to stab what the beasts cannot see. The hills come striding back toward the farm. Megyn's dog appears ahead of her, sniffing behind and between the beams of light. Breathing heavily, an older man, her father, in his dressing gown and outdoor shoes, laces flapping betwixt and between, has caught up with her. They cannot see somebody, startled and confused in the shadows, make the sign of the cross. They do not know now what to do. The bull means business and there is a man coming at them, too, from the other side. No one said it would be like this.

Something, somewhere, drops like a heavy cat and the moaning throughout the yard becomes louder. Mother of God. Someone is scared. The noise stops. Megyn's father suggests that there is fox. She doesn't think so. There are two or three deep throated groans from the farthest barn before all the others join in again.

All around them the bushes are squaring up as if for a fight. She looks around for her dog but it has disappeared. From a shadowed vantage point there is a twang that only a dog would hear. The animal responds immediately. It bounds through the farmyard, cuts between the sheds, then rushes back into the yard as if it is being chased. There is the sound of something jumping heavily. The dog becomes even more manic, leading its owner across the yard, farther into the farm and down toward the lower pens. Two angry guard dogs have been released sending Megyn's own dog back to the house. From the converted barns, others, a farm worker, a visitor, and a business woman emerge. Two children are looking from a bedroom window.

Then, in the arc of her phone light, she sees Ned, standing erect, like a sentry, in front of one of the barn's doors. His own torch is at his feet. He doesn't respond to the commotion. In her torchlight he doesn't move. His face is frozen.

'Fuck,' she screams.

A bolt holds his shoulder to the wooden doors. A dog rushes in front of her. In the torchlights, his head looks like a bucket rimmed with spear tips. He is prepared to launch himself on anything that moves. Her father drags the animal away while Megyn gets nearer to Ned. Someone tears toward the house to get more help while others call up the ambulance and police on their phones.

A motor bike chokes, splutters, chokes again, then roars. A dog seizes the rider's leg. Leather becomes flesh, becomes muscle, becomes a gaping wound. The rider cannot throw him off and their bike can't move. The dog momentarily loosens its grip and that is enough for the rider to make their escape. The dog returns with an even deeper bite before it is flung free like a frisbee. The bike speeds up into the hills. The dog has blood, cloth and lumps of flesh in its mouth. It is shaking terribly.

Chwefror | February 2017

Gwen is given a quiet funeral with all the proper prayers, rituals and hymns. It lasts an hour and more people have attended than Mary-Jane had expected. Many of them are her friends from the church and they have much that is positive to say about her. The priest mentions her devotion to the church, the choir leader her knowledge of music, and others her love of animals. No one mentions Ned, only Mary-Jane and her father. After the service, Mary-Jane travels with her mother to the crematorium.

Her mother is so light that the four pallbearers are able to lift her easily and carry her to the bed of metal rollers. They turn for a few seconds as if they are welcoming her. Mary-Jane steps in between the pallbearers, supplied by a local funeral service, and guides her mother's head into place. She positions the coffin exactly in the centre and mentally measures the space on each side. Then it is her turn to move back and watch.

There is a prayer and a reading before the rollers take her mother from her and she slips gently out of her daughter's reach as a curtain comes between them. Everything softly stops. The rollers do not move and Mary-Jane stands beside the pallbearers with her head bowed.

After a while, the pallbearers leave her in her own space. The curtains whisper again, momentarily, as they jolt together. Behind them the rollers will turn again, Mary-Jane knows that, but for now Gwen simply waits.

Mary-Jane thinks of her mother in the coffin, then sitting in her chair or lying in her bed in the care home. Like a ghost, her body seemed not to have fitted her any longer, and her clothes, only a frame, had more colour than was in her face.

Visit after visit, Mary-Jane had watched her mother retreating physically to where her mind had already gone. Darkness. Toward the end, Gwen hardly lifted her head off her pillow. She just lay there like a vegetable on a supermarket shelf removed from primary contact with everything that sustains life. She remembers the last card that a nurse must have bought for her and she could barely sign, her script a sequence of squiggly spiders.

The priest comes forward to guide Mary-Jane from the closed curtains, a loose shoe-lace teasing the solemnity of his steps. Together, they follow behind the small procession of wreaths and flowers into the mid-morning sunshine as the crematorium is left to its restful gloom, waiting another.

She thinks of Gwen alone, inside her box, protected by its wood from the cool draft from the open door. She imagines the curtains speaking to the silent, empty room ... or maybe to Gwen herself. She wants to go back.

After the funeral, there is food and drink, singing and table banging. All this is intended as a celebration of Gwen's life. But Gwen had long forgotten everybody there. Rival mourners fight and then cry and hug each other. Mary-Jane leaves as soon as she can.

'If you insult a Catholic priest you insult the Pope, and if you insult the Pope, you insult God,' someone says to her.

'Is that what you really think?' Mary-Jane responds, knowing it was what her mother thought.

As she turns from the reclaimed wreaths laid out next to their cards, she walks toward a man older than herself, heavily bandaged, and resting on a walking stick.

She has signed her name on her wreath without a hyphen.

He notices that but doesn't mention it.

'All done?' she asks.

He flinches. The pain is like claw marks down his face. He tries to keep pace with her. She slows down and he rests beside her.

'What now?' she asks.

He sighs heavily. 'It depends on the court.' They both look in the direction of each other but their eyes do not meet. 'I have done a deal. Well, I think I have,' he says.

'Will you go back to the farm, to Prothero ... if you can?' she asks, gentler than she has been with him the last few months.

He tightens his lips before answering and adjusts the sling that supports his arm. 'No. He wants nothing to do with me now.'

She nods. Mourners whom she can barely recognise pass her

like stragglers leaving a racecourse.

'They could have dressed respectably,' he says, noticing them too.

Then he continues with what he was confiding in her. 'If I can, I am leaving here. I have been a fool. Maybe I can start again. If it is not too late. And you?'

'One final piece of filming.' She sounds weary.

'Anything about Amelia?' he asks.

'No. I don't think I will see her again.'

She sounds as if she really doesn't want to. He makes as if to ask her something but stops in mid-breath.

She says take care, look after yourself, or something similar. Within a few seconds, she will not remember her exact words. There isn't much feeling in them.

***

The shop is filled with large photocopying machines, each has a bank of dials and buttons. Mary-Jane feels that she is inside an alien space ship from some 1950s science fiction film. The air is clogged with the smell of printing ink and hot metal. She cannot imagine how anybody could work here. Her arms are filled with envelopes and photograph albums. Each of the envelopes has clearly marked instructions in black felt-tip pen. Everything is arranged in carefully constructed columns and on each envelope they are positioned the same distance from the edges. It is hard for her to manoeuvre herself between boxes of paper, bottles of toner, and packets of cartridges, some of which are ripped and torn open reminding her of an eggshell from which a chick has hatched.

The assistant, who wears a lapel badge which identifies her as a digital technician, welcomes her and comes out from behind the counter to help. Mary-Jane is expected and has already talked through her requirements. Together they spread the packages and albums over the counter as if they are wedding presents at a reception. Mary-Jane draws attention to her notes and explains what is in each envelope with the technician touching them as if to bestow a blessing. She opens some of them to check the size and quality of the prints. Many of the smaller ones are black and white images of Mary-Jane's mother as a child, playing on swings or climbing frames which had no more structure than a gallows. How health and safety has evolved, Mary-Jane thinks to herself, while watching to check that the technician returns everything to its rightful envelope in their precise position. A few she has to adjust or push deeper into their packets. Her mother laughs and enjoys the camera.

'Is this your mother?' the technician asks.

'Yes. She was very photogenic.'

The technician cannot help taking a quick glance at Mary-Jane's face. She knows her from television and as a vet in the town but says nothing.

Mary-Jane is reminded of how serious her mother looks in the photographs where she is older, standing in her St Illtyd's school uniform between her parents. It is as if she is rehearsing her sombre face to meet the nuns who would teach her there. There are few photographs in which she seems to be having fun. One picture Mary-Jane has made a point of marking for inclusion in the digital album, it is one of her mother as a baby in the arms of her mother.

In many of the later pictures, her mother is often bent and holding her arms close to herself. She cannot remember having much tactile contact with her and wonders if that is a family trait. She can only remember hugs and kisses on special occasions. She knows that she takes after her mother in this respect. Did her mother withdraw from her or did she withdraw from her mother?

Photographs of herself and her father are different from those where she is with her mother. They are hardly ever posed, the camera catches them side-on, or from behind, as they run together, chase balls, play racquets or lead a little dog. The dog amuses her, she cannot remember it getting any larger or growing older. There are lovely photographs of her father being kissed by it in his face and of them both trying to out stare each other. She wonders who took these photographs and whether it were her mother. She has no memory of what happened to the dog. She suddenly disappears from the photographs. She wishes she could ask her mother, it has never occurred to her before to do so.

The technician mumbles something about Mary-Jane having spent a long time in the family archive. She can see that some of the photographs date from the early part of the twentieth century. Mary-Jane relates again the story of her mother's illness and how she wants to retain as much as possible of her life so that she would not be remembered simply as someone who had dementia. She does not want her life to be lost to the wider family as it has gradually become lost to her. The technician nods, as if she understands, and places the pictures together, as Mary-Jane has sorted them, in different folders. Mary-Jane likes the sense of order and she feels the technician understands the project. As she observes the photographs disappearing between covers which will eventually become digital files, resting somewhere in the google ether like gods in the clouds above Mt Olympus, it occurs to her that all she has now are scattered images from other people's lives. But maybe, she thinks, this is all that any life amounts to in the end.

As she collected them, she studied them and cross-referenced them. She had looked carefully into her mother's changing face and, in the few photographs there were, into the eyes of her grandparents and great-grandparents. There are pictures of two young people near the River Taff; a young man in a soldier's uniform; a girl performing a cartwheel; a child on the shoulders of her father; and a beautiful foal with Mary-Jane's father.

It took her a while to realise that what she was looking for was evidence of her mother's particular form of dementia. As she turned over one print after another, carefully checking the negatives where she had them, she began to see her mother's dementia as something that had been inside her all along, even as a toddler, and in her mother before her. All the time, she sighs, it was there, silently developing. All the time, she says to herself, it has been in me, too.

Chapter Twenty One
Closing Frames

Ebrill | April 2017

Mary-Jane pauses to take in the size of St Patrick's Catholic Cemetery. She has come to Leytonstone on the train and meets the camera crew at the gate. There is no historian with her or waiting to greet her this time. She will talk to the camera as if she were talking to herself. It is something she has done in her farming broadcasts in Wales many times, but she has not heard it referred to as the crew describe it, spontaneous, rehearsed outpourings of soul. The location of the cemetery is very different from the one near Llanrwst. A fast, wide-laned road circles it and it seems much more urban than even the location of the university. As they move beyond the gate, the camera is panning the immediate graveyard reminding Mary-Jane to follow the script. She had been prepared for a very different burial ground from Llanrwst but not quite for what confronts her.

'It is packed,' she says. 'I did not expect this. All the graves are so tightly close together. It makes me think of the space around Meic's grave. There are so many large memorials, ostentatiously so; statues of Jesus, Mary and angels, angels everywhere you look. The Victorians, and most of these burial plots are Victorian, certainly believed in angels. And it is so noisy, making a mockery of the numerous scripts about resting in peace.'

All the time she walks with the crew around her, the director speeding them up and slowing them down as the camera picks out the more innovative memorials, the inscriptions that have the most drama and those that speak for the new decade. Eventually, the director allows them to walk uninterrupted at their own pace to where the path divides.

'Mary Jane is not buried in this part of the cemetery but over there where there are fewer graves and much more space.'

They all tread slowly as Mary-Jane appears to scan the names and epitaphs. But they all know the grave she is heading for. At one point she stops, and focuses, as does the camera now, on a particular statue of the Virgin Mary. She is very tall and Mary-Jane blinks and screws up her face as she looks through the sunlight into the Virgin Mother's beautifully honed eyes. Around her, there are several kneeling women all looking up to the Virgin Mary's face and beyond to heaven. Mary-Jane comments on the beauty and spirituality of what everyone now is studying. How it reminds her, from her own Catholic upbringing, that we can only touch the perfect divine through the less perfect Mary, that she can intercede for us.

This is not in the script but the director is not displeased. Mary-Jane has added something of her own.

The director is not a Catholic herself, but she respects that Mary-Jane is speaking from deep inside the relationship she has established with her great-great-great-grandmother. Maybe she is uttering a prayer to the Virgin Mary, asking her to intercede on behalf of her great-great-great-grandmother. Or maybe she is asking for her great-great-great-grandmother to intercede for her own mother who has passed during the making of the programme and will be acknowledged, it has been decided, in the closing credits. Or maybe she is praying for her great-great-great-grandmother to intercede for herself.

Mary Jane's grave is considerably further on. The camera picks it out in the distance. It is the final location. As they make their way over the grass, Mary-Jane tells the camera that she is remembering her slow, grassy walk in her bare feet to Mary Jane's husband's grave in north Wales. She reminds viewers that the two may not have in fact been married but they were married in nearly every other respect. She also reveals how she believes that when the two were together, Mary Jane may have been at her happiest even though her relentless restlessness never allowed her to appreciate it fully.

As they approach the grave, Mary-Jane has the last-minute surprise which the programme has set up for her.

For the first few seconds, Mary-Jane says nothing but allows the camera to do all the talking. The director signals for the camera to move slowly out of close up which is Mary-Jane's cue to speak.

'Well,' she says. 'I did not expect this. On the gravestone is written 'Marie Jeanette Kelly.' This is the name which throughout historians have suggested Mary Jane preferred and may have seen as more reflective of who she truly was.'

'So, both their gravestones have a mystery in their inscription. MJ inscribed on Meic's stone,' she explains, 'and Marie Jeanette Kelly on this one. Who knew enough about her to suggest this? It makes us wonder about identity and selfhood for women which is what I see my great-great-great-grandmother's life was all about. Those moments, as here, when there was a glimpse of who she really was.'

The camera continues while Mary-Jane gathers her thoughts and appears to suppress tears, maybe from thinking about what she has just said or anticipating what is to come next. She wishes at this point that one of the historians were present. But the script had said that it has to come from her.

'Mary-Jane ... no ... Marie Jeanette ... is not thought to be buried here, at this exact spot. But that doesn't matter. She is buried in this cemetery, and in this side of it. I know I am the closest physically to her I have ever been and I now feel very near her spiritually. It is as if I could open a door and step into a room and there she is, my great-great-great-grandmother in her kitchen, cooking for Meic just home from the colliery. She has been searching for me all the time I have been searching for her and now I feel she has found me.'

The camera moves out of Mary-Jane's face into a pan of the wider cemetery.

'That gives me some relief. I am glad that I have learned, and imagined, so much about her life that she is no longer just the alleged fifth victim of an infamous Victorian serial killer. That would have been hard to live with and somehow, very unfair on her. It doesn't matter whether she was his fifth victim or someone else's. Someone took her life and so have many historians, so-called Ripperologists. I have bonded with her, as many women of her own time did. She is more than her ... death ... the brutality of her murder. We have given something of her life, her short-lived periods of happiness, her hopes and, of course, her suffering, back to her. There is so much in her life that teaches us something, brings us all together as women.'

There is a longer silence, contemplation, as the microphone picks up the moan of distant traffic and, overhead, a small aeroplane.

'But she and Meic rest so far apart, he in a remote rural graveyard in north Wales and she somewhere in a metropolitan cemetery in Leytonstone. I discovered that she does not have a grave to herself but is buried on top of five or so others, the way people might bury their pets ... So much distance, difference and incompletion ... As in Marie Jeanette's life itself.'

Tears are beginning to slip and slide down Mary-Jane's cheeks. People watching this scene will comment that they have never seen her cry.

Her final words to camera: 'I feel that I have brought them together once more.'

Mae'r nofel hwn wedi'i gyflwyno i Marie Jeanette Kelly (1863-1888)

Linden Peach was born and brought up in Cardiff and educated at Aberystwyth University and with the Open University. He was awarded the Personal Title of Professor of Modern Literature by Loughborough University and has published extensively on modern Welsh literature. He is a Fellow of the Royal Society of Arts and of the English Association.

www.ingramcontent.com/pod-product-compliance
Lightning Source LLC
Chambersburg PA
CBHW050121170426
43197CB00011B/1669